more praise for *Nesting*

"*Nesting* is a savvy blend of two current crazes—it's chick lit for the HGTV crowd. . . . The authors throw Martha Stewart-esque caution to the wind in this lifestyle guide with attitude . . . all with a can-do, girl power mind-set." —*Publishers Weekly*

"I have so many ideas from this book that I'm going to have to quit my job." —ADAIR LARA, author of *Normal Is Just a Setting on the Dryer* and *Hold Me Close, Let Me Go*

"There's literally something for everyone in this wacky compendium of wisdom, wit, and the hilarious experiences of our fellow chicks." —FRAN MCCULLOUGH, author of *The Good Fat Cookbook* and *Living Low-Carb*

"The mother hens of the chick movement bring home their take on style and female empowerment. . . . Funny, useful and hip, a sort of Bridget-Jones-meets-the home arts." —KNIGHT RIDDER

"At last a departure from perfection and the arrival of playful when it comes to decorating and celebrating. Full of permission to embrace our own unique style whether that includes paper plates or china! From great advice to vicarious adventures, *Nesting, It's a Chick Thing* will delight and inspire." —LISA HAMMOND, author of *Dream Big*, and founder of Femail Creations

"There's a decided go-girl twist to this creative, comprehensive tome on 'nesting' (i.e., homemaking, but with attitude) . . . the true focus of nesting is not on domestic goddesshood, but on sisterly solidarity." —AUTUMN STEPHENS, author of the *Wild Women* series

"Here's proof that chicks who enjoy, celebrate, and take time to compare notes with other like-minded chicks can create original homes and gardens worthy of nesting." —SHEILA ELLISON, author of *How Does She Do It? 101 Life Lessons from One Mother to Another*

"Even if you never throw a party, decorate a table or plant a bulb, you'll have a ball reading this spirited book. And these gals make it so easy, you'll soon be nesting with the best of them." —MJ RYAN, author of *Attitudes of Gratitude* and *The Power of Patience*

to ....

from ....

nesting

it's a
Chick Thing™

Ame Mahler Beanland & Emily Miles Terry
creators of *It's a Chick Thing*™

WORKMAN PUBLISHING COMPANY • NEW YORK

Library of Congress Cataloging-in-Publication Data

Beanland, Ame Mahler.
    Nesting : it's a chick thing / Ame Mahler Beanland & Emily Miles Terry
      p. cm.
    ISBN-13: 978-0-7611-3160-1; ISBN-10: 0-7611-3160-4
    1. Home economics. I. Terry, Emily Miles, 1967– II. Title.

TX158.B392 2004
640—dc22

                                   2004043488

Workman books are available at special discounts when purchased in bulk for premiums and sales promotions as well as for fund-raising or educational use. Special editions or book excerpts can also be created to specification. For details, contact the Special Sales Director at the address below.

Workman Publishing Company, Inc.
225 Varick Street
New York, NY 10014-4381
www.workman.com

Manufactured in the United States of America
First printing: June 2004
10 9 8 7

"It's a Chick Thing" is a trademark of Chick Ink.

This book is dedicated to

TOM MILES

Emily's beloved father and the chicks'
biggest fan, who taught us the power *of* love,
the importance *of* laughter, *and the* value
of integrity *and who always encouraged*
us to strut our stuff.

table *of* contents

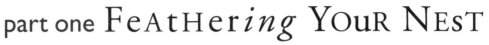

part one FeAtHer*ing* YOuR NEsT

Creature Comforts and Pretty Perches . . .

part two *fLocKing* TogetHer

Hen Hospitality and Fabulous Fetes . . .

part three CHicks *and* chow
Sweet Dishes and Hot Tamales . . .

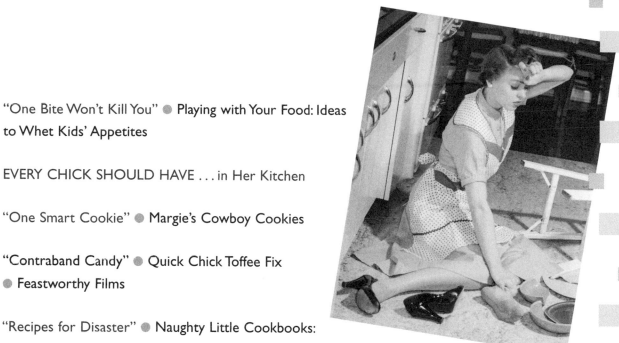

"Life is uncertain. *Eat dessert first.*"
—*Anonymous*

part four CHIcks *and* HOes

Scratching Around in the Garden . . .

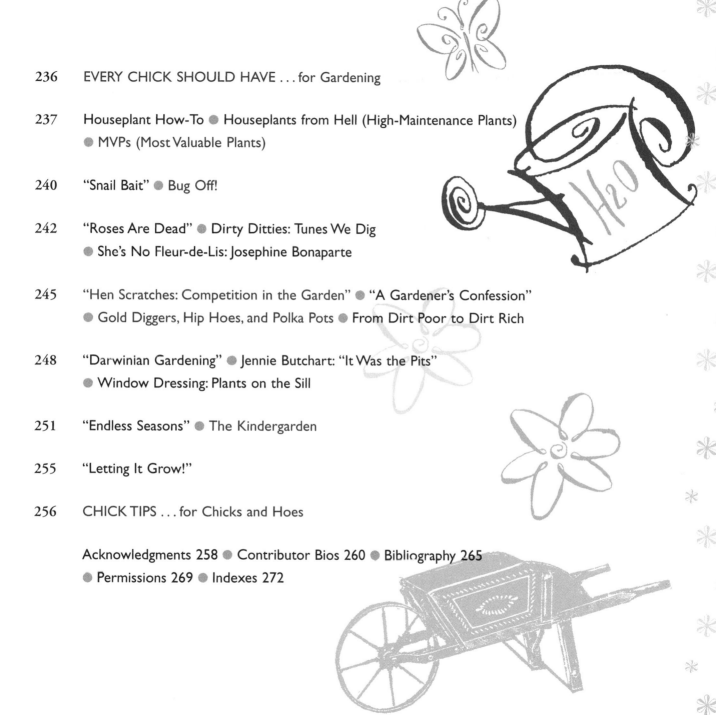

"*Birds of a feather* flock together."

iNtroDuction *nesting with attitude*

THIS BOOK WAS BORN OUT OF A SHARED OBSESSION. The two of us met about a decade ago at a small publisher's office on the West Coast, in the midst of the dot-com revolution. While the cool cats around us were spending their free time in cyber cafés, we chicks bonded during furtive conversations in our cubicles, pretending to discuss "home pages" when we were really talking about our homes. ("Domain name? Is that where I can get personalized door mats? Are they expensive?")

Frustrated with most of the complicated or conventional information out there on homes, we turned to each other for decorating inspiration, cooking savoir faire, or home-repair backup. We exchanged cocktail recipes and flea market shopping tips, relayed tales of decoupage disasters, and conspired to plant perennials that never made their way into the ground. Soon our little "chick network" of two expanded. We told two friends, they told two, and so on, and before we knew it we found ourselves loosely connected to about three hundred women—creative chicks who are generous of spirit, fearless with power tools, and more than willing to chip their nail polish in the name of home improvement. We'd become a posse of postfeminist domestic "experts," proving that what we lacked in time, experience, money, you name it, we could make up for with attitude and ingenuity.

Our own windows don't boast glamorous "treatments" and we don't serve fancy canapés at our parties.

As we write this, Ame's kitchen table is moonlighting as a potting bench, and the only thing Emily made from scratch at her last party was a martini. Like perfectly coiffed hair, perfect homes scare us. We believe that nesting well is about enjoying what you have, not stressing about what you don't. We find inspiration and satisfaction in simple things like line-dried sheets and ripe tomatoes dusted with salt. We love laughing until it hurts over a muddled recipe and cherish Crayola masterpieces created by three-year-olds. We're much more concerned with licking the frosting off the spoon than whether the spoon needs polishing. While we appreciate a delicious meal (or two), we think it's more important for a hostess to have a great time than to serve a perfect soufflé. And above all, we believe that the best advice, either hard-won or gut-instinct, comes from real-life people—namely, other chicks.

In writing this book we invited every woman we knew—and some we *wished* we knew—to share stories and tips about what we consider the four pillars of nesting: decorating, entertaining, cooking, and gardening. There are spring chicks who prowl the hot spots looking for the perfect cosmopolitan, shy homegirls who like to stay home and read *Cosmopolitan,* mother hens whose generation defined "cosmopolitan," and hip chicks who are *so* over cosmopolitans. Their voices span generations and cover the gamut of life experience.

Collaborating with friends and nesting with a passion that fuels your creativity are surefire ways to

"Style is what kicks in when charm fails." —*Annette Tapert and Diana Edkins*

keep the home fires burning. We want you to seek adventures in domesticity that are anything but domestic. Whether you're a chic apartment urbanite, first-time suburban resident, or practically a domestic goddess, we hope to embolden you to find and flaunt your true colors, both literally and figuratively. You'll find everything from encouragement to mix Grandma's heirloom china with your garage-sale trinkets and advice on room-by-room decor to the low-down on partying effortlessly through the year and creating the garden retreat of your dreams. While we've included some delicious recipes, we've also provided plenty of excuses for you to lay down your spatula and join the party. Inside these pages we've painted a picture of what we call genuine hospitality that doesn't require any floor mopping. And, after reading this book, even though you still won't have a perfect house, you'll be in good company.

All the tips, recipes, and crafts are chick-tested and mother-hen-approved gems that you can follow to the letter, modify to your taste, or, better yet, adapt to a totally different use. Make them your own and don't forget to share your discoveries with your girlfriends!

Our book celebrates the jubilation of a do-it-with-a-friend success, the mastering of an amazing recipe, the "aha" of a friend's laborsaving shortcut, the legendary party moment that still triggers hysterics, the garden resurrected with the help of a girl-friend green team—complete with the priceless stories of the foibles, dents, and spills along the way. Mix a little self-improvement into your home improvement—ditch the fear, embrace the fun, break the rules, and *nest with attitude.*

Ame & Emily

part one

"There is a terrific lot of hooey built up about decorating." —*Dorothy Draper*

FeAtHer*ing*
YOuR NEsT

Creature Comforts and Pretty Perches . . .

Building *ing a* LOve NEst

On first sight, anyone would have been hard pressed to believe that Stonehouse Farm could ever be the fruition of our fantasy. The front yard was buried under an array of lawn ornaments and broken-down farm equipment. There were more posts and wires running across this property than our entire city block. From the ancient windmill in the center of the yard the spokes of electric lines splayed to all points of the compass. And inside, what a sight to behold!

Our floors? Slanted. Our ceilings? Unbelievably low. With a touch of disgust mixed with sheer disbelief and not a little bit of delight, I describe them by saying, "I can palm every ceiling in my house!" The walls? Okay, let's just say that what wasn't covered in brown paneling looked like the pocked, irregular surface of the moon (pictures and mirrors keep my secrets). The bathroom? Almost functional and as deep and wide as a bathtub. The kitchen? Perfect, if you don't mind a sink that backs up, counters that induce back pain, and electrical wiring that sends your husband flying (isn't that right, John?).

Despite all of this, the house was blessed with several amenities—nice doors, ample closet space, a spacious dining area, a mudroom, and an abundance of delightful nooks and crannies. It's an odd and quirky house, but it is ours. John and I were thrilled to have our own canvas on which to experiment and dare, adding another layer of character to the house with the objects of our desires. A chandelier in our guest room looks as if many hands have tried to alter its surface, clay pots rubbed with rust and dirt look as if they were unearthed centuries ago, while a weathered, paned window frames a delicious handmade collage. These shards of rusted, worn, and damaged elements are brought together to create a thing of exquisite, even sophisticated, beauty.

To spice up the exterior of the house, we added gingerbread to the eaves followed by a white picket fence around the front garden. Turned wooden posts and railings were added to the porch. Inside, we chose our battles by priority. A bookcase covered walls that were cracked and unattractive

"To me, a home is a fantasy

while providing places for our many books and favorite collections. My crooked dressing-room floor was covered with fabric, braced to the floor with tacks. With paste and time, I papier-mâchéd our bathroom floor with paper leaves, concealing the mold that lay underneath. These small projects enhanced the cleverly painted walls to create a look and feeling that is our own. The satisfaction is all ours, the reward of hard work, best enjoyed in moments of leisure.

Since I cherish my time at home, I've had to let go of any yearning for perfection. As much as I try, there is always dog hair on the couches, hay scattered sparsely on the floor, scratches on the furniture, and cat hair on our clothes. I take comfort in a home that is cozy, warm, and welcoming to all who visit. Guests may dance in our living room. A spilled drink isn't a disaster, just an excuse to refill the glass. Every Easter, our families play a vicious card game of Spoons on our dining-room table. I don't wince each time a spoon slides across the table; instead I pray that I'm not left sitting without one. I love our home, for it is truly lived in and loved in.

We were recently discussing a wish list for the house, and John said that the stairs needed repainting. In a split second I blurted a horrified "No." I couldn't imagine covering up the years of memories contained in our steep and winding stairway. I painted them six years ago, and as time has passed, the layers have peeled away. The original red paint is beginning to show through and the memory of our home is coming alive. Looking back, I remember furniture that had to be hoisted through second-floor windows because the staircase wasn't wide enough. I think of our dogs, Gilbert and Alex, carefully and deliberately climbing each step to the security of sleeping at our sides. No, the stairs will stay for some time yet.

One of my greatest inspirations comes from being surrounded by all that I love—our home, our animals, our business, our friends. To look out of my studio window every day and see the beautiful expanse of land that envelops our home, and to watch Judge, my horse, holding court with all his witnesses—the sheep, the goats, and the miniature donkey, Rodeo Jack—to live, work, and play in such an environment, I'll take imperfections in my home any day.

Whether your home blesses you with bluebirds, bats, or both, try to appreciate its charms and flaws. I believe it's most often the unlikely, quirky, whimsical things about a home that make it so enchanting. If not, we are left with white canvases that search endlessly for true breaths of life.

—*Tracy Porter*

A little birdie told us . . . Before you refinish a dinged-up hardwood floor, try painting it. Simply sand it, clean it well, and roll on a paint made for floors or porches. Add a border, a pattern, or stencil detail in contrasting colors. Seal and protect it with a few coats of polyurethane and you've got a fresh look that'll floor 'em.

waiting to be revealed." —*Tracy Porter*

STARTING FROM SCRATCH What's a Chick to Do with an Empty Room?

We believe that the most memorable rooms aren't the result of gigantic budgets. Great decor, like a great personality, is uniquely inspired by attitude, creativity, and a sense of self. Sure, it's easier said than done, but based on some tips from the pros as well as heavy doses of advice from our talented chick gang, we've come up with some suggestions for how to tackle an empty nest.

"A house is just like a man—you ought to live with it at least a year before deciding on anything permanent. And even then it's a big gamble."

—*Katherine Anne Porter*

GET SOME PERSPECTIVE—YOUR OWN! Shakespeare's words, "To thine own self be true," might justly be applied to decorating a house. Before you can begin to make a room your own, you have to know and be comfortable with your own personal style. Be patient and figure out what you respond to when left to your own devices, *not* what the design magazines assert. What is your gut reaction to certain colors, styles, textures, and spaces? What moves you? In which rooms, houses, places have you felt most comfortable? Why? Take our little quiz on page 10 to get started on your path to self-decorating discovery. Shamelessly pillage your girlfriends' homes, favorite catalogs, Web sites, magazines, design books, and retail stores to get more ideas of what you like.

LET THE WALLS TALK. When faced with a gaping, empty space, our first inclination is to either choke or stuff it full of all the things we can get our hands on. Resist these urges and let your empty room sit for a while. It won't spontaneously self-decorate (drat!), but it will teach you a lot. Observe the light at different times of the day. Roll out a rug or blanket and experience it at night. Notice when you're most drawn there; and try to visualize what you and others might be doing in the room.

CREATE A STYLE "REMINDER-BINDER." Buy a large three-ring binder or accordion file. Divide it into sections for each room or area in your house and stock it with plastic page protectors. Begin to collect magazine clips, color swatches, fabric bits, sketches, and anything else that inspires your search. You'll begin to notice connections or patterns in your choices that will make it easier to translate your likes and dislikes into certain decorating styles. Down the road you can add actual fabric swatches, paint chips, and floor plans (see page 8) from your home. Whenever possible, bring your binder with you when you go shopping.

CALL UPON A MUSE. Whether it's a favorite piece of art, Grandma's teacup, a piece of jewelry, a rug, your garden, a textile pattern—find something that you love and use it to begin building your room. Look to your muse for color, texture, and style inspiration that you can translate into choices like wall colors, furniture, rugs, fabrics, and accessories. For example, we know a chick who loved Matisse's palette in *Harmony in Red* and hung a large framed poster of it in her living room. Inspired by its three primary colors, she painted the wall behind it a delicious raspberry and the adjoining den a French blue, accented by mustard yellow built-in bookcases. The effect? *Magnifique!*

GET TO THE POINT. Every room needs a focal point or place of immediate visual interest. In an empty room, it's often obvious—a fireplace, a lovely window, or an intriguing architectural detail. If the focal point is not obvious, then you need to create one. A piece of art, an interesting piece of furniture, a beautifully painted wall, an ornate mirror, an artfully displayed

Edith's case of empty nest syndrome was so severe, she could not even muster the strength to *catalog*-shop.

collection, a bold pattern in upholstery, or a rug—all are great ways to give your room focus.

SPACE OUT. Use a tape measure to calculate the dimensions of your room and draw out a scaled floor plan on grid paper. Imagine the furnishings you'll need and experiment with "arranging" them on your plan. For a more literal experiment, use tape to mask off areas on the floor to get the feel of how a large piece of furniture, like a couch or a dining-room table, will feel and look in the room. Stacking boxes (plentiful if you've just moved) is another good way to get a feel for how things will fill the space. Don't be afraid to angle furniture and don't immediately default to pushing everything up against a wall. Furnish according to your day-to-day life—not to the needs of entertaining or hosting a family reunion. Ensure ample seating for yourself and a few friends, but don't overdo it. Make sure there's plenty of space to move through the room and around furniture—a good rule of thumb is to leave about twenty inches between objects. Remember to include things like rugs and lighting fixtures in your plan, because these details really define and distinguish a room.

OPEN UP TO YOUR OWN FABULOUS FRIENDS. Now that you have a better sense of your design direction, seek input from friends whose taste you admire. Invite a gaggle over for coffee, throw down some pillows in your empty room, and start an uncensored design brainstorming session. Take notes and provide pens and notepads for anyone who wants to sketch ideas.

MAKE THE FIRST MOVE. After you've put in the time with your shopping research, you'll eventually fall in love with something and actually bring it home. Much like your muse, this first item—whether it's a rug, a painting, a couch, or a table—will help set the stage for ensuing pieces and design decisions. Choose it carefully, but don't obsess. You're decorating—nothing is permanent. Buy something because you love it, and it will always look great somewhere in your home. Go for quality in your larger pieces like sofas and chairs, which get more use than something like a coffee table. Try to keep larger, more expensive, upholstered pieces of furniture neutral, or at least in solid colors. That way you can update or change the look by simply changing accent pillows or throws instead of doing a costly reupholstery job. Alternatively, go ahead and choose a bold pattern for a chair or ottoman for a brave, surprising element.

COLOR OUTSIDE THE LINES. Nothing will make a greater impact in your space than painting the walls with a palette of your choice. There's no right or wrong way to choose color (and we'll argue with anyone who says there is), but there are smarter and more elegant ways to put things together. Consult a design book that has a color wheel explaining the way colors contrast, harmonize, or complement one another. A color wheel will help you understand why you like certain colors together and can help you combine colors with confidence. Then, armed with a few choices in mind, head to the paint store and pick a few shades to try out on your walls. (See pages 14–17 on how to paint.)

MIX IT UP. Never, never one-stop-shop when decorating a room. You'll wind up with a hypercoordinated, boring space. Instead, mix high-end investments with flea market finds for a personalized "collected over time" look.

REMEMBER, A HOUSE IS A WORK IN PROGRESS. Interesting houses, like interesting people, evolve, so take your time and enjoy the process. Keep building your room off the special things you've chosen, the palette you've established, and the personal style you're developing. Never try to do a whole house at once. And remember that in decorating, as in life, the rules are meant to be broken.

"I am a *marvelous* housekeeper. Every time I leave a man, *I keep his house.*"

—*Zsa Zsa Gabor*

A little birdie told us . . . The ideal distance between the bottom of a light fixture and the top of a dining table is thirty to thirty-six inches.

What's Your Style~Q?

The key to successful decorating is simple—you have to know what you like and confidently exercise your taste. Adopt the nesty chick's mantra, "Decorating is not forever." You never know until you try a new look, change a paint color, inject a piece of artwork, or roll out a new rug whether or not it will work. And, contrary to what the fashion mags tell us, style cannot be dictated, defined, or owned. No one knows what you like except you, and that makes you the undisputed expert. The trick is turning those unique likes and dislikes into confident, solid decorating choices in your home. This quiz will help you focus on the decorating styles you are most drawn to.

1. A dinner party is . . .
   a. A few close friends, a homemade meal, and a bottle of wine
   b. Four perfectly paired couples chatting over sparkling crystal and candlelight
   c. Lounging with your best buds over some tasty take-out and the trendiest new cocktail
   d. Sushi and champagne served on your new square dishes

2. Your library has to have . . .
   a. Hardcover editions of your favorite children's books
   b. Well-worn, leather-bound copies of the classics
   c. Beat poetry, the *Guinness Book of World Records,* and Jane Austen's *Emma*
   d. The latest dishy memoir or fast summer read

3. You're perched on a bar stool, what'll it be? . . .
   a. A glass of chardonnay
   b. A champagne cocktail
   c. A *mojito*
   d. A martini

4. When it comes to organization, you are . . .
   a. A piler—just get it all in one place
   b. A hider—out of sight, out of mind
   c. A flinger—let things rest where they land
   d. A gatekeeper—clutter doesn't even get through the front door

5. Your beauty potion of choice . . .
   a. A luxurious hand and body cream
   b. Red lipstick
   c. Shimmery body powder
   d. Aromatherapy bath oil

6. First-date attire . . .
   a. Jeans, a V-neck tee, and a soft cardigan
   b. A body-skimming black dress with sparkly accessories
   c. A vintage dress and high-heel boots
   d. A sleek suit and a crisp white shirt

7. A beloved sends you the perfect flower arrangement . . .
   a. Garden roses and hydrangeas
   b. Long-stemmed white roses in a ribbon-tied box
   c. Gerbera daisies and twisted willow
   d. Calla lilies

8. Your response to a red wine spill on your sofa . . .
a. "Don't worry about it. This happens all the time."
b. "Let's hope my cleaner can work a miracle."
c. "Wow, that's the same color as my throw pillows!"
d. "Leather wipes off in a flash."

9. An irresistible place to curl up and dream . . .
a. Sleigh bed with a plump feather mattress, cozy duvet, and a plethora of pillows
b. Four-poster bed with an ironwork canopy dripping with silk
c. Tufted-upholstered headboard beneath a tent of gold tulle and Chinese lanterns
d. Sleek, floor-skimming black frame with luxurious linens in three shades of white

10. Your friend needs a new lamp. You take her to . . .
a. The flea market
b. Your favorite French antiques store
c. A salvage yard, then the hardware store
d. Your trendy online source

IF YOUR ANSWERS TEND TO BE MOSTLY *A* . . .
COUNTRY CHIC CHICK You are drawn to the patina of age and the charm of a little wear around the edges. You would never compromise comfort for looks, and your home is a cozy, welcoming nest filled with sentimental treasures and make-yourself-at-home hospitality. Your recommended splurges: quality upholstery pieces that look and feel divine, unique accessories with vintage flair, and sturdy wood pieces that are painted or beautifully distressed. Subscribe to: *Country Living, Old House Journal,* and *Country Home.* Shop: Pottery Barn (stores, catalog, and online at www.potterybarn.com), Eddie Bauer Home (stores, catalog, and online at www.eddiebauer.com), and Sundance (catalog and online at www.sundancecatalog.com).

IF YOUR ANSWERS TEND TO BE MOSTLY *B* . . .
CLASSY LASSIE You create timeless, graciously appointed spaces that make all your guests feel like VIPs. Your home is elegant, fresh, and always in good taste. Your recommended splurges: traditional, antique-inspired furniture in balanced arrangements; accessories that evoke classical forms; and architectural details. Subscribe to: *Martha Stewart Living, Traditional Home,* and *Veranda.* Shop: Ballard Designs (catalog and online at www.ballarddesigns.com), Restoration Hardware (stores and online at www.restorationhardware.com), and Horchow (catalog and online at www.horchow.com)

IF YOUR ANSWERS TEND TO BE MOSTLY *C* . . .
BOHEMIAN BABE You weave a nest filled with character, whimsy, and in-your-face personality. You are an adventurous decorator driven by impulse and confidence, and your home is vibrant and interesting as a result. Your recommended splurges: original artwork, unusual imported furniture, and gorgeous rugs. Subscribe to: *Elle Decor, House and Garden,* and *Lucky.* Shop: Urban Outfitters (stores and online at www.urbn.com), Anthropologie (stores, catalog, and online at www.anthropologie.com), Z Gallerie (stores and online at www.zgallerie.com), and Crate and Barrel (stores, catalog, and online at www.crateandbarrel.com).

What's Your Style~Q? *continued*

IF YOUR ANSWERS TEND TO BE MOSTLY *D* . . .
MODERN MILLIE You love clean lines and uncluttered spaces. You tend toward rich neutrals and soft monochromatic schemes that create harmonious environments. Your recommended splurges: a great sofa with clean, architectural lines; soft, textural fabrics; and artful light fixtures. Subscribe to: *Metropolitan Home, Dwell,* and *Architectural Digest.* Shop: West Elm (catalog and online at www.westelm.com), Ikea (stores, catalog, and online at www.ikea.com), Design Within Reach (catalog and online at www.dwr.com), and GoMod (online at www.gomod.com).

A COMBINATION OF *A, B, C,* **AND** *D* . . .
ECLEC-CHICK You like to mix styles, eras, and patterns. Your decorating choices are driven by emotion and you buy first, find a place to put it later. You have a knack for spotting the diamond in the rough or discovering a brand-new use for a tired old item. Your recommended splurges: primitive antiques, vintage glassware and textiles, and one-of-a-kind art objects. Given your gusto for embracing different looks, pick a few mags or shopping destinations from the lists above—you have options!

> "Once your eye is trained to something, it reveals itself, and everywhere you go, you latch on to more of it."
>
> —*Ellen O'Neill*

DecOraTion *of* InDepeNdenCe

HOUSES, NO MATTER HOW HUMBLE OR GRAND, come and go and ultimately do not define us. Home is an attitude that has to do with love and caring, thoughtfulness, honesty, and authenticity. It is our lives, our families, and our souls that need to be housed. But if you seek contentment by continually decorating your house, it may forever elude you. I've seen people compulsively decorate and redecorate, which I think betrays a restlessness that tells me that person's *spirit* has not found a home. I've also seen the most compulsively *decorated* house, but have glimpsed no life *behind* the decorations.

Interesting people create interesting houses. By being *ourselves,* we can break through the limitations imposed by place and circumstance. It is the expression of well-lived lives that creates beautiful spirit and charm in a house, not the beautiful furnishings. I've seen the homeliest houses transformed into havens of affection and joy by fascinating, high-spirited people. An architecturally elegant, symmetrical structure doesn't automatically translate into a relaxing, comfortable atmosphere in which we want to spend time alone and share our love of life with others. . . .

[Decorating], when not approached as a natural extension of who you really are, can be harmful, especially when it becomes so enslaved to status and fashion that it becomes artificial. If more people would live their lives honestly, putting the things they love around them, I believe Americans would be far less anxious and disappointed. The art of living in today's world requires us to reach inside ourselves and search for the answers. As long as your home and the choices you make for it work for you, who cares what anyone else thinks? How you choose to live is really no one else's business. In fact, the more eccentric, personally defined, and quirky it is, the better. "You can't do that" is something you don't have to hear in your home. You darn well can. It is this absence of confidence in our own abilities to make the right choices in our lives at home that causes unnecessary pain, expense, and unease. Have fun. . . . Don't force anything. Don't rush. Living is a process. Everything will flow together in good time.

—*Alexandra Stoddard*

PAINTING LIKE A PRO

Nothing transforms a room faster and more economically than a fresh coat of paint. Be it pink or orange, stripes or stencils, knowing how to paint is a must for any nesting chick. Painting a room may not be rocket science, but it's not as easy as dipping a roller and gliding your way to the color of your dreams either. With preparation, the right tools, and a systematic approach, you, too, can paint like the coverall-clad professionals. There are lots of good how-to paint guides out there. We recommend *Paint Your House Inside and Out: Tips and Techniques for Flawless Interiors and Exteriors,* by Bonnie Rossier Krims and Judy Ostrow, or visit www.thisoldhouse.com for tips from the pros.

SOLVE THE COLOR QUANDARY. When you head to the paint store, never go empty-handed. Take something with you for inspiration—a piece of fabric that's in the room, a magazine clipping, even something as quirky as a piece of fruit—anything that inspires a palette for your room. Select a bunch of chips, and if you particularly like one hue, get a few of that color and tape them together so you get a better sense of what the color looks like beyond one tiny square. Tape the chips to your walls and live with them for a few days. Narrow it down to two or three colors, then go back to get a quart of each and paint them on the wall in at least two-foot squares in various places around the room. Take the time to see how they look in different light.

PAINTING IS ALL ABOUT PREP. Now take a deep breath and accept the fact that you will spend much more time getting ready to paint than actually painting.

PREP SUPPLIES
Drop cloths
Spackling compound
Putty knife
Paintable caulk
Ladder
Painter's tape (ordinary masking tape is too sticky and can damage surfaces)
Fine sandpaper
Screwdriver
Bucket and rags
Tack cloth

Empty the room as much as you can, leaving yourself at least three feet of clear space away from each wall. Cover any furniture left in the middle of the room with drop cloths. Take down all the switch plates and remove all picture hooks and nails from the walls. Fill any nail holes or cracks with spackling compound, using your putty knife, then let it dry. Sand the repairs smooth. Tape off the moldings, window and door casings, and baseboards to protect them from paint. Cover the floors with drop cloths and open the windows to get as much ventilation as possible.

PRIME TIME. If you're painting a room that's in good shape (it's been painted before, you didn't have to do too many patching repairs, etc.), it's usually safe to skip this step. But if you're painting over a contractor's finish, crayon marks, or unfinished wood, or you're putting a light color over a dark color, a coat of primer will be your best friend. Consult with the hardware store to select the appropriate primer. Make it even easier for yourself and ask them to tint the primer close to your chosen color.

GET READY TO ROLL—AND BRUSH. Choosing the kind of paint you want for the surface is simple when you know the facts. Check out our little guide at left for details.

What kind of paint do I use?

Savvy chicks know that quality paints are worth the investment. If you cheap out, you'll just wind up painting again much sooner than you planned—and who wants that? You have two basic choices in paints: latex, which is water-based, or oil-based. Latex paint is easy to clean up with soap and water, has less noxious fumes than oil-based paints, and is quick-drying. Oil-based paint requires solvents for clean-up, has a strong odor, and dries more slowly but also more smoothly. Experts recommend oil-based paint for applications where there is heavy use; for example, floors or cabinets that are touched frequently. To complicate things even further, all paints come in four finishes—flat, eggshell, satin (or semi-gloss), and gloss (or high-gloss). Check with the pros at your local hardware store to see which is best for your room. (Be sure to tell them the condition of the walls and how much use the room gets.)

PAINTING SUPPLIES
Paint can opener
Paint for ceiling
Paint stirrers
Three 2½-inch sash brushes (invest in soft, high-quality synthetic brushes)
Paper or plastic cups to hold paint for "cutting in"
One 6-pack of disposable 8-inch rollers (longer nap for textured walls, shorter nap for smooth walls)
Roller pan
Six disposable roller pan liners
Telescoping painter's rod for the rollers
Regular handheld painter's rod for the rollers
Paint for trim and moldings
Paint for walls
Plastic wrap
Inexpensive sponge-pad brushes
Hat or bandanna (to protect your hair from drips)

PAINTING LIKE A PRO *continued*

The best way to paint is from the top down: ceilings first; then walls; finishing up with the moldings and window and door casings; and baseboards last. Dip your brush in the paint only about one third of the way, then scrape it against the can to remove a little more paint for a neater stroke. "Cut in" the ceiling at the edges and in corners with a sash brush. ("Cutting in" refers to painting a surface at the edges where the roller can't reach, carefully avoiding adjacent surfaces.) Then finish up the ceiling with a roller using M- and W-shaped strokes. The last step is to untape the baseboards and window and door casings and finish up painting those with a sash brush.

If you don't complete the paint job by the end of the day, tightly wrap your wet paintbrush or roller in plastic wrap and store it in the refrigerator. It will save you clean-up time (just don't let them sit there more than twenty-four hours).

A little birdie told us . . . Many of the major paint companies make ceiling paints that are a pastel tint when wet, yet dry to a white finish. They help you get even coverage by making missed spots obvious.

Do I Know Hue?

We've all been "green with envy," "red-faced mad," "feeling blue," or, our own favorite, "tickled pink." Scientific studies have now confirmed the power of color to influence our moods and alter our perceptions. When decorating, color is the fastest way to set the tone or change the feeling of a room. And there are some pretty predictable emotions associated with colors. In general, colors from the warm end of the spectrum (red, orange, yellow, and yellow-green) are stimulating. Colors from the cool end (green-blue, green, blue, violet) are calming. The pros say that a warm color scheme needs a little bit of a cool color injected for balance and a cool color scheme has to have a dab of warmth for energy. Warm colors advance and cool colors recede, so if you want a room to look larger, paint it a cool color. To cozy up a large room, go for a warmer color.

Who knew a bucket of paint held such power? The bottom line is, don't overthink it when choosing colors. Go with your gut and pick a palette that speaks to you. Below are some qualities and emotions commonly associated with different colors:

Red: excitement, passion, vitality, ardor

Orange: warmth, order, comfort

Yellow: energy, cheerfulness, brightness

Brown: contentment, earthiness, masculinity

Green: nature, balance, harmony

Blue: calm, tranquility, relaxation, peace

Purple: royalty, luxury, serenity, ease

Pink: youth, innocence, happiness, femininity

Black: boldness, sophistication, modernity, simplicity

White: cleanliness, purity, spaciousness, naïveté

WALLS THAT SING

If your walls could talk, would they say, "I'm bored"? Next time you paint, give them a personality boost with a simple graphic pattern—stripes, diamonds, or dots. You can keep it subtle by using two muted colors, or go for drama with high-contrast combinations. For an elegant look, try using the same color in two different finishes—one flat and one with more sheen. Metallic paints are fun to make patterns with, too. This is a great trick for chicks who love designs but aren't fans of wallpaper. Plus, it's inexpensive, relatively quick, and yields big impact. Here are some ideas for walls that are worth talking about.

STRIPE IT RICH. Choose two colors of paint and apply the lightest color to the walls first. Decide what width stripe you want. Then do some simple math: measure the perimeter of the room and divide it by your stripe width. Take half of that and you'll have the number of stripes you'll need. Now, using a ruler and a pencil, go around the room and make marks where the wall meets the ceiling in whatever width you want. It's best to begin behind a door or in a less conspicuous part of the room so that if adjustments are needed you can fudge the measurements in a discreet area. After you've marked off the increments around the room, it's time to make vertical guidelines from floor to ceiling. Use a chalked snap line (available at any hardware or home-improvement store) to snap straight vertical lines from ceiling to floor. Be sure to ask for washable chalk so any residue can be wiped away. When you've got all the stripe lines chalked in, go around the room and make an X with your pencil wherever you'll be painting a stripe. Next, use painter's tape to mask off the area of the stripe to be painted. After you've taped off the areas to be striped, use a brush to cut in the top and bottom of the stripe where it meets ceiling and baseboard. Fill in the main body of the stripe using a roller. Remove the tape and voilà! Perfect stripes!

DIAMONDS ARE A GIRL'S BEST FRIEND. Choose two colors for your diamond pattern and start by applying the lightest to the wall. Begin by considering how wide and how tall you want your diamonds to be and when you've decided, make a template using posterboard. Using the template, carefully measure around the room, mapping out the placement of your diamonds. Once you get the spacing marked, tape off the diamonds with painter's tape and then fill them in for a jewel of a room.

SEEING SPOTS. Choose two colors and start by painting your walls the lighter shade. Then, using a plate, make polka dots on the walls randomly or create a pattern. If you're very steady of hand, you can simply trace around the plate with a pencil and then fill in the circle. Or, to be safer, create a stencil: Trace the plate onto stencil material and cut out the circle. Secure the stencil to the wall with low-tack double-stick tape and fill it in with a roller. Do the polka.

Tag—You're It!

Y RETAIL AVERSION WAS BORN OF NECESSITY. We had a one-bedroom apartment in New York City, and in our home money was even tighter than the square footage. But I was longing to decorate, so I scoured every tag sale and secondhand store I could find. I sought any piece of furniture—as long as it was cheap enough that I could place against the four vacant walls of our apartment. And my mission paid off as, one by one, a bedroom set, coffee tables, side tables, and a couch fell into place. And although my successes were many, I did have a certain weakness for three magic words when uttered in connection with any piece of furniture—"twenty-five dollars." Regardless of condition, size, era, even complete uselessness, if a piece of furniture bore the price tag of $25, I was automatically its new owner. Yet despite that minor flaw, as my apartment filled I became more discriminating and better at bargaining, and a lifelong hobby (some say obsession) was born. Upon seeing my bargains, friends commented that I had an "eye for the diamond in the rough." Though my furniture looked more like cubic zirconia to me, I was proud of my comfortable, solidly furnished apartment and above all, my frugality.

I bought our first dining-room set before we even had a dining room. As I watched the baby, my husband braved a windy day and smug Park Avenue glances as he single-handedly strapped an old table, six chairs, a sideboard, and a server onto our small Japanese-made car and brought them home. That's the problem with tag sales and secondhand stores—delivery is rarely included.

And so it continued, even as our space and our income grew—our one-bedroom apartment evolved into a two-bedroom, and the apartments eventually gave way to the relative spaciousness of our own home in the Connecticut suburbs. Now our nest is filled with the treasures that I've hunted and gathered over the years—and each treasure has a story. "Remember where that one came from? Remember lugging it home in the rain? Remember the price?

The mere thought of paying retail made Miranda's head throb.

Twenty-five dollars!" A coffee table made from the hatch door of a ship. My signed Boulanger lithographs. Our cherry dining room table, with two leaves and six chairs. The old binoculars in a well-worn leather case. I have no regrets, though my husband still talks about the "Greg Brady Nightmare" lamps—three-foot-tall, pyramid-shaped, acid green lamps that I bought as a temporary solution to a dire lighting shortage. It was $25 for the pair!

Now that I have a fully furnished home and a garage filled with hundreds of tag sale cast-offs, I have become the self-appointed personal tag-sale shopper for my friends, neighbors, and family. Armed with my cell phone, I ring up prospective takers from estate sales and front lawns. "Do you need wicker bar stools?" "Didn't you want a set of Nancy Drew mysteries?" "There's a table here that would look great in your foyer." They receive my calls good-naturedly, and sometimes allow me to bargain and obtain a treasure for them. And you can bet someone has a surprise gift coming whenever I hear those irresistible three magic words.

—*Josephine Phillips*

A little birdie told us . . . For a romantic and whimsical touch in a little (or big) girl's room, revamp an old chandelier by spray-painting it white and entangling it with silk flowers and French ribbon.

Decorating by the Book
The Nesty Chick's Library

Decorating books are one of the best ways to get fresh and inspiring ideas for your home. Whereas magazines can make your head spin with their constantly changing trend alerts, books usually offer a more grounded and lasting take on the subject. The best part—they can become a sophisticated part of the decor on coffee tables or at bedsides.

Bedrooms: Private Worlds and Places to Dream, the editors of *Victoria* magazine

Contemporary Decorating: New Looks for Modern Living, Elizabeth Wilhide, Joanna Copestick

Cottage Style Decorating, Cynthia Overbeck Bix

Country Living Country Chic: Country Style for Modern Living, Liz Bauwens

Creating a Beautiful Home, Alexandra Stoddard

Designers in Residence: The Personal Style of Top Women Decorators and Designers, Claire Whitcomb

Designing Women: Interiors by Leading Style Makers, Margaret Russell

Eclectic Style: Decorating with Your Treasures, Collectibles, and Heirlooms, Connie Duran

Gardenhouse: Bringing the Outdoors In, Bonnie Trust Dahan

How to Decorate, Martha Stewart

Jane Cumberbatch's Pure Style Living, Jane Cumberbatch

The Shabby Chic Home, Rachel Ashwell

Tracy Porter's Dreams from Home, Tracy Porter

19

SAVVY CHICK FLEA MARKET SHOPPING

Everything old is indeed new again when it comes to furnishing your nest. While we might not find ourselves interviewed on *Antiques Roadshow,* flea markets are a great place to find inexpensive accessories and furnishings and an immediate and fun way to inject personality into your surroundings. While hunting and pecking through yesterday's junk is a national pastime, flea markets can be completely overwhelming —with aisles and aisles of cast-off stuff, pushy shoppers, and savvy dealers. Over the years we've learned a thing or two about flea marketing and we've combined that with some tips from the experts.

THERE ARE TWO SCHOOLS OF THOUGHT when it comes to flea market shopping. The "early bird gets the worm" approach gets you a great selection, but the "last woman standing" technique gets you the best deals. So if you have a specific item or need in mind, get there early—and we mean early! Arm yourself with a flashlight because the sun may not be fully up and you want to be able to carefully scrutinize potential purchases. If you are more in the mood to stroll and just see what strikes your fancy, saunter in after noon and scavenge for those end-of-the-day bargains.

RECRUIT A FRIEND WITH A TRUCK. You'll need at least an SUV and a helping hand to cart all those great deals home; and be sure to load some rope and blankets in the back for securing your treasures. Wear super-comfortable shoes, bring a dolly or cart for transporting things, and swap your purse for a comfy backpack. You'll keep your hands free yet have a place to carry fabric and paint swatches as well as a list of items to be on the lookout for. Otherwise, in the heat of the moment, you might walk right by a rusty watering can that would be a perfect addition to your collection. Always bring a tape measure and a floor plan with measurements. Before you grab up that steamer trunk, measure it; it's only a find if it fits. And most important, bring cash; cold, hard cash can make the difference between getting a good deal and a downright steal.

IF THE PRICE IS RIGHT. When you run across an item that has a no-brainer bargain price and possesses some experimental potential—buy it. You can paint it, distress it, transform it, and if nothing else, write it off as "nesting research." If you aren't happy in the end, you can resell it, give it away, or donate it. The thrill of the deal, paired with a lot of imagination and elbow grease, has yielded some of our favorite furnishings.

INSPECT, INSPECT, INSPECT. This will cue the seller that you are interested, communicate a respect for the object, and make her think you are truly a discriminating chick. Don't point out imperfections right off the bat—that's rude. When you really get down to talking price, politely pointing out any flaws will help you justify asking for a lower price.

Mirror, Mirror—Off the Wall

We've rarely met a mirror that we can't salvage—except maybe those hideous three-way mirrors in dressing rooms. Almost any mirror can be a fast way to add sparkle to a room, create a feeling of spaciousness, or fill boring wall space. Scour garage sales and flea markets for ornate framed varieties and never underestimate the power of spray paint to transform. A gaudy gold, plastic abomination becomes a shabby chic treasure with a coat of white spray paint and a dry brushing of dark furniture stain. A flat, unframed mirror is a prime candidate for a mosaic border that you glue right onto the glass and grout. That 1980s black lacquer mirror? Spray the frame pewter and you've got a sleek, modern mirror that will look great in practically any setting. Collect small mirrors and unify them by painting the frames to match for a fashionable wall grouping. Or use them as trays to display candles, costume jewelry, collections, or even hors d'oeuvres. An ordinary back-of-the-door mirror makes a great alternative to the usual table runner when you gild the frame and display a row of votive candles and flowers. And if you tilt your mirrors downward a bit, they will reflect the whole room instead of just the opposite wall.

Instead of hanging mirrors above a mantel or shelf, try leaning them against the wall for an elegantly casual touch. Layer artwork in front and behind for an even more laid-back style. If you must hang a mirror, try something new. Add a French ribbon suspended from a glass knob or decorative hook. Buy a length of small chain at the hardware store and use it to hang your mirrors for a charming retro look. Glam up a mirror by painting a stencil or freehand design on the frame or the margins of the mirror itself.

You might want to give your boring medicine cabinet mirror or closet door mirror a shot in the arm. Using glass-etching cream, found at any craft store, make a design or pattern around the edges. Or "editorialize" your viewing experience by writing along the mirror's edge with a paint marker, "Hello, Gorgeous!"

"We don't see things as *they* are, we see them as *we* are." —*Anaïs Nin*

YOU ARE NOT A HAG IF YOU HAGGLE. In a professional tone, ask the dealer, "Is this your best price?" Or you can simply make an offer of about 20 to 30 percent less. When they tell you the price, a good response is, "Is there any way you would consider 'X' dollars?" You may not haggle every day, but the vendors do, and they expect it. Take a deep breath, and go ahead.

BE PREPARED TO GO OUT ON A LIMB. Flea markets offer a potpourri of lovable one-of-a-kind objects, and the fun is in finding something out of the ordinary that speaks *to* you and *of* you. You want to be discriminating, but not to the point of missing an opportunity to weave a little drama or whimsy into your nest.

The Bold and the Beautiful

DOROTHY DRAPER, OR DD, as she was referred to in her heyday, was one of the most sought-after interior decorators in America from 1925, when she founded Dorothy Draper Inc., to 1960, the year she retired. Dorothy lived large and decorated in extremes, proving that women could be homemakers in every sense of the word. Fearless and attention-seeking, the iron heiress hung blue satin curtains lined with chartreuse in the Whitney Museum of Art in New York, suggested that socialite C. Z. Guest's French paintings might be enhanced with fiery red borders, and adorned a premier casino and hotel with tropical flowers the size of stop signs. DD adored grand, oversized architectural details like massive mantels and wide, ornate moldings.

Though she decorated primarily for tycoons and artists with blockbuster-size wallets, Dorothy's greatest influence and best advice went to American housewives. "Your home is the backdrop of your life, whether it is a palace or a one-room apartment," she decreed, "it should be honestly your own—an expression of your personality. So many people stick timidly to often uninspired conventional ideas, or follow some expert's methods slavishly. Either way they are more or less living in someone else's house."

DD pleased those who could not afford her services by emboldening them to take their own risks. She suggested that American housewives use blue denim, bath mats, and horse blankets in place of expensive fabric and upholstery, urging, "Use your wits and you'll never want." While her great mass appeal and wide influence did offend some of the well-heeled and well-connected—Frank Lloyd Wright called her an "inferior desecrator"—DD always held her head high, once quipping, "There is a terrific lot of hooey built up about decorating."

Decorating According to Dorothy

"Give your man room and make him comfortable. It's all very well to feed the brute, but if you want him to stick around the house after dinner, think of him when you plan your living room."

"If you can't decide what color to paint something, paint it black, and it will disappear like magic."

"The wider the curtain, the bigger the cushion, the smarter the effect."

"No room can be called perfect unless it has real comfort."

"Don't be in the least disturbed by trends or fashions, or anyone else's advice. They are probably wrong. Be critical—never humble."

"If it looks right, it is right."

Defying tHe DiNing RoOm

I DON'T THINK I'VE EVER "DINED" IN MY LIFE. Don't get me wrong, I eat—I even pig out or binge on occasion—but the whole idea of "dining" is pretty foreign to me. "Dinner" was "supper" in our house, and we chowed down in the kitchen around an old veneer table with chrome and wicker seats. (Yes, I grew up in the seventies.) My parents and I cooked together and enjoyed the cozy kitchen where we made meals and ate family style. And our small condominium in southern California didn't even have a dining room.

For a long time I yearned for this elusive room. In my mind's eye the dining room was impeccably decorated with fine furnishings, sparkling crystal, and heirloom china. Such a room would require a person to walk more carefully and speak more distinctly. It boasted unique architectural details, luscious fabrics, and fancy chandeliers. It gleamed and sparkled with tables set with engraved silver and sterling dessert platters. But it was always something I didn't have.

When my husband and I bought our dream house, I was over the moon about the separate dining room. Just describing it to others would make my heart race: crown molding, chair rails, antique chandelier, and a bay window! The possibility of furnishing it with a formal dining-room table and sideboard sent my head swirling. Colonial style in a rich cherry wood? Mission-inspired, with Tiffany lamps? French Provençal, accented with yards and yards of toile?

But once we had moved into our home and begun to live there, we realized we loved eating and congregating in our open kitchen or in the adjacent sun room. So the dining room stood empty and formal, and I couldn't understand why I hadn't jumped at the chance to fill this coveted room that I'd finally acquired. As the weeks rolled by and the dining room remained empty, the flaw in my vision became clear to me. When I thought of dining rooms I had always thought of the *things* inside them, never the people. In all my daydreams, the lovely chairs around the hand-carved table had been conspicuously empty. My husband and I discussed it, and agreed that the room was a fantastic space; a fantastic space that would eat up thousands of dollars from our furnishing budget and get absolutely no use.

So instead we turned our dining room into a showcase for our artwork and collectibles. We don't have Picasso originals or Tiffany lamps. On our walls you'll find a funky signed poster by pop artist Peter Maxx next to an original oil painting by my husband's uncle. A framed Matisse print ▶

from the Tate Gallery in London picks up the magenta sunset colors of a landscape by New Mexico artist Inger Jirby. In the bay window, pieces of artisan pottery and glass sparkle in the morning sun. The only piece of furniture in the room is an old chest of drawers that belonged to my great-grandmother—the perfect surface where friends can rest a drink while they enjoy looking at some of the things my husband and I cherish most. Guests love to mingle in this room, and the art is an instant ice breaker. When we entertain, we set up a couple of folding tables in the center of the room and cover them with nice tablecloths for appetizers and desserts, and our "dining" room becomes a vibrant space.

It is also the perfect setting for our daughter's tea parties. She comments on the vivid colors and textures of the room, and it's the space in our house where she's inspired to color and create.

We love our dining room—and you rarely hear anyone say that. I often find myself pausing as I pass through it. It provides something that every home should have: a room where you just want to hang out for a while. And if you call munching on animal crackers and sipping juice boxes "dining"—well, then, we do that in there too.

—*Jill Bauer Dunne*

"The essence of taste is suitability."

—*Edith Wharton*

A little birdie told us . . . If you want a craft room, create one by covering your dining-room table with a glass top and using it as a place to scrapbook, sew, or organize your collections. The drawers in your buffet or hutch are the perfect place to store supplies.

The Original Domestic Diva

NEXT TIME YOU EASE BACK into your recliner, flip the handy electric light switch on the wall, sip a Pink Lady cocktail, nestle into a boudoir pillow with arm rests, or cozy up with a snazzy quip-embroidered pillow, think of Elsie de Wolfe, who invented all these things. She was the original "life-style" guru and the first person to market a decorative look for the homes and gardens of the masses.

A tough-talking New York "goil," Elsie rose through the ranks of both American and European society as *the* arbiter of good taste and chic decorating. The Chintz Lady, the First Lady of Interior Design, the Ultimate Hostess, Best-Dressed Woman of the American Stage—Elsie was all that and more. She coined the term "interior decorator" when, at age forty, she left her role as an actress and embarked on a newly invented career—charging for the decorating advice she'd been doling out freely for years. "I believe in plenty of optimism and white paint!" was Elsie's motto. She replaced the dark draperies and claustrophobic furniture arrangements of Victorian style with light, fresh colors, delicate patterns, eighteenth-century French- and English-inspired furniture, and breezy chintz fabrics. *The House in Good Taste* was packed with clever money-saving, do-it-yourself tips on attaining high style without high prices. No fuddy-duddy when it came to new technology, Elsie was the first designer to consider electronics in furnishing the modern home. She built special cabinetry to stylishly accommodate phonographs and said, "My first thought in laying out a room is the placing of the electric light openings."

While Elsie always grounded her decorating style with a nod to eighteenth-century influences, she had a flair for the eccentric and always leaned to the informal and comfortable. Cabbage roses and chintz easily gave way to zebra stripes, leopard prints, and black lacquer should the urge strike her. The bathroom in her Parisian apartment was so fabulous—ridiculously spacious and luxuriously appointed with animal skins, velvet, and mother-of-pearl chandeliers—that she served coffee to her party guests in it. "I have such joy out of my bathroom that it is difficult for me to speak of it in measured terms," she declared. As for developing taste, Elsie put it best: "How can we develop taste? Some of us, alas, can never develop it, because we can never let go of shams. We must learn to recognize suitability, simplicity, and proportion, and apply our knowledge to our needs."

"I have always lived in enchanting houses. Probably when another woman would be dreaming of love affairs, I would dream of the delightful houses I have lived in."

—*Elsie de Wolfe*

my BarBie DreAm HOuSe *Sweet Home Alabama*

REMEMBER THOSE BARBIE DREAM HOUSE DAYS? Those carefree afternoons of having Barbie lounge poolside on a pink chaise, or brushing her silky hair while she gazed into the mirror at her pearlescent purple vanity set? Well, I don't remember because for me the Barbie Dream House was just that—a dream. My mother convinced me that only bored and boring little girls needed to have their mothers shell out good money for pink plastic boxes. She claimed that if I used my imagination, I would realize that I already had everything I needed to create a palace fit for my eight-inch queen. So under the guise of encouraging my creativity and artistic expression—and, oh yeah, grossly insufficient dream house funds—I was robbed of the pleasure of owning that pink confection of a house.

That is how my Barbie came to stiffly inhabit a cardboard box decorated with quilting scraps, duct tape, and buttons. Too bad they didn't have Homeless Barbie back then! A little fire-burning barrel and mini newspaper duvet would have complemented my Barbie's residence perfectly. If necessity is the mother of invention, I should have retained a patent attorney. I was a nine-year-old recycling, shabby-chicing, trash-to-treasure genius. I made tables out of paper plates and toilet paper spools; I created place settings with button plates and tin foil goblets. My Barbie even had a telephone made of twist-ties, beading wire, and masking tape. I logged hours coloring pictures for Barbie's walls, framing them with Popsicle sticks and hanging them with thin ribbons. Barbie's rooms were painted and faux-finished with crayons, eye shadow, and just about any other medium I could sneak out of my mother's makeup drawer. It may not have been a 90210 address, but my Barbie's house was a designer original and she seemed quite comfortable living in it. Thank goodness my best friend Justina's parents would not take on the dream house mortgage either. Can you imagine the humiliation if my Barbie had had to pull her soda-can roadster up to a fancy pink house to visit her friend Skipper?

Justina and I spent many dreamy hours playing with our fashion dolls from the wrong side of the tracks. When they weren't relaxing with their feet up on thread spool ottomans, or redecorating their rooms with magazine cutouts, our Barbies headed for the great outdoors. We'd fashion swimsuits out of deflated balloons and pretend that our dolls were the fancy Malibu Barbies that frolicked during commercial breaks between the Saturday morning cartoons.

As for transportation, who needed the pink Corvette? Our dolls commandeered GI Joe's Jeep from Justina's older brother and tore up the dirt track in her backyard. And they got *dirty*. By summer's close, my Barbie had dreadlocks, a farmer tan, and a heart tattooed on her shoulder thanks to a laundry marker we found in a kitchen drawer.

Now, when I recall that little girl dramatically pleading with her mother for a pink plastic dream house, I barely remember the disappointment. What I do remember, in great detail, is the fun and excitement of building that little nest. I remember how a few discarded shoe boxes, fabric scraps, and cast-off sewing notions, markers, paints, and assorted knickknacks could hold magical powers. I learned that watercolor paints and crayons don't mix (a fundamental fact of decorative painting technique), that denim makes a great bedspread, and that you can never have too many throw pillows. I also learned that doing anything with a friend doubles the fun. Little insights translated into far bigger lessons.

So when my mother reads this and gets that tingly, smug "I told you so" feeling, I can credit her for imparting the most important lesson of all—that dream houses don't come prepackaged and neatly stacked on shelves. They unfold slowly, with faith, effort, and the help of good friends.

—*Ame Mahler Beanland*

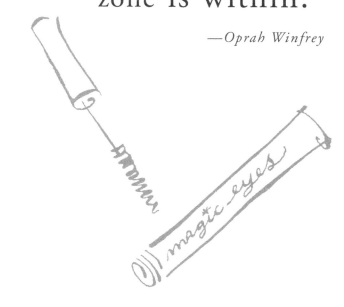

"The *ultimate* comfort zone is within."

—*Oprah Winfrey*

magic eyes

It Takes a Flock to Make a Nest
SEVEN CHICKS EVERY HOMEGIRL NEEDS

Forget DIY—Do It Yourself—and embrace DWC—Done With Chicks. It's so much easier—and much more fun—to get your girlfriends in on the act of nest improvement. You can build a dream house with this dream team on your bench.

THE JACKIE. This chick can tell you immediately whether toile is out and silk is in. She knows how to match colors you didn't even know existed and her elegant flair for coordination would shame a Hollywood stylist. She can convince you to give your old heap of a sofa the old heave-ho without hurting your feelings, and she has the ability to help you accentuate the positives. When you need a remedial style course, she's your teacher.

THE GREEN GERTIE. She has ten green thumbs and toes to match. This organic chick can clear a rosebush of a thousand voracious aphids, save your dying oak tree, and get rid of those pesky rodents using only her trusty squirt bottle and a secret potion. She can tell you where to put it, how to grow it, and when to cut it back. Flowers seem to blossom bigger just because she smells them. When it's time to get down and dirty, call on Gertie.

THE MARTHA. With a little nip and tuck she can rework a plain curtain so that it's worthy of Versailles. With a slight furniture rearrangement she can create space you never knew you had. A little cluck-cluck over a recipe, and it's instantly gourmet. She practices the domestic arts with the intensity and diligence worthy of an Olympic athlete. Don't even think about making a nest without her advice.

THE BARGAIN BETTY. She can smell a good deal a mile away and then squeeze an even deeper discount out of it. Her gracious demeanor belies a shrewd deal-maker and treasure-seeker with an eye for the fabulous amid the foul. With her touch a roadside reject can be refashioned into a gleaming showpiece. Whatever your heart desires—goose-down pillows, heirloom-quality antiques, wall-to-wall carpet—she can get it for you at the absolute best price. This gal should be a regular on *Antiques Roadshow,* but you're lucky she's not famous yet and is free to shop with you.

THE FIX-IT FANNY. This chick has a tool belt that takes do-it-herselfing to new heights of fashion. She might prefer Prada to Levi's, but she can hammer out a solution to your domestic problems without putting a nick in her French manicure. A real power chick with the tools to match, she can take on projects that would make Bob Vila call for reinforcements. From the gutters to the basement, this gal's got you covered.

THE NEIGHBORLY NELLIE. The original girl-next-door, she is the best thing about living in your neighborhood.

Her door is always open to help you with those last-minute emergencies—an egg, a cup of sugar, a spot of milk, even a shoulder to cry on. She's like having your own marriage counselor and handyman in one. You can't get your fire alarm to stop blaring? Run to her house! If you don't have one of these chicks on your block, consider moving.

THE MOTHER HEN. A veritable fount of wisdom, this chick was home improving when DIY was just a twinkle in Home Depot's eye. Always there to offer up loving, or pointed, advice when you need it, she knows it goes down easier with a spoonful of sugar. Whether she's soothing your ruffled feathers, swooping in to rescue a recipe gone bad, or doling out fix-it advice, she's the one you can call on any time for good, honest, down-home counsel.

"Remember, if you ever need a helping hand, you'll find one at the end of your arm . . . [and] as you grow older you will discover that you have two hands. One for helping yourself, and the other for helping others."

—*Audrey Hepburn*

GrandMa StyLe

My SENSE OF STYLE CAME FROM MY GRANDMOTHER. Her decorating sense shaped me as much as my mother's did not. Don't get me wrong: I love my mother. I just hated the furniture she chose, and I didn't even know it until I was looking for my first apartment with my husband-to-be.

"You know the kind of place, with towers and things, long windows? Old bathroom? What's it called?" I asked my husband, when we were trying to figure out what we liked.

"Sure," he said, nodding, smiling. "Old."

It wasn't until we actually found it—a second-floor one-bedroom in a mustard yellow Queen Anne Victorian in West Philadelphia—that we knew what we liked and that we liked the same thing. This place took my breath away. There was a bay window in the living room, an archway leading to the tiny kitchen, black and white tile on the bathroom floor, a stained-glass window in the bedroom, and an arched alcove perfect for a dresser. I sighed with happiness as I unpacked my wedding gifts, finding just the right spot for everything. It reminded me of my grandmother's place in Brooklyn, a fact I did not realize until she had died and someone else pointed it out to me.

We relished the task of finding furniture that would suit our new home. Over and over we were drawn to particular items. An Art Nouveau dresser with a sinewy mahogany mirror spoke to me and we purchased it for $35. One week later, as if by magic, a wardrobe in a similar style appeared in the same store, hidden by rows and rows of yellow wood tables stacked upside down and on top of each other. The wardrobe had a worn keyhole but no key; we paid $65 for it. We followed our instincts and together we decorated our splendid, tiny castle, thus beginning a lifelong tradition of uncovering "junque" and giving it new life.

My mother would visit my homes—so many over the years, but always essentially the same. Old. Victorian. Weirdly shaped rooms, stunningly beautiful mantels, the faint smell of past lives. I strove for elegance, above all else. But somehow I never got there. I always ended up with comfortable, soft, pleasing. Maybe even funky. Mom would look at my things with a puzzled expression. I could almost hear what she was thinking: Is this okay? Where did she come up with this stuff? Mom, whose first house was decorated in "Danish Modern," with its unforgiving straight lines, bold geometric shapes, sharp angles. Mom's house was smart, sophisticated, the sixties personified. Mom was expressionistic modern dance. I was a Tchaikovsky ballet.

Where did I come up with this stuff? From her mother. "Mama," we called her. My grandma was beautiful, with wavy white hair, a strong jaw, and a slim figure. Her smiles were hard-won but worth it. Her Brooklyn apartment featured high ceilings, an ornate lobby, a white forties kitchen, big windows, and the best of all, a claw-foot tub that allowed for very deep baths. Her closet smelled of perfume and lipstick. She had rows and rows of beautiful shoes, a long dressing table, real jewelry (at least it looked real to me!), and dresses of tulle, satin, silk. Furs. Designer labels. I could try it all on, parade around in it all day. She didn't care.

I am certain that my sense of style comes from Mama, a woman from the shtetl who managed always to live well and look good, to turn an ordinary old Brooklyn flat into a classy joint. She knew how to find beautiful bargains. She knew how to make fake seem real. Her stuff was probably junque, too; who knows? The impression of grandeur, with mostly ordinary things found and revived. But always beautiful, tasteful.

And yet . . . if you look real closely at my pretty rooms, sprinkled in among the strategically placed lace runners, the softly shining silver, and the tasteful though gently worn mahogany, you can spot the imposters—the occasional peek of a brassy base metal beneath silver plate, the hooked rug whose regular pattern gives away its machine-made origins, or the chips and dings in my vintage crystal collection. Still, I think Mama would approve.

—Sue Senator

> "*Adornment* is never anything except a reflection of the heart."
>
> —*Coco Chanel*

A little birdie told us . . . Old people are hot! Take those black-and-white pictures of Grandma and Great-Aunt Ethel out of storage and display them in silver frames for instant ancestry and family-tree chic.

Designing Divas Sound Off

If you've ever tried to keep pace with the most current trends in home decorating, you've probably realized the perfect use for the expression "when Hell freezes over." It's simply not possible to stay hip, in fashion, or trendy, because the whole point of these fashion conventions is to keep us changing our minds and buying new things. On the other hand, there are so many trends and fashions to choose from that it makes it easy to keep your home fresh and stylishly vibrant. Here are quotes from some of the hottest home decor trendsetters and designers—both historic and contemporary. Their decrees are emulated by the masses and yet, as you can tell, they hold very different opinions of what a home should look like. Pick the advice you feel most at home with, forget when the chick said it—true style is ageless— and let it inspire you to boldly strut your stuff.

"I find an overabundance of decorative objects to be completely distracting and excessive. My own style is fairly minimal, understated, and architecturally driven. In fact, I could be the poster child for the adage 'Less Is More.'"
—Sheila Bridges (2002)

"More is more. This is the effect I love the most. I may need a resting place from time to time, but for the most part, just keep it coming! Layers, textures, colors, and patterns make me a little wild. Once I get going, it can be hard to stop."
—Tracy Porter (1998)

"The drab age is over. . . . Until very recently people were literally scared out of their wits by color. Perhaps this was a hangover from our Puritan ancestors. But whatever the reason, browns, grays, and neutrals were the only shades considered safe. Now we know that lovely, clear colors have a vital effect on our mental happiness. . . . Be sure your colors are honest, fresh, and clear."
—Dorothy Draper (1939)

"Because I prefer a subdued look, every room is done in a monochromatic scheme of muted and sun-bleached floral prints. . . . White walls are the most classic, clean foundations for any room. Acting as a sort of blank canvas, white complements and contrasts with a variety of colors, tones, and textures, and serves well as a backdrop for all styles of furniture."
—Rachel Ashwell (1996)

"Use color fearlessly. Have confidence in your choices, even if others don't."   —Muriel Brandolini (2001)

"Simple, honest materials usually age with grace: concrete is very forgiving, marble develops a lovely patina, and the first scratch on stainless steel is the worst—the surface becomes more beautiful with time." —Page Goolrick (2001)

"[In the dining room] pairs and sets of things are most desirable. Two console tables are more impressive than one. There is great decorative value in a pair of mirrors, a pair of candlesticks, a pair of porcelain jars, two cupboards flanking a chimney-piece . . . when things pair logically, pair them! They will furnish a backbone of precision to the room." —Elsie de Wolfe (1913)

"[Dining room] walls can be decorated with old wooden fencing, a pleasing fancy that stimulates recollections of field trips in search of wildflower meadows and picnic spots. . . . Garden hand tools, rethought and embraced as significant cultural artifacts rather than mere work implements, may be displayed for their fundamental beauty. The table may be a rough-hewn shed door turned horizontally to serve as a dining surface; a metal bistro table, a little rusty but still serviceable; or a finely crafted wooden groaning board." —Bonnie Trust Dahan (1999)

"When people keep telling you that you can't do a thing, you kind of like to try it."

—*Margaret Chase Smith*

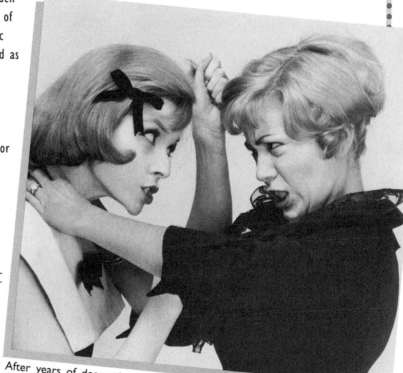

After years of decorating tension and nesty competitiveness, Edna finally snapped when Stella refused to concede that orange was the new pink.

Women's Work

INTERIOR DESIGNERS AND NESTY CHICKS ALIKE owe a great debt to Candace Wheeler. Heralded as the Mother of Interior Decoration, she is all but unknown today, yet in the late 1800s her name was at the top of every New York decorator's and wealthy client's list. More important, she spearheaded a movement that paved the way for women to turn their creative talents into a profitable career.

In the mid-1800s, middle-class women had but one way to showcase their decorative skills—hobbies. Women artisans were relegated to their drawing rooms, to paint pretty pictures and embroider lace for their homes. The male-dominated worlds of art and design were virtually devoid of a woman's touch. Candace bucked this system. Skilled at embroidery and painting, she studied her "hobby" and became a textile designer.

In 1876, at the age of forty-nine, she attended the Centennial International Exhibition in Philadelphia and had a life-changing epiphany at the booth for London's Royal School of Art Needlework. It wasn't so much the beautiful tapestries that impressed her as it was the idea of women-owned and -operated businesses. The Civil War had left a wake of struggling widows who were untrained for the workforce; Candace saw a way for them to parlay their domestic skills—from embroidery and knitting to painting and cooking—into profitable services and products. She returned home to New York and founded the New York Exchange for Women's Work, where women could consign their wares. The Exchange is still in business today, selling women-made arts and crafts, from hand-knit sweaters to heirloom-quality quilts.

At the same time, Candace's own talents were being recognized by the New York design world. Louis Comfort Tiffany invited her to join his decorating firm, where she designed patterns and directed installations in some of America's most prestigious residences. Buoyed by her success, she achieved her dream of founding her own company in 1883. Associated Artists, an all-woman textile design and manufacturing enterprise, created everything from inexpensive cotton prints to lavishly embellished wall hangings.

Inspired by nature, the women of Associated Artists created an iconic style with their sophisticated interpretations of native American plants and flowers arranged in sinuous, flowing patterns that have become part of our country's visual history. While at the helm of her prosperous business, Candace also took on the occasional side project that appealed to her—such as the seating design for the 1893 World's Fair library, which showcased more than seven thousand books authored by women.

NESTING NO-NOS

We all have our pet peeves when it comes to decorating, and we nesty chicks have occasionally walked into a room and had to restrain ourselves from digging our claws into it. A potentially beautiful space is a terrible thing to waste. Regardless of individual style or taste, there are a few nesting no-nos that even the most decor-challenged chick can keep an eye out for.

"NO MORE WHITE WALLS!" Okay, we won't go Joan Crawford on you if you've intentionally chosen a frosty shade for your walls. We accept the fact that white is technically a color, and we won't tongue-lash you for choosing it, as long as you don't automatically default to it or accept it only because it was there when you moved in. Walls that are infused with color, whatever the shade or intensity, beckon and embrace. If you must have white, limit it to one room or one wall, never the whole house.

NOTHING PERSONAL. Sometimes you walk into a home that's clearly been well planned, beautifully appointed, and obviously fussed over, but something is "off." Next time you get that feeling, look around. We bet you'll be hard pressed to find anything —a knickknack, a collection of photos, a sentimental collection, a quirky piece of art—that ties it intimately to its inhabitants. Homes should speak volumes about the people who live in them, so make sure yours has something interesting to say by sur-

rounding yourself with the things that inspire you, comfort you, and make you happy.

IT'S NOT NATURAL. Rooms that do not have some organic element or touch of nature feel sterile and jarring. Enliven your nest by incorporating natural textures into your rooms. Fresh or dried flowers, plants, a vase of twigs, a sisal rug, wooden or woven furniture and accessories—all bring a touch of the outdoors, which adds a certain vitality to any room.

CLUTTER, CLUTTER EVERYWHERE. As strange as a home can feel when devoid of personal touches, a space that's packed with tchotchkes can be even worse. You might be attached to your old issues of *House Beautiful,* but if you want your house to be beautiful, find an out-of-the-way spot for the pile. Don't overdo it with the knickknacks, exercise discretion, edit often, and display objects in collections as opposed to sprinkling them around. Try rotating them, putting a few away every few months.

TECHNOLOGY ABOUNDS. You might be proud of your flat screens, but wires and electronic components are not decorative items. Whenever possible, camouflage the television, computer, or stereo equipment and conceal, organize, and properly attend to unsightly wires and cords. Discreetly securing the wires to the back or legs of furniture with tape will prevent them from creeping out.

AM I IN THE MALL? Let's face it, we all have our favorite home-furnishing stores. Just be careful that your nest does not become an homage to your favorite retailer. "Oh, your house looks just like the catalog" is not really a compliment. Beware of "home*ogenizing*," which can happen when you over-shop at one retailer or overdo one very distinctive style of furniture or accessory. When you try too hard to make a statement, you often end up with a room that's well decorated but lacks the personality that is the true essence of style.

FLUFF AND FOOF OVERLOAD. Decorating guru Christopher Lowell once called an overly feminine room "the land of precious." You know the look—lace, ribbons, silk flowers, dolls, foof, foof, foof! Achoo! We are big fans of girlie spaces, but don't take it to an extreme. A well-designed room has a little yin and a little yang to keep things comfortable for all kinds of chicks as well as those gentlemen callers and dwellers.

SCENE IN A BAD LIGHT. Nothing makes a room shine like well-planned lighting. The well-lit nest has a balanced mix of lighting for various tasks and for general ambience. Fluorescent bulbs and bright lights are designed for task-oriented spaces like offices, reading nooks, and kitchens. Keep them out of the other rooms of your house. Always consider the sources of light and generate some from above (with ceiling fixtures or recessed lighting) and some from below (with lamps, candles, and uplights). Use light to create a sense of drama, highlight plants or artwork, or enhance mood. Try pink lightbulbs in rooms where you might want face-flattering soft light. When entertaining, use candles wherever you can, then dim the overhead lights so you have just enough light to navigate around the furniture and find your food and glass.

"One sits uncomfortably on a too comfortable cushion."

—*Lillian Hellman*

A little birdie told us . . . People tend to hang their pictures far too high. Rule of thumb, hang your artwork at the average person's eye level—the focal point of the art should be about sixty-eight inches from the floor.

MarTha

MARTHA—like Cher, Madonna, or Barbie—is a national icon and needs no surname. Love her, hate her, eschew her, emulate her—whatever your feelings about Martha Stewart, a book on things domestic would be remiss without her. A self-proclaimed "maniacal perfectionist," Martha has garnered legions of fans and detractors alike with her detailed instructions for homemaking projects from the mundane (how to sew a button) to the extravagant (gold-leafing your own faux Fabergé eggs). And with her phenomenal success has come a big side of scandal. Whether you cheer her or jeer her, you gotta give the chick credit. She empowered American women to be their own decorators, to stretch their homemaking skills (sometimes to the breaking point), and to elevate the things of everyday life to an art form.

Good Things from Martha

Her publications, especially *Entertaining*, the definitive book on hosting elegant parties.

Her relentless stream of ideas for keeping holidays fresh and creative. The chick can carve a pumpkin 200 ways and make 65 recipes from the seeds alone!

Her ability to translate high style into affordable prices and make it available to everyone.

Her Web site, with the recipe-finder feature. You'll never lose that macaroni and cheese recipe again.

Her macaroni and cheese recipe.

"The 'homemade,' the 'handcrafted,' the 'heirloom,' and the 'keepsake' have always been for me the real essence of the holiday season."

—*Martha Stewart*

the WalTer Mitty of real EstAte

"I'LL TAKE MY COFFEE ON THE MASTER SUITE BALCONY," I say. Emerging from my sunken tub (with jets), I grab my robe (size small), hanging neatly in the ample walk-in closet (with built-ins). As I lean against the wrought-iron railing overlooking the back garden, the warm sun dries my hair, tinting it a natural blond.

I am pampered, organized, relaxed.

Wait a minute. This is not my house. This is not my life. This is an open house, with a For Sale sign in front. I have no intention of buying this house or any other. But I am an open-house addict, on the circuit Saturday 1–4 or Sunday 2–5.

My home is supposed to be my sanctuary. But sometimes, on a weekend afternoon, I find a stand-in. When I take off my shoes at a stranger's stoop and wander from room to room, I become the Walter Mitty of real estate. I daydream that somehow, in this particular space—a paneled study here, a workout room there—my life would be different. I would be different. More content maybe, more creative definitely, thinner absolutely. If only.

My real house is sixty-five years old and has a master bedroom with two tiny closets and a bathroom off the hall with a broken shower. I'm the mother of two preschoolers who have their own rooms, only one of which we've fixed up so far. My day often begins in a rush with a handful of Frosted Flakes and a squirt of Clairol's Touch of Sun on my roots.

My husband and I bought our home in San Jose in 1999. The house had *Sunset* magazine's singular requirement for true California living—a kitchen overlooking the backyard, with ready access to a barbecue. It didn't seem to matter at the time that the kitchen was a 1970s remodel with heavily grained, dark oak cabinets and countertops made of fake butcher-block laminate.

But a house in need of updating gave me an excuse to hit the open-house trail, and I've been on it ever since. There's a whole brigade of us out there "just looking." We greet each other with that same furtive, shameful nod, as if caught peeking in someone's medicine cabinet. Some people mutter excuses about snooping into other people's lives: This one's friend is thinking of buying a house, that one's sister is moving to town. Some are unapologetic about sizing up the crystal in the china hutch, or checking the Viking range to see if it has actually been used.

We open-house addicts call ourselves "lookie-loos."

I used to think we were essentially just a bunch of nosy neighbors. But I've come to realize that the roots of this fixation are deeper than mere voyeurism or practical market research. The fascination comes from the way a house both reflects and defines a person's identity. A wall of windows overlooking the courtyard of a Carmel open house makes me imagine myself a famous novelist with a salon of literary friends who drive down to the famous Nepenthe restaurant in Big Sur for inspiration and a Cosmo. A curving stairway in the grand entry of a $3.5 million San Jose house makes me imagine the charity benefits I could throw there—and the housekeeper I could afford to clean up after them.

Is it so hard to believe that living in a great space can be not only inspiring but even life-transforming? Maybe I picked up that romantic notion from my father, an architect, from whom I learned to appreciate natural light, open spaces, flow. Or from spending a summer as a tour guide at Hearst Castle, where I watched the sun sink into the Pacific from the Celestial Suite.

After reading *Under the Tuscan Sun,* I became convinced, like thousands of other people, that the greatest dinner parties are only a remodel away. So if we can't buy the dream house, we try to improve the ones we have. I do love my house—the large bedrooms, the screened-in porch, the hardwood floors. Yet when my husband leaned against the old electric stove last year, wrapped his arms around me and asked, "Will we be happier if we have a new kitchen?" I didn't know what to say.

Well, we have a new kitchen now. And, in fact, we have thrown some fabulous dinner parties. Yes, instead of the wood floor I wanted, we have new linoleum. And while I love our limestone counter, it is tile, not granite. But when we stand next to our new Viking range with the seasoned griddle, my husband hugs me just the same as he always has. And the kids still spill the Frosted Flakes.

Now if only I had that sunken tub.

—*Julia Prodis Sulek*

"Whether I've lived in a one-bedroom apartment or on a sprawling estate, my gift to myself has been to make my home a sanctuary— *a place that rises up to meet me every time I enter the front door.*"

—*Oprah Winfrey*

A ROOM OF ONE'S OWN

Some say retreat is a state of mind. That's fine in theory, but when a chick needs to get away, there's nothing like the right space and a few props to jump-start your self-imposed time-out. Though a "country house" sounds wonderful, it's hardly commonplace and not what we mean when we say a retreat. We think the best spot requires no commute, no mortgage, zero upkeep, and is ready in an instant. Sound impossible? Not if your retreat happens to be within your own nest. Treat yourself to a quiet space all your own to which you can escape and recharge when you need to.

POSSESSION IS NINE TENTHS OF THE LAW. So find a space within your home and stake your claim. Make it as private and removed from the goings-on in the house as possible. This is *your* space—although you might choose to invite others in, don't let anyone else dictate how you design, use, or feather your retreat.

IT'S ALL ABOUT YOU. Personalize your haven with colors, fabrics, furniture, candles, and objects that are chosen with only one chick in mind—you. Consult *The Nook Book: How to Create and Enjoy the Coziest Spot in Your Home,* by Karen Hansgen, or *A Room of Her Own: Women's Personal Spaces,* by Chris Casson Madden, for some creative ideas.

KEEP IT SOOTHING BUT CREATIVE. Fill your retreat with things that help you to relax and restore—favorite books, magazines, art supplies, beauty potions, nail polish, music. Keep out objects that remind you of work, chores, or other mandatory "to-do's."

MAKE A STANDING APPOINTMENT. Your retreat may be the place you go to meditate for fifteen minutes before starting your day, to read the Sunday paper once a week, or to recline nightly with a crossword

Tinker Bell's Apartment

"But there was one recess in the wall, no larger than a birdcage, which was the private apartment of Tinker Bell. It could be shut off from the rest of the home by a tiny curtain, which Tink, who was most fastidious, always kept drawn when dressing or undressing. No woman, however large, could have had a more exquisite boudoir and bedchamber combined. The couch, as she always called it, was a genuine Queen Mab, with club legs; and she varied the bedspreads according to what fruit-blossom was in season. Her mirror was a Puss-in-boots, of which there are now only three, unchipped, known to the fairy dealers; the washstand was Pie crust and reversible, the chest of drawers an authentic Charming the Sixth, and the carpet and rugs of the best (the early) period of Margery and Robin. There was a chandelier from Tiddlywinks for the look of the thing, but of course she lit the residence herself. Tink was very contemptuous of the rest of the house, as indeed was perhaps inevitable; and her chamber, though beautiful, looked rather conceited, having the appearance of a nose permanently turned up."

—from *Peter Pan,* by J. M. Barrie

Marie's Petit Retreat

Marie Antoinette was known for living extravagantly, yet few give her well-deserved credit for living well. More girl than woman when she was crowned queen of France, she still had the savvy to realize that in order to maintain her sanity, she needed a place to escape the oppressive rituals of the French court and the elaborate palace, Versailles, where she was under constant scrutiny. Though she had many getaways at her disposal, Marie Antoinette's favorite retreat was Petit Trianon, a house in the gardens of Versailles. Her husband, King Louis XVI, gave it to her as a wedding gift, saying, "This pleasure house is yours." As a child, Marie Antoinette had enjoyed a country house with imaginative gardens, and she sought to re-create those at Petit Trianon. In later years, rumors flew that the queen had "plastered" her retreat with "gold and diamonds," yet in reality, Petit Trianon was decorated relatively simply, with objects and portraits that held special meaning for the queen. Her favorite family portraits were hung on the walls and the rooms were decorated with soothing pastel fabrics in apple green and cotton toile.

More important than the decor, however, was Marie Antoinette's attempt to create a separate world for herself—one less complicated and more creative than her majestic realm. At Petit Trianon, guests were allowed to serve themselves; children were warmly included; and amateur theatrical performances were staged in which the queen enthusiastically participated. Later, in her ongoing attempt to keep this world both whimsical and delightful, Marie Antoinette had a model village built in the garden. This *hameau* included twelve cottages surrounded by a mill, an aviary, and an elaborate henhouse adorned with a thousand white porcelain pots (monogrammed with her initials) and filled with flowers. Who knows? Perhaps there was a little cake, too.

puzzle. Whether it is daily or weekly, make sure you commit to spending regular time in your retreat.

TAKE IT OUTSIDE. A hammock, a special seat in the garden, an outgrown playhouse, or a tree house—all make fabulous getaways for busy chicks.

HANG OUT THE DO NOT DISTURB SIGN. Negotiate a deal with your family. Let them know that your retreat time is sacred and make sure they respect both your space and the time you spend in it.

"I vant to be alone."
—*Greta Garbo*

CReaTuRe ComfoRTs And PRetTY PeRcHes ● 41

❋ A room pulled together with the help of her girlfriend gang

❋ A soft and cozy blanket or throw to cuddle up with

❋ An heirloom of her own choosing

❋ A well-stocked toolbox for emergencies, do-it-herselfing, and attending to creative whims

❋ Framed baby pictures of herself and pictures of family and friends on display

❋ Something pink in a place of prominence

❋ A room with no television and beautiful music

❋ Fresh flowers

❋ A room painted her favorite color

❋ A reading nook, with a library of beloved books and an ultra-comfy, just-my-size chair to curl up in

❋ A room with a decor she doesn't take so seriously—a place to experiment, have fun, and let loose

❋ An item that she splurged on and loves

❋ A souvenir from a special journey or memorable adventure

❋ A chandelier

❋ Luxurious soaps and potions sink- and tubside for aromatherapy and pampering

❋ A pair of paint-splattered, well-worn overalls—for when she wants to really get down to nesting

HaNd Me *a* ScreWdriver *(and hold the vodka)*

I'M STANDING IN MY FRIEND MONICA'S BATH-ROOM, staring at the swath of pea green paint that I've just applied to the formerly white wall. I glance at the paint chip I left on the floor and then back at the wall. These two colors bear no resemblance to each other. I'm no expert, but it is clear that the paint on the wall has a scary yellow undertone, while the one on the chip has more blue and is much less offensive. Surmising that Monica does not want to wake up to an artificially jaundiced face each morning, I put down my roller, pack up the paint can, and set off for yet another trip to the home-improvement store.

The next night I'm still in the bathroom. After spending all day stripping and sanding the floor, I'm ankle deep in adhesive, trying to neatly apply squares of linoleum without gluing myself to the floor in the process. And the weirdest thing is—I'm enjoying it!

This burst of home repair on a home that isn't even mine was brought on by the TV program *Trading Spaces,* in which two pairs of neighbors switch houses for two days and, with a thousand-dollar budget and an expert designer, completely redecorate one room in each house.

For our exchange adventure, Monica and I scaled it down a bit. We had two days and two hundred dollars to transform each other's bathrooms. As with many of our schemes, this one had our friends worried about what we'd gotten ourselves into. Okay, they were worried about what Monica had gotten herself into. She's an artist with great taste, an elaborately decorated house, and a fully stocked toolbox. I'm no artist, it took me a year to buy curtains for my house, and when I ask for a screwdriver I mean a cocktail. Let's just say I'm not known for my home improvement flair. I don't think, for example, that it is all that important to, say, hang a picture straight. When I asked Monica if she was worried about what I'd do to her bathroom she said, "I know whatever you do will be better than the way it is." Not exactly a ringing endorsement.

Monica's bathroom was pretty much a blank slate—primarily white, accented by the previous owner's kitty-cat border. I had a blank mind until a couple of days before the ▶

"And the trouble is, if you don't risk anything, *you risk even more.*" —*Erica Jong*

room exchange, when I hit the creative jackpot. I knew Monica hated the white linoleum floor with its pink-and-blue-plaid design. I decided to replace it with a black-and-white checkerboard-patterned floor. It was still linoleum, but it fit my budget and would, as they say in the design world, make a statement. After tracking down the floor, I lucked out and found black-and-white accessories, including square picture frames (which I used to make a big checkerboard square on one wall), a soap dish, a soap dispenser, and a toothbrush holder. Before I knew it, I had a theme.

Though I wasn't so surprised at my shopping ability, I was downright shocked by my sudden burst of handiness. I guess it had been lying dormant all these years. Standing alone in Monica's bathroom, I knew I had no choice but to dive in. There was no one to ask for help, no one there to tell me I wasn't doing it right. Left to my own devices I became a virtual home-repair maven. I painted. I measured and cut the flooring. I wielded a drill like nobody's business. I dismantled and installed towel racks. I even hung the pictures straight.

Monica loved the finished product, and I loved what she did to my bathroom—robin's-egg-blue walls and new wainscoting in linen white. She accessorized with candles and apothecary jars and, so it wouldn't be too girly, accented it with two rubber duckies sporting devil horns. She even made collages from paint chips and framed them—cheap and pretty art.

Our friends were amazed at both of the bathrooms. I'm sure they would have been horrified if they had actually seen the way I tore up the floor, not to mention my highly unorthodox painting methods. In fact, those things scared me a little, too. I made some mistakes, but I learned something very important about home decorating—most things can be fixed. I also learned that I can be the woman to fix them.

—*Kate Dube*

A little birdie told us . . . The Do-It-Yourself Network Web site is an awesome source of information on everything from specific project steps to detailed tips on choosing the right tools. Visit it at www.diynet.com.

The Chick's Starter Tool Kit

A chick's gotta do what a chick's gotta do. Whether it's finding a stud or wrenching a nut, chicks need the tools to get the job done. Don't be afraid to try your hand at fixing something before you call in the professionals—just do a little research first. For specifics on repairs, Home Depot has a line of how-to books for many different types of projects, or you can check out *Dare to Repair: A Do-It-Herself Guide to Fixing Almost Anything in the Home,* by Julie Sussman and Stephanie Glakas-Tenet. Here are some recommended items to get your tool kit started for all those do-it-herself projects.

BRIGHTLY COLORED PLASTIC TOOL KIT. May we suggest pink?

MEASURING TAPE(S). We recommend both a small one with thin tape (10–15 feet) and a monster-size one (25 feet or more).

SET OF SCREWDRIVERS. Go with a set that has a variety of flathead and Phillips models for all types of jobs. Depending on how much use they get, you may need to replace them, as we chicks tend to wear them right out.

HAMMERS. Invest in a couple of basic claw hammers—a heavy, full-size one for big jobs when you need driving power, and a smaller one for tick-tick-ticking in nails or more delicate projects.

DRILL AND DRILL BITS. When purchasing a drill, go cordless, and don't wimp out on the power and size. A 9.6-volt cordless drill is good for everyday, light to medium use, but 12 to 14.4 volts will give you awesome power for practically any job. (Another plus to more powerful drills is that they have a longer battery life.)

LEVEL. Get a small one (6 inches) and a 2-foot carpenter's level; for certain projects a laser level is worth the investment.

STUD FINDER. These will get the job done, even if you have a great guy around.

WRENCHES. Buy a small set with various sizes, as well as a self-adjusting wrench that can accommodate many nut sizes and has the added benefit of locking into place when you squeeze the handle.

PLIERS. Stock your box with three kinds: needle-nose for delicate or precision gripping, tongue-and-groove pliers that adjust to fit different-size nuts and pipes, and locking pliers that can be tightened viselike around an object.

HOT GLUE GUN. For ultimate flexibility, add a dual temperature glue gun to your holster. You can use the low setting for fragile materials like fabric, paper, ribbon, and Styrofoam and turn up the heat for applications that involve glass, plastic, wood, and metal. And for the crafty chick who likes to roam free, splurge on a cordless glue gun.

BOX-CUTTER

WIRE CUTTERS

YARDSTICK

ReStOraTion

I LEARNED HOW TO "HAMMER IN THE MORNING and hammer in the evening" from my father. From my mother, I learned how to take those handy skills and add the spice of creativity. And in addition to handiness, my parents also schooled me in the arts. Besides ballet classes and clarinet lessons, I studied piano. My classmate Melinda and I had the same piano teacher, so we shared the spotlight at recitals as well as grade-school functions. We went on to attend high school together. Yet even with all that close proximity, our lives never really crossed until ten years after graduation, at our high school reunion. I was in the middle of a crowded room; perhaps it was a fortuitous, simultaneous turning toward each other that initiated what I remember as our first conversation. In the eleven years since that reunion, Melinda and I have become best friends.

Soon after the reunion, my husband and I purchased a craftsman bungalow home in Arkansas and I spent the ensuing several years repairing walls, installing wainscoting, painting, removing paint, and restoring a home in the craftsman tradition. Melinda, who remained in my hometown of Birmingham, loved hearing about my home project stories on the phone and when I went to visit her. After I convinced her to purchase a home, Melinda bought her own Craftsman bungalow and hosted a house-warming dinner where our parents had the opportunity to meet again. Though it had been many years since they'd spent time together in the PTA meetings and recitals of our youth, they picked up right where they had left off. Our mothers, surprised to learn that they both suffered from similar heart ailments, renewed their friendship that evening with a strong bond of support and understanding.

Among other things, Melinda and I share a love of home projects and this "nesting instinct" has been the impetus for our developing relationship over the years. She, as a librarian, possesses book knowledge about renovation, and I have provided the go-get-it attitude and skill that helps her pictures become reality. I travel often to Birmingham to see my family, and, of course, to help Melinda with what she calls "Lindsley doing my projects while I take well-timed naps." One of her most famous (and most well-timed) naps was at a crucial moment when half of her wallpaper was secured to the wall and the remaining half was dangling and dripping over my head.

When Melinda lost her mother to heart failure, I was there for her. A year later my mother's heart gave out and Melinda was there for me. With my mother gone, my visits to Birmingham to see my father became more frequent and seeing Melinda and her bungalow's progress was always a cheering note. On one of those visits I was pleased to see that she had initiated a handyman's task on her own, stripping paint from the wooden mantel in her living room. Her goal was to transform her drab, all-white living and dining areas into true Craftsman-style rooms, with dark wood trim and golden walls. She admitted sheepishly that she'd been at it for two months and that there must be an easier way.

I suggested an alternative for doing the trim, a technique that I developed when experimenting with the steel front door on my house. (I had painted on a medium-brown colored oil paint, let it dry, and then streaked red oak stain over it using a wood-graining tool to make it look exactly like stained wood.) She agreed to let me experiment on a small, hidden corner of her room. When I finished with the small corner, she looked at her piece of wood, looked at my section of trim, looked back at her piece of wood, and exclaimed, "Let's do it!"

Given the recent loss of both of our mothers, this behemoth project provided us with a much-needed, bittersweet connection. We stayed up the entire night and into the early morning, working our way around the room. With our hands engaged, our hearts opened, and we experienced the amazing gift that girlfriend home-improvement projects can hold.

We already had such wonderful shared history that had taken place in these rooms—of catching up on our lives, of the dinner where our mothers had renewed their friendship. But this time was different. As we worked at transforming and restoring those rooms, we restored a little bit of ourselves, too. Amid the ebb and flow of easy conversation and quiet contemplation, we felt unity and comfort in our shared losses. We laughed and teased one another as we methodically painted and stained. We learned the value of comfortable silence in the presence of a true friend, something that comes more readily when one's mind is task-oriented. That night, while feathering Melinda's nest, we felt we were surrounded by the eternal wisdom, guidance, and love of the women who had raised and comforted us in nests of their own making. The four of us—Melinda, the spiritual and enlightening presences of our mothers, and I—engaged in home improvement of the highest order.

—*Lindsley Armstrong Smith*

WAITING FOR THE DUST TO SETTLE How to Survive Construction

Be it a simple remodel or a full-scale reconstruction, home improvement projects seem to go better with a little support and some advice from chicks who've been there, done that—and lived to tell.

1. To prepare yourself, and your family, plan a Renovation Movie Night. Watch *The Money Pit,* with Tom Hanks, and *Mr. Blandings Builds His Dream House,* with Cary Grant. Scenes of special note include Tom Hanks falling through the hole in his floor and Mrs. Blandings giving her contractor her paint colors. Later on, when you're experiencing the same building nightmares off-screen, try to remember how "hysterical" these movies were.

2. Don't be the first one to "view the damage" post-demolition. Have someone who won't be irreparably damaged by the sight of flying dust, dented walls, and dirtied sinks do it. Cajole your spouse, good friend, or cleaning person to view your place first and tidy it up before you see it, to soften the emotional blow.

3. Get a library card and familiarize yourself with the hours at your local branch. It makes a perfect retreat where kids can do homework and you can do research, thumbing through the latest overpriced home decorating magazines for free or reading a trashy novel without having to listen to a chainsaw in the background. You might even sneak in a ten-minute nap amid the stacks.

4. A chick never leaves any design decisions up to her contractor. Never say, for example, "Towel racks? I don't know, surprise me!" Men wearing tool belts can invent new versions of ugly that boggle the imagination.

5. Stop reading the WANTED DEAD OR ALIVE signs at the post office. The power of suggestion will lead you to positively swear that the same murderous gang is hanging the Sheetrock in your family room.

6. Meet your new best friend—Lysol. Stock cans in the bathroom and douse your toilet generously throughout the day. Better yet, invest in a Porta-Potti rental. Sure, the neighbors will moan, but they don't have to share their throne with ten strangers daily. A chick has to draw the line somewhere.

7. Carry on with your own maintenance. There will be days when you'll need a little reminder that you are still a chick, even though you are living in a dust bowl. The walls may not be painted, but your toes can be.

8. Develop the patience of Job. Anyone who's undergone a renovation or house project remembers that naive statement, "Oh, I'm sure they'll be done by the holidays. They promised." It's not that contractors are dishonest by nature; they simply hold the illusion of being in control. Key word: illusion. So give it up, Pollyanna, and resign yourself to numerous delays and missed deadlines. It will be worth it in the end.

fix~Up~Your~Nest fests

Everything's easier when it's shared with friends, and we love it when practical tasks take on the air of a party. Recruit some of your nearest and dearest and convene in the name of home improvement, organization, and, most important—fun.

READ 'EM AND EAT. Freshen up your library with an annual book exchange party where every guest brings a few good books to swap and a tasty dish to share. Have each person inscribe her name and the date of the party inside the front cover with a sentence-long review before passing it on.

STITCH AND BITCH. Quilting, knitting, and sewing aren't just for grannies. Recruit a crafty gal to give a private lesson and fellowship in cozy style while you spin yarns and get caught up over a pot of homemade soup and warm libations. Toss in a few neglected tasks, like sewing on buttons, mending, and other repairs, and you will feel downright industrious. Consult *Stitch 'n Bitch: The Knitter's Handbook,* by Debbie Stoller, for more ideas.

DESIGN INTERVENTION. Whether you just moved in or are simply decor-dumbfounded, make a hearty brunch for your trusty decorating divas and get their advice on ways to spiff up a neglected room or banish those white walls. Daytime is best: All the hardware stores and home improvement warehouses are open and ready to equip you with the means when inspiration hits.

TRASH BASH. Do you have a room with a congested pathway, a crammed closet, or a cluttered bookcase? Order an extra-large pizza, invite your most ruthless recycling rowdies, close your eyes, take a deep breath, and let them help you clean up your act. Be sure to take before and after pictures.

THE PAINT PARTY. Nothing brightens a nest like a fresh coat of paint in a color of your own choosing. And nothing makes it easier to do than having a crew of people to help you. Bribe your buddies with promises of hearty food, rockin' tunes, and good company in exchange for their brushing and rolling expertise.

BEFORE AND AFTER RENOVATION. Hold an open house to get in good with your neighbors before the construction begins. The noise and inconvenience may be easier for them to take if you've primed them with hospitality, food, and drink beforehand. When the dust settles, invite them back to celebrate the finished product.

"I'm going to need a glue gun, some pinking shears, and five yards of grosgrain ribbon. That should do it."

—*Elle Woods, in* Legally Blonde 2

SEASON'S CHEATINGS Making Holiday Decorating Easier

Chicks love to celebrate, but nothing takes the fizz out of a good time like a long list of chores and a heap of have-to's. Try some of these chick-tested ideas to simplify your decor for holidays, special occasions, and celebrations year-round.

1. Organize your decorations by holidays (Halloween, Thanksgiving, etc), or at least keep them all together in one big plastic bin for easy access and cleanup.

Everyone looked forward to December, when Millicent unpacked her balls and baubles.

2. Less is more. Eschew extravagant, labor-intensive decorating and opt for a more spare approach with small touches like fresh greenery, pillar candles, and a few special decorations displayed in prominent areas.

3. Give your decorations a longer shelf life by starting in the autumn with arrangements made of leaves, twigs, gourds, and pumpkins and making minor tweaks and additions at Halloween, Thanksgiving, and on through the December holidays.

4. Choose a color scheme or decorating theme that will take you through the holidays and into the New Year—a palette of all white or a color that's already part of your decor. You'll be able to decorate sooner and enjoy it for longer without feeling rushed to clear it out after the big day.

5. To add glow and sparkle throughout your home, use tea lights, in simple clear glass votive holders. Cluster them on mantels, on a table, or use them to line a walkway or add twinkle to a staircase. When you change the color and type of candles, you change the look.

6. Forgo expensive wrapping paper: Use painter's masking paper, purchased in rolls at the home-improvement or hardware store. Typically you can find it in craft brown, sage green, or rose colors. Dress it up with raffia, twine, pinecones, or berries for a natural touch, or add elegant ribbons and ornaments. Embellish it with craft paint and rubber stamps, metallic pens and flowing script, or kid-friendly stickers. Have fun, and go wild—it's your blank canvas!

7. Enlist help. Invite friends over to bake treats and trim the tree.

8. Go natural. Twigs and branches are essential to a well-decked nest. You can twine some white lights amid twisted willow branches along a mantel or in a tall vase. Use flowering bulbs and seasonal plants to give your home a cozy holiday touch. Create pretty displays with bowls of apples, pears, oranges, and lemons interspersed with greenery.

9. Dress up chandeliers with a swag of greenery, ribbons, or dangling ornaments.

10. Go for the gold, or the silver. Create an easy and elegant mantel or centerpiece by spray-painting pinecones, apples, pineapples, walnuts, twigs, or magnolia leaves with metallic spray paint. Or use metallic craft paints and dip the tips of items, or sponge on thin layers for a subtle gilded touch. Coat twigs with spray adhesive and dust them with glitter for a magical effect. Group your gilded treasures in bowls, or arrange them with candles and votives for a luxurious holiday touch that looks like a million bucks.

11. Use your memories as decorations. Pull out pictures from holidays past and use a photocopier or picture enhancement machine to blow them up. Frame and display them prominently on tables, mantels, or shelves to get you in the spirit.

12. Act like a kid. String popcorn or cranberries, cut out snowflakes, make a dreidel from a little milk carton, build a snowman, bake and decorate sugar-cookie ornaments —indulge in something that reconnects you to the innocent wonder of the season.

DecOrat*ing* fRenZy

I'M DYING TO TURN SOMETHING ON ITS SIDE. Or upside down. And I can't stop thinking about the possibility of distressing something—anything! Sitting in my home office, I look up from my laptop when I ought to be writing, and my eyes light on an innocent wooden crate—a crate that has been waiting all its life to play a bigger role as my bedside table.

And those bookshelves. They look so tired—so sick of standing upright, so bored with holding books. Wouldn't they be thrilled at the chance to take a load off, to lie down under my bed, to try their hand at storing my extra bedding, a bag of sex toys, some Kama Sutra oil, an earthquake kit?

I've been prowling around my house lately, hunting for the end table that is longing to become a kitchen cabinet, the basket that is dreaming of reincarnation as a colander. In my relentless search, I leave no nook or cranny unturned.

It's an obsession that is fast becoming an embarrassment. It messes up my carefully wrought M.O. The me I purport to be is a latte-sipping, literary sophisticate—a hip, intellectual gal who prefers *The New Yorker* to *House & Garden*, *Harper's* to *House Beautiful*. I am (aren't I?) the epitome of the untamed, undomesticated feminist who spends her time running a home business, not running to Home Depot. I have a master's degree in poetry, not potpourri!

But never mind that. Let me tell you, I was thrilled out of my mind when I transformed the piano bench into a coffee table. "Why, that's simply BRILLIANT!" they would say on my favorite BBC television show, *Changing Rooms*. I watch this show religiously (channel 162), along with its knock-off American version, *Trading Spaces* (channel 50). Small bubbles of foam appear at the corners of my mouth as the designing crew commences with the painting and hammering. And speaking of foam—the other kind—what a wonderful invention! Sort of the decorator's Miracle Bra. You can stuff it into so many flat, needy places—it plumps things up and fills them out in an instant. Last week I cut a piece of foam into the shape of my bay window seat to

"Serious is a word you want to *completely avoid* when it comes to decorating."

—*Kathryn Ireland*

make a cozy sitting nook. Covered it with a $6.99 cotton shower curtain from McFrugal's, and voilà! To tell you the truth, I think I'd rather spend an evening with a slab of foam than go to the theater.

I'm mesmerized by the potential to make everything over. I have Big Plans. I'm going to hang my rugs from the ceilings, turn my rarely worn high heels into bookends, my bookends into doorstops, and my doorstops into mobiles for the baby's nursery. My baby is long gone, but that doesn't stop me. Nothing can stop me!

Frequent excursions into the realm of household rejuvenation have become my most sacred form of meditation. Strip, sand, polish! Paint, glaze, sponge! Staple, tack, glue! Uncover, re-cover, slipcover! These are my mantras. I feel certain that if I focus all my excess energy on the fine art of redecoration, I will attain enlightenment. One of these days I'll drape a mosquito net over my bed to make a canopy, and my third eye will awaken. Or I'll unearth an antique wicker ottoman from somebody's basement,

and my crown chakra will explode, right through the top of my head, transforming me into a torchère for the den.

The other day I dressed up the television in an old kimono and actually got dizzy from the satisfaction. Last night I turned a ladder on its side and lugged it toward the bathtub, my armpits sweaty with excitement. Behind me, my couch was emitting pheromones. I vowed to hurry back to the couch later, just as soon as I was done with the ladder. When the overhead light fixture in my bathroom broke, I stuffed an old basket with Christmas lights, hung it over the broken fixture, plugged in my creation, and almost had an orgasm.

I know I'm buying into the ridiculously rampant redecorating trends of the day, but I don't care. I've been renewed by the promise of stenciled flower borders, enthralled by the allure of my trusty glue gun, and seduced by the call of the wild armoire. Ah, the ever versatile armoire! Someday my television is going to outgrow its kimono—and when it does, I will be ready.

—*Jane Underwood*

DECOUPAGE (from the French word *découper,* to cut out) is one of our favorite chick crafts. It's easy, it's cheap, and it enables a crafty gal to transform just about anything from mundane to marvelous. Terracotta pots, garage-sale furniture, cigar boxes, lamp shades, wooden crates, plates, serving trays, picture frames, art canvases, cylinder vases—all are great foundations for decoupage projects. Victorian chicks elevated it to an art form with the intricate patterns, painterly effects, and sweet collages they devised. That's a lovely sensibility, but if your taste ranges more toward the mod, don't let decoupage's sweet reputation deter you. Invent a contemporary design or pattern that expresses your style and get gluing. Below is an easy craft that adds a puff of personality to any powder room or boudoir. (Note: The basic decoupage steps apply to any project.)

I Wanna Tissue All Over

(Decoupaged Tissue Box Holder)

Before you begin, cover your work area with newspaper or a plastic tablecloth.

You'll need:

Wooden or cardboard tissue box cover from a craft supply store, or an old one you want to restyle

Acrylic craft paint (Choose a color for the background of your decoupage collage; depending on your design, you'll see a little or a lot of it.)

Modge Podge craft glue

1-inch-wide paintbrush

Artwork (color photocopies, magazine clippings, decorative paper napkins, color photocopies of fabric, words clipped from magazines or printed yourself)

Scissors

Newspaper or vinyl tablecloth to protect your work surface

Paint the box and let it dry thoroughly. Begin your collage by cutting out your images and loosely planning your design. Dip the brush in glue, coat the back of the artwork, and place it on the box. Brush over it again with more glue, using strokes that begin in the center of the art and brush toward the edges. Keep doing this until your design is in place and the box is covered. Let it dry. Then apply a generous topcoat of glue to seal it.

The secret to successful decoupage is the number of coats you have the patience for applying. (The more coats, the smoother the surface.) The glue dries quickly—in about thirty minutes—so we typically leave the project out and apply at least four to six coats over the course of a day or two.

You can further embellish your work by lightly sanding it, adding a crackle glaze and aging it with varnish, or gluing on buttons or fabric trims. One of our favorite tissue box designs is to paint the box hot pink and decoupage the message "Bless you!" that has been typed or written in calligraphy on a white piece of paper with torn edges.

You can decoupage almost any flat surface. If you are working on a porous object—such as a terracotta pot—start with a coat of exterior polyurethane to seal it before gluing on your design, and finish up with two more coats. Protect furniture from scratches by sealing it with two coats of interior polyurethane as a final step.

A little birdie told us . . . Love that ultra-coordinated look but hate the high price? Take a piece of fabric, color-photocopy a detail from it, cut it out, and decoupage it onto lamp shades, serving trays, storage boxes, wastebaskets—you name it.

Nesty Little Secret

Everyone poaches—it's a great way to borrow ideas, solve design problems, and glean inspiration—but you should poach graciously and creatively. If you're pilfering an idea from a friend, ask first. Try a sweet, "I love the color in your dining room so much that I'd like to try it in my foyer. Would you mind sharing the mix?" Or take an idea and make it uniquely yours by altering it in some small way. And the cardinal rule of poaching: Always give credit where credit is due!

"No amount of training or schooling can teach you this. *Either you have flair or you haven't.*"

—*Rose Cumming on the "artistic alchemy" that makes a house a home*

CURTAINS FOR YOU

Flounces, jabots, pinch pleats, bishop's sleeves, valances—we shutter to think of the many costly, intricate options for dressing a window. Call us curtain rebels, but we are just plain tired of the compulsion to swag, gather, and drape fabric around all our windows in the conventional manner. After years of outfitting them in costly, predictable fashion, we've decided we'd rather dress ourselves.

SOMETIMES THE CURTAIN HAS TO COME DOWN. If you have nice casings, detailed moldings, or beautiful architectural details, consider going curtainless. Play up pretty windows with contrasting wall colors or paint the moldings in an accent color. Install a simple shade for privacy, and let the sun shine in. One word to the wise—while we are all for recycling those old drapes, the curtain ensemble trick works only for one fair chick, Scarlett O'Hara.

REFRAME IT. To highlight or add interest to a window, try stenciling a design, monogram, or quotation over it. Accent a view and emphasize height by hanging a floral arch or wreath above a window, or swathe it in rustic fashion with dried grapevines or twisted willows. Surround the window with a collection of plates, artwork, tiles, or decorative initials.

BOTTOMS UP. Enhance a window from the floor up by flanking it with two tall arrangements of bamboo, palm trees, lofty topiaries, or small branches.

FROM PRE-FAB TO JUST FAB. An inexpensive pair of store-bought curtain panels can be dressed up in countless ways. To lengthen them or to give them personality, add a coordinating fabric to the bottom. Sew on fringe, roping, ribbon, or other trims for a designer look. A row of mismatched buttons at the bottom, or up the sides is a charming detail. Replace

or embellish tab tops with ribbons or a contrasting fabric. Add sheer pockets and tuck silk flowers or leaves inside for a touch of color and whimsy.

SHEER BRILLIANCE. Romance a pair of store-bought sheer curtains by tacking on silk rose petals or leaves with a needle and thread. Or make them sparkle by adding shiny sequins or beaded embellishments in a scattered arrangement. Buy beaded garlands or ribbons at après-holiday sales to use as tiebacks or, for a luxurious effect, dangle them from the rods on the sides of panels.

DON'T GET HUNG UP ON HANGING THEM UP. Often a simple, easy-to-install rod from the hardware store is all you need. If you want a different color or finish, look to the spray-paint section and customize the color. For a unique look, consider hanging your curtains on cables (kits can be found at hardware stores), or use decorative drawer pulls to suspend them.

CONSIDER THE VIEW FROM THE STREET. That red and green stripe might look great in the room, but from the street it may look like a pizza parlor. Lining all your curtains with inexpensive fabric is a good way to keep the look consistent from the outside of your home.

NOT JUST FOR WINDOWS. Use curtains to create a nook for curling up in—in a bay window or between rooms for drama and cozy effect. Or use them to conceal a messy bookshelf or cabinet.

A little birdie told us . . . To make a small window look larger, hang your panels just beyond the window edges. Hang valances high, so that the bottom only covers an inch or so of the actual window.

"Although I look like a drag queen's Christmas tree on the outside, *I am at heart a simple country woman.*" —*Dolly Parton*

bam-BOo-Hoo

IT HAD BEEN ONE OF THOSE PROVERBIAL DAYS. You name it, I'd had it—spilled milk, a load of dark wash mysteriously spotted with bleach, garbage pilfered by the dog, a black cat crossing my path, and my two-year-old opening an umbrella in the house. I was anxiously waiting for a mirror to break, and looking for a ladder to walk under just to round things out. After a two-hour read-a-thon I'd finally gotten my little one down for a nap, and decided to seize the moment and clean my neglected bathroom.

This is not as bad a job as it sounds. I love my bathroom. It's spacious, with windows opening to a view of a beautiful Japanese maple with delicate green leaves. It has marble floors, thanks to the ostentatious taste of the previous owners, and white tile that's impossible to keep clean but gives me brief delusions of spa-like serenity. I have a row of huge starfish hanging above the shower and my beachcombing collection of shells and stones displayed in an apothe-

cary jar; a pair of vintage seashell etchings round out my beach house fantasy. Best of all, there are no plastic tub toys. In a nutshell, it's the last stronghold of adult life that my husband and I cling to in our very kid-friendly house.

My most beloved fixture in the bathroom is a vase of tall, twisted lucky bamboo anchored in a base of sea glass and polished stones. I know this probably sounds incredibly dated—lucky bamboo is so "over" with fashionistas—but long after all my hip friends had tossed their bamboo or neglected it to death, mine was tall, leafy, and the same lovely shade of jade as the Japanese maple outside my window. Just looking at it made me feel lucky.

I was taking my usual few minutes to dust the leaves when I saw it—a lighter green spot on the trunk that looked a little shriveled. I simply couldn't deal with one more sign of bad luck, so I responded appropriately—I denied it. After a distracting and vigorous scrub-down of the shower, and near chemical asphyxiation, I inspected the bamboo again: This time I saw two leaves clearly tipped with brown. This must be the source of my unlucky day.

By the next day, the two brown leaves were yellow all the way to the trunk. Not good. In the meantime, I had overdrawn my checking account, forgotten a dentist's appointment, and dinged my car door. Clearly, something had to be done. Desperate to restore my chi, protect my karma, and stave off certain ruin, I consulted a book on feng shui.

It turns out that caring for lucky bamboo imported from Taiwan does not get a lot of airtime in tomes dedicated to the ancient art of seeking harmony and balance in your environment. A turn to the Internet yielded similar results.

"I'd rather *shop* than eat." —*Wallis Simpson*

By the time the bamboo had drooped over on itself and begun to look fuzzy around the roots, I accepted defeat. Now I'm definitely a "survival of the fittest" kind of chick, and any other languishing plant in my home would have gotten a guilt-free heave-ho, but this was no ordinary plant. I presumed some protocol must exist for laying a lucky bamboo to rest, so I drove to the nearest nursery for some advice. The woman behind the counter smirked in disbelief as I posed my question, about how to dispose of a dead plant. When I said "lucky bamboo," however, her smirk gave way to wide-eyed concern. She warned that I could not, "under any circumstances," bury or let the plant touch the ground. She proceeded to educate me on the invasive nature of some bamboo varieties, painting a cataclysmic picture of my entire town, the whole county, possibly even the state becoming a massive bamboo forest growing at astronomical rates, choking out all native crops, plants, and trees.

I thanked her for her time and quickly left. But as I drove home, I began to question the credibility of my Nostradamus of the nursery. If what she said was true about lucky bamboo, where was the warning? Wouldn't my bamboo have come with a label like you see on rat poison, Tilex, or hydrochloric acid? Wasn't she being a tad bit overdramatic?

But something about her condescending smile kept nagging at me. I knew I had let the superstitious side get the better of me, but to have another person openly witness and then sneer at my gullibility was downright embarrassing. Like all people, I simply want good fortune and harmony in my life and that lucky bamboo had seemed like such a good idea—until it died. Look, I'm not certifiable—I know those green curly stalks hold no particular power. Or do they? They sure had me investing my time and energy into resurrecting them.

It made me think about why I get so caught up in the gadgets and *gizmos du jour* that get hocked to me. I guess it's part superstition and part indulgence. But mostly it is that these things remind me of something that I either want more of in my life, or that I already have and fear losing. I rationalize that the trendy tchotchkes are tangible symbols that help me focus my energies, manifest my wishes, and count my blessings. That and, oh yeah, one more thing—I'm a compulsive nester, and I love to shop.

As for the ultimate fate of the lucky bamboo, I unceremoniously laid it to rest in the trash can—not in the green waste bin, where I feared it might stage a hostile takeover. And then and there, in the alley, I decided that it was the *bamboo* that was unlucky, not me.

—*Ame Mahler Beanland*

WABI SABI The Art of Imperfection

Next time a visitor catches you in the midst of a home-improvement fiasco—or just a less than pristine house—greet him or her with a sweeping, "Come on in, and don't mind the mess. We are avid disciples of *wabi sabi,* so it's all good," and offer them some tea. While they are scratching their heads, or before they suddenly excuse themselves for another appointment, you can confess that your messy house far from exemplifies *wabi sabi,* then enlighten them on the hottest Eastern design principle to sweep the West since *feng shui.*

IF FENG SHUI WERE A CHICK, she'd be Grace Kelly—elegant, self-possessed, and always classically put together. The *wabi sabi* poster girl would be Drew Barrymore—beautiful yet unpredictable, poised yet charmingly flawed. Whereas *feng shui,* the ancient Taoist art of harmonious arrangement, upholds the laws of balance and careful order, the Japanese aesthetic of *wabi sabi,* a centuries-old practice founded by Zen monks and based on the tea ceremony, is all about the beauty of imperfection and irregularity.

WABI MEANS AUSTERITY OF DESIGN without severity, and *sabi* refers to an object's patina, or broken-in quality. *Wabi sabi* is a philosophy that values things that have borne the test of time—and the marks, dings, wrinkles, and scratches that come with it. It's like comparing a perfectly cut, flawless diamond to a sand-worn piece of beach glass and trying to argue which one is prettier. Conventional wisdom would go for the diamond, but proponents of *wabi sabi* would say that the beach glass, in all its natural glory, is a far more impressive object, for true beauty resides in the

When the Joneses first moved in it was French country, then neo-gothic, followed by Danish modern, and now shabby chic—at this rate Marilyn was never going to be able to keep up.

unique marks left by experience and use, rather than in the unmarred or pristine. *Wabi sabi* reveres natural objects and respects materials for their irregularities, simplicity, and lack of pretension. But this feel-good philosophy goes beyond a decor aesthetic. The real power of *wabi sabi* is tapped when you extend its forgiving concepts to your life, your relationships, and your self.

INCORPORATE A LITTLE *WABI SABI* INTO YOUR HOME by cutting clutter. Decorate with objects that are multifunctional—items that are meaningful, useful, and attractive. For example, play up the beauty of worn wood floors by cleaning and oiling them instead of refinishing them to cold perfection; decorate with simple bowls, artful lamps, and candles; or display family photos and heirlooms with altar-style simplicity and reverence. Bring touches of nature into your home with natural fabrics, wooden or stone accents, and organic, muted colors.

If you are hankering for a bigger dose of *wabi sabi,* try wading through *Wabi Sabi: The Japanese Art of Impermanence,* by Andrew Juniper. Be inspired by *Wabi Sabi Style,* by James and Sandra Crawley.

A little birdie told us . . . Instead of using a headboard, hang a distressed old door, a wrought-iron gate, a folding screen, or a set of shutters behind a bed.

Wabi Sabi in a Teacup

TRUE BEAUTY IS FOUND IN THINGS THAT ARE:

Imperfect • Impermanent • Incomplete • Modest • Humble • Unconventional

NEST NEGOTIATIONS Decorating Together

What do you do when you crave a velvet chaise and he loves the leather recliner? Or he insists his subwoofers make a stunning focal point for the living room? Or you say "silk," and he says "corduroy." Short of moving out, there's only one thing to do—find a way to compromise. This is what nesting is all about—weaving the stuff of your lives together to create a home that delights you both. Before you start packing your bags (or his), try some of these approaches to striking a style accord.

IT'S BETTER TO HAVE DECORATED AND LOST THAN TO HAVE NEVER DECORATED AT ALL. When faced with clashing design sensibilities, people often give up on decorating altogether. Decor standoffs usually have ugly endings—a bland, uninspired room or a mess of random furnishings and mismatched styles. If you are in a style stalemate, make the first move: Start a conversation about creating an environment that's more pleasing to you both. Plan an outing to a home furnishings store where you can each point out things you like, look for common ground, and get ideas. Flip through some design magazines or books together at a coffee shop. Taking the initial conversation out of your shared space will keep it from becoming personal. Sitting in the house, picking on each other's things, and attacking each other's style is not a productive way to get the creative juices flowing.

RETIRE FROM THE DESIGN POLICE. In almost every couple there is one person who's more concerned with decorating than the other one and is also, shall we say, a little less than diplomatic in the delivery of his or her comments. If you are the offender (and the fact that you are reading this book sort of blows your cover), make a greater effort to listen to the other person's point of view. Decorating is a creative expression, and nothing stifles creativity like fear. Your partner might be holding back some fabulous ideas because he fears your criticism. You may be so infatuated with one style that you've become afraid to try anything new. There is no right or wrong way to decorate—just different approaches based on individual preferences. So check your predisposed notions at the door, turn your badge in, and welcome the perspective of another person.

BIRDS OF A FEATHER FLOCK TOGETHER. You've wound up in the same nest together because you were obviously drawn to each another. If you are butting heads over a decorating decision—a new sofa, for example—give the debate a break and take a trip down memory lane. Reminisce about how you met, a vacation you've taken together, a special celebration you've shared. Connect on a deeper level, then take up that sofa debate again. Spending a little time remembering why you are together in the first place can soften you both up to the idea of compromise.

EMBRACE ECLECTIC. If you love sleek, contemporary design and pop art, yet your housemate is wedded to English antiques and primitive pottery, there is an answer—eclectic. Eclectic decor is the blending of myriad styles for a look that is vibrant, surprising, and easy to live with. Envision a room with a sleek leather sofa flanked by antique end tables, a simple mantel displaying rustic pottery pieces with a colorful painting hanging above it. Because eclectic design allows for a little of this and a little of that, it is very forgiving and fun-spirited. Remember, if the two of you can live in harmony, so can your stuff. Check out these books for eclectic-style inspiration: *Eclectic Style in Interior Design,* by Carol Meredith; *Breaking the Rules: Home Style for the Way We Live Today,* by Christy Ferer; and *Bohemian Style,* by Elizabeth Wilhide.

EVERYONE NEEDS A LITTLE CARTE BLANCHE. Each of you should have a space in your home that's yours alone. Negotiate an area, a corner, a bookshelf, or a room that is yours to decorate as you please. Another way to give yourselves equal opportunity at decor is to take turns displaying your creative flair in the more prominent places—like the fireplace mantel or the coffee table.

SPEND SOME TIME TOGETHER ON THE OLD COUCH INSTEAD OF FIGHTING OVER THE NEW ONE. Sometimes a design deadlock is just a smoke screen for some underlying issue. Perhaps your partner is being stubborn about painting the room because he doesn't like change and he just needs a little reassuring that you're not going to go overboard. Or you're attached to that antique coffee table because it belonged to your dear Aunt Edna. Call it Freudian Furnishing, but objects hold powerful symbolism to people, and sometimes it takes a bit of gentle prodding to understand what's really going on. So before you throw up your hands in resignation, talk it through and see if you can get to the bottom of your design dilemmas together.

"It's like magic, when you live by yourself, all your annoying habits are gone." —*Merrill Markoe*

The Chick's Eye Versus the Cock's Eye
A Bird's-eye View of Domestic Life

TO THE CHICK'S EYE	TO THE COCK'S EYE
taupe	brown
hydrangea	a flower
a pile of recycling material	prized collector's editions of *Sports Illustrated*
sateen 500-thread-count sheets	a great place to get lucky
dormant azalea bushes	weeds
space-hogging eyesore destined for donation	favorite recliner
lavender sprig, perfect for tucking atop a gift	garbage
a parrot tulip	a flower
eyesore of tangled wires	proof he's got a big set
fabulous handmade decorative pillows	useless objects that hide the remote control
a Casablanca lily	another flower
vintage lace tablecloth from Grandma	fussy old rag
a hand-painted porcelain umbrella stand	a garbage can
a cardboard box	a perfectly functional footrest
an antique cachepot	an old flower pot

"*Marrying a man* is like buying something you've been admiring for a long time in a shop window. You may love it when you get it home, but it doesn't always go with everything else in the house."

—*Jean Kerr*

NOt reAdy *for* priMe Time

MY HUSBAND, MARK, AND I LOVE TO WATCH those home-improvement TV shows where a man and a woman remodel a house together. They help each other out, exchange witty repartee, and, at the end, survey their handiwork. How sweet. Of course, it's a total crock.

That's because the couples that host these shows aren't actually married. And that piece of paper makes a big difference; it means that you work on the house together not because you get paid to, but because, in a moment of weakness years ago, you vowed that you would tolerate each other day in and day out forever, even during home renovations. At the time of our wedding, I imagined that we'd one day have a sink in our bathroom. And Mark imagined I'd be of some practical help when we finally got around to fixing up the house. Ah, innocent love.

If Mark and I had our own home-improvement show, viewers could see that in real life, disagreements are to be expected, and that little spats—some resulting in stony silences lasting up to three months—are a natural part of the renovation process. I've developed an outline for our show. In episode 1, we don't do any work per se. Instead, I spend the entire half-hour persuading Mark that he'd have more fun in the hallway hanging Sheetrock than in the woods stalking the elusive white-tailed deer.

By episode 5, work has commenced and Mark has framed in much of our master bedroom. However, due to an incident in which he rejects my idea for built-in drawers but later welcomes the same suggestion from his brother, much of our repartee must be bleeped out.

By the final episode, in which I accidentally drop Mark's brand-new tape measure into a gallon of enamel paint, the show opens with the disclaimer "This program contains scenes that may be disturbing to younger viewers. Discretion is advised."

Theoretically, we make a great redecorating team: Mark has years of carpentry experience and lots of tools, and I have stacks of decorating magazines. But because he has some freakish aversion to working at home after he's already put in a full week somewhere else, he lacks the drive to turn my interior design visions into reality.

When he does take on a project, he gives no warning. At 7:00 A.M. on a Saturday, he'll march into the bathroom while I am showering and say something like, "I'm framing in that stupid closet you wanted in the guest room. How big do you want it?" He sounds cranky because, being a man, he ranks closets low on his list of design needs, somewhere between gold faucets and hand-painted ceiling frescoes.

I don't remember having asked for anything particular in the guest room, but I know better than to pass up the offer of a closet. With no idea of how dimensions translate into actual space, I wing it. "Three feet by five feet?" (Eight by twelve? Does he want it in metric? I need a cup of coffee.)   ▶

"but it can't change a lightbulb." —*Gilda Radner*

"Five feet?" he says. "Are you crazy? You don't know what you're talking about."

That part is true. As far as construction goes, about the only things I'm good for are fetching tools and sweeping up sawdust. Even then, I don't know the names of the tools. Occasionally, Mark will send me out to his trailer for something like a three-eighths-inch Morton's shank cotter grappling wrench "in the red toolbox." He fails to mention that he owns seven red toolboxes, all of them filled with hundreds of unfamiliar implements. Since I only know from "hammer" and "screwdriver," I have to guess what he is talking about.

I bring back the closest thing I can find that is definitely neither a hammer nor a screwdriver, and hand it to him with what I hope comes across as casual confidence.

"What? I said three-eighths-inch! This is a five-sixteenths!"

As I try to decide whether I should go back to the tool trailer and find the right tool, or twist off Mark's nose with the wrong-size wrench, I can't help wishing we were on TV. At least then we could cut to a commercial.

—*Jessie Raymond*

A little birdie told us . . . Revamp your kitchen and bathroom cabinets by simply changing the hardware. For a retro feel, try glass knobs; go modern with sleek chrome; pewter is classic; brass adds a rich sparkle to the room.

In *My* Dreams

I HAVE A CONFESSION TO MAKE. Deep inside my "mommy-self" there is a place that wants—really, really wants—my house to look like one of those homes you see in the design magazines. You know what I mean—impeccably appointed furniture that matches; delicious colored sheets that don't have crumbs on them; rugs free from cat hair, food particulate matter, and other unmentionable stuff—basically no *things* to clutter up the overall composition.

My mantel would feature one candle, a wooden sailboat, and a slender vase of enigmatic blooms—cherry blossoms, I think, would be nice. There would be no Tinkertoy robots, no wooden widgets, and no baked-dough creations obscuring the elegant simplicity of my fireplace still life.

Everything would be milky white, delft blue, and gently faded red—well-worn but casually elegant colors that provide a striking yet soothing balance. There would be no tiny green plastic chairs leaning against the hearth. No Little Tykes art desks in bold blue, red, and uncompromising yellow shoved against the wall, behind the couch, or next to where the computer sits. And there would be no computer.

The hardwood floors would be lustrous, thick old planks—and when the sunshine fell upon their magnificent buttery expanses, no silhouettes of crust, size one shoes, or dribbling tippy-cups would break the swath of gentle light. Furthermore, the ornamentation—consisting of a few very fragile, very tasteful objects—would not be relegated to the top shelf of the bookcase, away from the probing of curious little hands.

Our parlor would have matching tables flanking a pale cream sofa—each with one knickknack of interesting and expensive persuasion, perfectly positioned. Perhaps there would also be a photograph, elegant black and white, framed in silver; it would *not* depict anyone with food on her face holding a birthday candle in the shape of the number one.

I would wander barefoot from room to room in my house—my feet thrilling to the various sensations of wood, wool rug, and the thick and thirsty bath mats that would be neatly placed in front of the clean, white claw-foot tub. The bath mats would match perfectly, or blend fetchingly, with the ballet-slipper-white bathroom—including the towels, the face cloth, the tumbler, and the crisp curtains hanging in the ▶

> *"Everyone* can keep house better than her mother *till she trieth."*
>
> —*French proverb*

> "At the worst, a house unkept cannot be so distressing as a life unlived."
>
> —Rose Macaulay

clean window, and the matching shower curtain. A pristine, rectangular bar of honey soap would perch sinkside, and it would never even cross my mind to scrutinize my toothbrush before using it as I lifted it from its color-coordinated holder.

My bedroom would have a quilt: a big, folk-art Americana flag quilt, a real handmade one, with crimson stripes, morning-glory blue bands of off-kilter stars, and linen-white lines. It would be soft and muted and would accent my heavy four-poster bed beautifully. My bed would sit in the center of the room on a floor painted milky white, brushed with a coat of pale blue wash. The plaster walls would be encrusted top and bottom with heavy white mold-

ings. And when I awoke from my nine hours of uninterrupted rest, I would not have to avoid crushing a sleeping two-year-old who had clambered from his toddler bed to wedge himself into the minuscule space between my husband, the four-year-old (who had climbed in with us at 3:00 A.M.), and me.

When people come to my house they would not say, "So, you have three kids?" Nor would they say, "How interesting," or "What an efficient use of available space." One day—*one day*—I'd like somebody to come into my home, look around for a breathless moment, fix me with an admiring gaze, and say: "Juleigh, your home is simply lovely."

—*Juleigh Howard-Hobson*

CHICKS IN THE NEST DECORATING FAMILY STYLE

Nothing strikes panic into the heart of a decorating diva like the arrival of a little brood of chicks and the ensuing bushels of plastic that seem to ooze from every container. Little plastic, big plastic, munchkin-size plastic furniture and playground equipment—there's no end to the size and variety of the kiddie accoutrements. And the primary colors they insist on coming in clash horribly with every tasteful color scheme known to woman. Just how *do* you incorporate the Easy Bake oven into your French country living room? If we could answer that question, we'd be filthy rich, but alas, we can't help you there. The bottom line is, when you have kids, it's impossible to hide that fact from other people when they enter your home. That said, we think it is possible to compromise. You need not live in an elfin explosion of Technicolor plastic toys and stuffed animals if you practice some smart toy containment techniques, or, as we like to call it, "how to hide future landfill."

THE BEST THING ABOUT TOYS IS THEIR DURABILITY. Thankfully, toys don't have to be carefully wrapped to put them away. You can just toss, throw, even hurl them into the appropriate containers and slam down the lids. And since you will find yourself doing this with mind-numbing frequency, it's nice not to have to dwell on the details. Outside of random electronic utterances from toys that refuse to go quietly (these talking, chirping, beeping, singing monstrosities should be banned from the planet), you won't hear from them again until—maybe 5:00 A.M. on Saturday?

DISGUISE TOY BOXES AS OTTOMANS, COFFEE TABLES, OR CHESTS. They can blend into the general decor and function beautifully as toy-hiders. If the hinges aren't kid- or tired-mommy-proof, you can find the slow-closing variety at your hardware store and just replace them. Colorful baskets or cubes, with or without lids, make attractive toy containers as well, and can be stacked or arranged on shelves. Or put an over-the-door shoe rack (the kind with pouches) in your laundry room to tuck stuffed animals and small toys in. Clear a drawer or shelf in a kitchen cabinet for art supplies and coloring books. Create as much storage space as you possibly can, but remember to purge at least twice a year or all your efforts will be in vain.

Baby Chick Decor

These days, the extravagance of some kiddy decor can make even the most enthusiastic mother hen panic and head for the hills. We're all for living it up, but remember, these are kids, and kids need to be able to act like kids. Adult chicks can appreciate a divine hand-hooked rug, but its finer points are lost on a three-year-old who simply wants to play tea party and decorate the dog with strawberry yogurt. So spare yourself the experience of crying over spilled milk and take some cheep-cuts to creating inspired children's spaces that leave lots of room for imagination.

1. Frame illustrations from your kids' favorite books. Purchase an extra copy of the book and use your utility knife and a straight edge to carefully remove the pages you want to frame. Or just scan or photocopy the pages you want to frame onto photographic or other high-quality paper.

2. Frame their own artwork. Nothing is better than having an original created by your child. They'll swell with pride when you treat their creative efforts like bona fide art, complete with mats and frames. It's a great way to decorate on the fly and sneak in a little esteem-boosting as well.

3. Create a mural. Even art school dropouts can manage this with a little hand-holding, a simple stencil kit, or foam stamps. Remember, it's a kid's room, so have fun with it. Paint a wall light blue, add a few strokes in varying shades of green to make "grass" spring up from the baseboard, and pop in a few bugs or butterflies for instant personality. Rent or borrow an overhead projector and use it to project a coloring book page or simple illustration onto the wall where you can trace it. Let the kids in on the act: Create a unique border of their handprints dipped in bright colors. Look for wallpaper transfers from a company called Wallies for everything from fairies to tree frogs to adorn your walls. Check them out online at www.wallies.com.

4. Decorate with their toys. Some kids' toys, plush and even plastic, are downright adorable, and you probably have a few lying around. Put them to work by arranging them on a bookshelf or on dresser tops. Depending on your child's enthusiasms, set up themes (dinosaurs, ballerinas, mice, puppies, etc.). They'll be noticed and played with soon enough, but that's the whole point.

5. Hang up a clothesline for displaying artwork, spelling out their name on construction paper, making paper pennants, or creating holiday artwork displays. (If you have younger kids, be sure to hang it safely out of reach.) Our friend Donna uses a clothesline for "curtains" in her little girls' room. As they outgrow favorite dresses, she adds them to the display.

6. Install a chair rail along the length of one wall and paint the bottom half of the wall with chalkboard paint. Then put up a ledge to hold erasers and colored chalk and actually let your kids draw on the walls.

7. Decorate the ceiling. Paint it a pretty color and add glow-in-the-dark stars, wispy clouds, or a planet mural. For older kids, drape tulle or netting from hooks for a princess's retreat or a jungle lair; suspend a kite or dangle airplanes, monkeys, or butterflies from sturdy fishing line.

HOME SWEET HOME

Any homebody worth her sniff knows the power of fragrance to sweeten a home. But, lest you fall prey to artificial, made-in-a-science-lab bastardizations of aromatherapy, always opt for naturally derived essential oils. If you must go faux, you can still go for high quality. Cheap out on the potpourri and you'll end up with an aroma that smells more like the backseat of a cab than a lavender field in Provence.

POTPOURRI. Display natural potpourri in dishes or small bowls throughout your home. Blend your own with natural ingredients like lavender buds, dried rose petals, dried citrus peels, cloves, nutmeg, etc. You can find recipes and purchase potpourri ingredients, pre-prepared mixes, and essential oils from the San Francisco Herb Company (www.sfherb.com, or call 800-227-4530). The mass-produced, prescented potpourris are far more heavily perfumed, so use them with restraint. Some good brands include Crabtree and Evelyn, Slatkin & Co., Claire Burke, Smith and Hawken, and Aromatique.

SCENTED DRAWER LINERS. These are musts for every chick's lingerie drawer, but don't limit them to the bedroom. Use them in unexpected places, like the sideboard in your dining room, the laundry room, or wherever you store table linens. Bundle potpourri or fresh herbs into hankies and tie with ribbon to make drawer sachets.

CANDLES. As with potpourri, scented candles run the gamut from the nauseating to the enchanting. Remember that whatever a candle smells like unlit will only intensify when it's burning, so don't overlook delicately fragranced candles. For a unique aromatherapy blend, light several complementary essential oil-scented candles at once; for example, lavender, rosemary, and lemon verbena. Some of our favorite scented-candle makers include Archipelago Botanicals, Illume, Illuminations, Trapp, Votivo, Kiss My Face, and Aveda.

CLEANER CLEANING PRODUCTS. Whether all you do is use lemon or orange oil to dust your furniture or you indulge in the plethora of aromatherapy cleaning products on the market, this is an excellent way to breathe some fresh air into household chores. Companies like Caldrea (www.caldrea.com),

"Smell is a potent wizard *that transports us* across thousands of miles and all the years we have lived." —*Helen Keller*

Mrs. Meyers (www.mrsmeyers.com), The Good Home Company (www.goodhomeco.com), and Williams Sonoma (www.williams-sonoma.com) all offer good herb-scented cleaning products.

SOAPS AND LOTIONS. Keep a freshly scented liquid hand soap and lotion sinkside for an après-chore pick-me-up. We are big fans of the Common Sense Farm liquid soaps that come in orange, mint, lavender, and almond (www.commonsensefarm.com). Pair one of these with a tube of Crabtree and Evelyn's Gardener's Hand Therapy and you've got the ultimate hand-washing experience. A dish of triple-milled French soaps in delicious scents like honey, *herbes de Provence,* and muguet (lilies of the valley) will sweeten a small bathroom with their very presence.

FRESH FLOWERS AND HERBS. Line the path to your home with fragrant flowers like star jasmine, lavender, or *Rosa rugosa.* Place sweet-smelling flowers like rubrum lilies, tuberoses, or lilac in your entryway or stair landings. Incorporate herbs into your landscaping: Grow woolly thyme between your stepping stones for a fresh scent every time you walk out the door. Plant basil, sage, lemon verbena, rosemary, scented geraniums, and lemon balm in your window boxes and containers. Or bring a fresh scent inside by growing a pot of mint on your windowsill.

SCENTED VACUUM POTPOURRI BEADS. Drop these into your vacuum cleaner bag for a cleaning experience that doesn't suck. The Good Home Company's (www.goodhomeco.com) lavender scent is our favorite.

A little birdie told us . . . Give guests (and yourself) fresh, "line-dried" sheets without the extra work by spritzing them with lavender-scented linen water and tumbling them in the dryer for a few minutes before you make the bed.

dreAm HOuse

At
a certain
age, about this
one, you stop saying •
Driving through neighborhoods of
Victorian homes • With bay windows,
turrets, wraparound porches, • "There's my
dream house." Because at this stage • your
dream house damn well better have been this
one • in which you gave birth to three of
your children, • watched them and the
cracks in walls grow, • this house with trees
whose branches meet and mingle • (like
fingers of lovers) over the street, this street
where you • watched old neighbors grow
older and die, • watched new ones move in
and have children • younger than your own,
this house to which • they will expect to
return once a summer and • for Christmas
until you are no longer standing, or it is. •
And if it hasn't been your dream house, •
You may as well keep quiet about it • because
it has been the house • where new dreams
were dreamed, • and nobody's asking you
anyway. 🍂

—*Maureen Tolman Flannery*

MOV*ing* DAy

BOSTON—IT IS MOVING DAY. In honor of the occasion the temperature has risen to 90 degrees. Fine weather for moving, a good purging number.

By four o'clock, I am standing in the middle of what was once my living room. The room is empty of living now. I am alone except for the fine vintage dirt that was hidden behind an old Victorian chest for nine years.

I am too tired for more nostalgia. That too has been purged by the heat. Still, there is something stunning about the speed with which three men can suck all the living out of rooms and into a truck.

There ought to be a ceremony for moving day. There ought to be some ritual more formal than the one that faces me now: a mover holding an old Playskool giraffe, relic of a child's childhood, and asking, "Is this going too?"

The list that I'll sign in a moment itemizes in exquisite detail every Thing that was collected for this space. One by one, Things were placed here. Walls, floors, cupboards were filled. Now, the structure is all that remains, as if left behind by a hungry vacuum cleaner.

Soon we will be filling rooms a mile away. They were emptied by a woman shedding fifty years of habit and habitation for an apartment. Our old house in turn will accept new belongings, new belongers. So will the old house of the people who are buying ours. There is a chain of homes being emptied and filled along this lineage.

The week before, on the other side of the country, in San Francisco, my great-aunt Polly died. She had a passion for collecting, this tiny woman who kept track of all of us. The things that she had gathered around her over nearly nine decades are also being packed: china that was carefully selected, furniture chosen deliberately, jewelry with its own history, expressions of her own taste. These Things will be divided.

I have today a sense of some universal pulsation. Homes emptied and filled, Things collected and divided. Each little universe, expanding and contracting and expanding. My great-aunt was the curator of her collection and her clan. Without a center, people cannot hold forever. Universal laws apply to families, too. Some will inevitably be drawn to other galaxies. Which will in turn expand.

Once, at an antiques show, I bought a nineteenth-century photo album that still had family pictures in it. Someone had carefully pasted in all the photographs of people who were important to her or him. What had happened to that family? Were there no heirs, no one interested in these photographs?

I emptied that small house of its people and replaced it with my own. This album, too, is in transit today, between homes.

There's something like this in the way we live our lives. My great-aunt accumulated platters of Meissen china, but also memories. We all do that. Our lives are museums of private experiences. Some we give a prominent place in our display cases, some we put away in crates, some we try to forget.

But we each have catalogs full of events, impressions, ideas. We acquire them over time, becoming more complex, elaborated, crowded.

We distribute some of these things before we die. We disseminate an idea, contribute a gesture, an attitude, a memory. We also leave behind empty space.

The room that I am standing in, the room which once was a living room, echoes today. It seems smaller, not larger, in our absence, already contracting.

Tomorrow, between owners, it will be cleansed. Next week this house will begin again. So will we. Our minds are already expanding the new house. And yet I have the sense of cycles, always cycles.

The mover hands me the itemized list. I sign it. It's hot in this house and beginning to pour outside. Time to leave.

—*Ellen Goodman*

Instant Karma
Making It Your Own

Settling into a new nest can be a bit like wearing a pair of jeans for the first time. Things don't feel quite right. Part of the discomfort is just plain logistics ("Where the heck is the such-and-such or so-and-so?"). But the other part is feeling that, although the stuff in it might be yours, the house still belongs to its former residents.

Time to make it your own. For instant karma, here are six things to do within the first week:

1. Fill a vase with your favorite flowers. If you can't find a vase, or a table to place them on, improvise. They'll brighten your home and make you feel better instantly.

2. Light your favorite scented candles.

3. Invite some close friends over for a box-opening ceremony; ask someone to bring the wine and plastic cups.

4. Set up a radio or boom box to play your favorite tunes (if you can find the CDs).

5. Get rid of the most odious item left by the previous owners—a horrible light fixture, putrid drapes, whatever it might be. Even if it leaves a giant hole in your wall or the neighbors see you in the buff for a week—it's got to go, and now is the time.

6. Put some family photos up on the refrigerator.

CHICK tips ... *for feathering your nest*

We've all met items that "speak to us." If you fall in love—buy it, make it, fake it, or just take it.

Go out on a limb. Don't be afraid to make a mistake; experiment, and try something new. You can do-it-yourself and you can undo-it-yourself.

Sit tight. Live with an empty room. Get to know your space, and spend time with it before you furnish and decorate. With enough time, it will speak to you.

A good house is never done. Keep your house vibrant by changing things when the spirit moves you and allowing your personal style to evolve.

Be touchy-feely. Give each room a touchstone, a soul—some special item, color, or quality that represents something you love and cherish.

Create elements of surprise. It's the unexpected that engages you with a space—a pool table in a dining room, an iron gate as a coffee table, an easy chair upholstered in polka dots.

Don't nest to impress, but to please yourself and your family.

Make every room a living room. Stake out the little-used areas and inhabit them—eat dinner in the dining room without company, read books in the formal living room, have drinks on the front porch.

Don't nest to excess. When in doubt, resist the urge to add; try subtracting instead.

When decorating, always consider both form and function. Good-looking but useless? We've made that mistake before! Don't do it.

part two

"Never fear being *vulgar,* just boring."

—Diana Vreeland

fLOCKing TogetHer

Hen Hospitality and Fabulous Fetes...

the Worst Party *ever*

I'LL NEVER FORGET THE WORST PARTY I EVER GAVE. It was 1969, my husband and I had just gotten married, and we were living in North Carolina. I decided to have a big Sunday brunch, and I wanted it to be fabulous. My first mistake was to invite twenty people I hardly knew. The second mistake was to spend a week getting ready, so I was exhausted before the first guest arrived. Worst of all, I decided to make a fresh omelet for each guest. Was I crazy?

As each person arrived, I had to run to the kitchen to fix a drink. Then everyone sat in a big circle in the living room while I spent what seemed to be hours at the stove making omelets, one at a time. There wasn't a sound from the living room—no talking, no laughter. But how could there be? I was the hostess, but I was in the kitchen! It seemed like the longest day of my life, and I think it took me a year to build up the courage to give another party.

I knew immediately what I'd done wrong. A good party is not about the food, it's about the people. Now I invite friends I really want to see. I make sure the music is fun, to get things going. I plan a menu that is more about assembling food than cooking. And finally, I make sure everything is ready before my friends arrive so I can be a guest, too.

That fancy brunch has evolved into Sunday breakfast. I have hot coffee in thermoses out where people can help themselves. The table is set with baskets of fresh bread, sour cream coffee cake, and raspberry and honey butters, and there are big platters of fresh fruit. Scrambled eggs and asparagus are passed, and we're all together at the table. We have a fun, relaxed morning, and I'm happy to have the time to spend with people I love.

—*Ina Garten*

"A clever hostess *always* has something up her sleeve." —*Dorothy Draper*

HOW TO BE A HOSTESS CUPCAKE

Who isn't wowed by the charms of a wonderful hostess and entranced by her indefinable *"je ne sais quoi"*? Was it her perfume? Her smile? A secret ingredient in the punch? After throwing and going to many parties, we believe that great hostessing is not about impressing guests—it's about genuine hospitality. Here's a little inspiration to bring out the hostess in you:

MAKE THE INVITATION IRRESISTIBLE. Hostess Cupcakes know how to get people excited about partying. You don't have to spend a lot of money on custom-printing and engraving, but do spend time creating a warm, thoughtful, and truly inviting invitation. (See page 85 for more on invitations.)

DON'T GET CAUGHT WITH YOUR APRON ON. Your guests will remember your laughter more than a perfect soufflé. Get things fired up in the kitchen and the table set well before they arrive. You can smile your way through a mediocre meal if you have warmly attended to your guests beforehand.

DON'T STRIVE FOR PERFECTION. When a Hostess Cupcake is good, she is very, very good, but when she is bad, she is great. Don't aspire to be a domestic deity by buffing the floors or creating complicated table-settings. Remember, no one wants to hang out with a Martyr Party Girl, so loosen up and don't even start to obsess. You want to have enough food ready beforehand, yet be able to leave a few tasks undone for eager guests who offer to help with the cooking or candle-lighting.

HAVE ONE WOW FACTOR. Whether it's an eye-stopping cake from a bakery, funky candles, an interesting centerpiece, or a fabulously fun appetizer or drink, have something to make your guests feel this is a special occasion.

CREATE A CHICK CHEAT SHEET. Write a list of all the food you're serving and tack it up where you'll see it so that in the heat of the moment you don't forget the salad stored in the basement fridge or the side of carrots that's hanging out in the microwave.

LET THEM EAT, DRINK, AND BE MERRY! Provide guests with a steady flow of food and drink from the start to the finish of your party. Stock ample backups in case your guests consume more than you anticipate, and serve bottles of sparkling water with dinner so your guests are well hydrated the next morning.

CONSERVE YOUR ENERGY FOR WHAT REALLY MATTERS—PARTYING! Get the shopping and most of the food preparation done a day before so that you aren't worn out on the big night. Premade, frozen appetizers or platters from grocers are great alternatives to home cooking.

DON'T BE AFRAID TO INVITE THE NEW KID ON THE BLOCK. Keep your parties interesting and unpredictable by introducing new faces each time, or by adding people you think other guests will like.

PAMPER THE PARTY GIRL IN YOU. Wear a new get-up or hostess ensemble. Indulge in a bit of special preparty maintenance like a pedicure or the ultimate luxury, a nap. And when kind guests offer to help by bringing a dish or loading your dishwasher —graciously accept.

TUNE IN, THEN TUNE OUT. Set up music selections that will offer an upbeat random selection or assign a friend to be D.J. (see "The Party Pantry" on the facing page).

SET UP A "BYOB" (BE YOUR OWN BARTENDER) BAR. In addition to having wines and nonalcoholic offerings, put out the fixings and tools for a couple of fun cocktails and provide large, framed copies of the recipes so guests can help themselves. This will allow you more time to mingle, and it gives your guests a fun opportunity to mix it up amongst themselves.

DIM THE LIGHTS. Bright overhead lights are draining and stressful to both you and your guests; always defer to candlelight and softly lit lamps in the areas where guests will be entertained.

"Sexy lighting in a powder room is how you get your guests to feel good."

—*Kelly Wearstler*

A little birdie told us . . . Don't be afraid to extend an invitation to an accomplished and experienced hostess—she will probably be the most appreciative guest at your party.

The Party Pantry

Party chicks pride themselves on stocking up beforehand. Always be on the prowl for odd finds and funky favors to add to your entertainment cache. Ethnic markets, import stores, and flea markets are great places to hunt and peck, as are après-holiday sales where you can stock up on next year's paper plates, napkins, and decorations at huge discounts. Some of our party pantry standards are:

GLASSES AND DRINK ACCESSORIES, including sets of wine, martini, and basic drink glasses; one or two drink shakers; an ice bucket with tongs; and festive cocktail picks.

GAMES to spice things up in a pinch. Twister for more limber crowds, Trivial Pursuit for the thinkers, Balderdash for the tall-tale set, Scrabble for a literary crowd, Pictionary and a good deck of cards for all ages.

PAPER GRAPE LEAVES for lining platters and dressing up a boring cheese plate.

A STASH OF NIBBLES that will mollify drop-in guests until the main event begins. An assortment of jarred olives, nuts, pretzels, frozen filo appetizers, and wheat crackers fill the bill. There should also be salad dressing and vegetables in the fridge to toss into the mix.

CANDLES to set a mood, infuse the house with a pleasant scent, or to obscure the dust on the mantel. Birthday candles, for those guests who happen to mention that it's their birthday today, as if it were no big deal. Hah!

MUSIC to set the mood. Nothing sinks a gathering faster than the wrong tunes, or worse, no tunes at all. So put some effort into cultivating an eclectic musical library for myriad situations and tastes: romantic couch cuddling (Josh Groban), dinner with your parents (Frank Sinatra), a chick's night in (the Go-Gos), a swanky cocktail party (Norah Jones), a play date for the kiddies (Raffi), pizza and beer with friends (*Dixie Chicks*) . . . you get the idea.

FESTIVE PAPER NAPKINS, PLATES, AND CUPS for various occasions and plenty of plastic forks, spoons, and knives for those big bashes.

DISPOSABLE FOOD CONTAINERS or take-out boxes so you can send your guests home with leftovers.

PAPER GUEST TOWELS for the bathroom.

MAKE 'EM AN OFFER THEY CAN'T REFUSE

Put out your party come-hither with style, by crafting a special invitation for your next fun get-together. There's nothing like a personal, mailed invitation to get your guests excited and set the tone and spirit for the occasion to come. Hostess Cupcakes aren't fettered by rules about presentation, wording, addressing, etc., so don't fret over breaching etiquette. A heartfelt invitation is always in good taste.

And a party invitation is a great way to express your creativity. Whether you use technology or choose to go the old-fashioned way, with charming handwritten invitations, let your imagination soar. Think color, think texture, think mixed media.

Push the envelope by sending out invitations in a mailing tube. Or craft an invite that fits inside a small box, wrap it in brown paper, and mail it. Imagine a beach party invite that includes seashells and a vial of sand, a Halloween party complete with cobwebs and a plastic spider, or a New Year's Eve bash announced with confetti and a noisemaker.

Invitations should be mailed so that your guests will receive them at least two weeks in advance of the party. For weddings or holiday gatherings, three to four weeks ahead of time is better. If you want to assure a crowd, consider sending a "save the date" announcement six weeks in advance to pique their interest and really get 'em revved up to party speed.

LET'S PARTY!

"Lack of charisma *can be fatal."*

—*Jenny Holzer*

A little birdie told us . . . Carefully unfold and flatten an existing envelope and use it as a template to transform old calendars, maps, magazine covers, almost anything, into a unique envelope. Use a pretty label for the address.

THE TEASE
Set the tone with a clever headline, quip, or piece of art. Inject a bit of personality to get them looking forward to the event.

THE WHEN
Give the time and date, and spell out the day of the week. If you want the party to end by a certain time, give the time range.

THE WHO
Make it easy for people to respond by giving a phone number and an e-mail address. Or provide the ultimate no-brainer—a self-addressed, stamped reply postcard. Never say "regrets only." You want to be sure your guests got their invite.

Chicktails, Anyone?

Fluff your boa, primp and preen, prepare to strut your stuff.

Come eat, come drink, and merrily celebrate with us.

OUR NEW NEST

Saturday, May 15
Jack and Jill's House
555 Swanky Avenue
Hipsville, CA

7:00 o'clock until . . .

COCKTAIL (OR CHICKTAIL) ATTIRE
RSVP no later than May 10th to
555-555-1970 or jill@youremail.com

In lieu of gifts, please help us warm our new home by bringing a recipe, tip, or other bit of "domestic wisdom" to include in our guestbook.

THE WHAT
Clearly state the reason for the party and who's hosting it.

THE WHERE
Give the complete address of the party destination. If it's new to your guest, include a map.

THE WEAR
If appropriate, give a cue as to how to dress.

THE SCOOP
Give any special info regarding gifts, parking, accommodations, etc., that will put guests at ease.

tHe SecreTs of SAffrOn

EVERY CHILD HAS A MASTER TEACHER BESIDES HER PARENTS, and Mrs. Coogan was mine. The Coogans lived at the top of our street in Philadelphia in a row house just like ours. But they were different from everyone else in our working-class neighborhood because the parents had not only gone to college but were both writers of some note. When they moved into the neighborhood, they had two children—a boy, Kevin, and a girl, Nell, who became my best friend. Forty years after they met, my mom would still tell with astonishment the story of Mrs. Coogan's audacious first visit to our house. One afternoon the doorbell rang, and my mom opened the front door to find standing on our stoop a tall, large-boned, handsome woman with the brightest shade of fuchsia lipstick freshly painted on her generous mouth.

"My name is Jean Maria," Mrs. Coogan announced in her breathlessly girlish voice. "I just moved in up the street and I've heard your husband is a college graduate and that you're a great reader. Well, we are too, and I'd like us to be friends because I really don't understand how I'm going to live here if I don't find someone to talk to. . . ."

The Coogans gave a lot of parties. It doesn't seem to me now that Mr. Coogan was a very social man, because he was always in his study writing, but they had a wide circle of friends, and Mrs. Coogan liked the excitement a party brought to the house.

She often heightened the excitement by taking to her bed in the days or hours before the party, resisting the cleaning and shopping a party requires. At the very last possible moment, when everyone else had given up hope, Mrs. Coogan would burst from her room and, in a whirl of activity, somehow got done what needed to be done. What she did love was the party itself—the hosting and the greeting, talking and laughing with her guests, drinking and eating and talking some more until well into the night. Their house appeared always to be in a state of animation, with a party being planned or just hours away. The only time all seemed quiet was in the suspended hush of the "day after," when our parents remained in bed and Nell and I would make a game finding all the small silver bowls of nuts and mints and half-empty glasses hidden about the messy rooms. . . .

"Patty, sweet puss, do you think you can help me with this?" she asked one day when my mom wasn't around. Mrs. Coogan had called me from the yard where I had been playing with Nell. She helped me up on a stool beside the counter to show me a magazine spread of something I had never seen before—a bowl of golden rice.

"We need to make enough for twenty and the recipe is only for six. So I guess four times everything?"

That sounded good to me, and when she put four green peppers down in front of me and asked me to cut them up, I thought that was pretty good, too.

"I would urge you to *be as impudent as you dare,*

I was not allowed to touch knives at home, but her faith in me was complete, and I boldly took the small paring knife from her hand and began to cut the strips of pepper as carefully as I could. Mrs. Coogan kicked off her shoes and disappeared into the living room; when she came back, she was carrying a martini glass and rowdy music suddenly exploded around us. I cut the peppers. She chopped onions. Nell came in from the yard, asked if she could cut something too, but quickly grew bored with all the peppers. Her eyes watered from the onions, and she soon wandered off. Mrs. Coogan took a sip from her glass and began to sway her hips to the music as she sautéed the veg-

etables together in an enormous black skillet. She didn't seem to mind, or even see, the bits and pieces of onions and peppers that splattered to the floor, for she kept up a lively patter between us and continued to stir the vegetables in the pan. I can't imagine what it was we talked about, but it was thrilling to feel all her interest zeroed in on me, on whatever it was I was telling her. Best of all, after I opened some cans of tomatoes for her, she whisked me down from the stool and, to a particularly raucous tune, swung me across the floor in a lively, all-the-way-down-to-the-ground-and-up-again manic version of a twisting jitterbug.

When we had finished dancing, I climbed back on the stool and she dug around the cupboard until she found a glass tube full of red threads. She pulled the cork from it and put it under my nose.

"Smell," she commanded. I took a big whiff and reeled my head away from the cold acerbic scent that curled from the vial.

"Now look at this." Mrs. Coogan shook the tangled ball of threads out into her palm, dropped a few into a coffee cup, added a little hot water, then stirred the mixture with her finger. The threads seemed to swell and burst open, bleeding yellow across the water like the sun setting behind a still lake. The scent rose lightly off the water, almost sweet but as citric as a lemon. Before she poured the threads into the rice, she told me to dip a fingertip into the water and place a drop of the liquid on my tongue. ▶

be bold, be bold, be bold, be bold."

—*Susan Sontag*

"Isn't that something?" She laughed at the frown I made as the taste melted like warm metal across my mouth. As she stirred the water into the rice, the white kernels began to turn yellow—first a pale creamy shade and then a darker, almost orange hue.

When I got home later and excitedly told my mom about what Mrs. Coogan and I had cooked, my mom appeared horrified. I thought it was about the knife or the funny stuff Mrs. Coogan let me taste. But a few minutes later when my dad arrived home from work, I heard her talking about the single bowl of rice that would feed the party that night. My dad opened a bottle of beer and said something about making a snack. My mom shrugged her shoulders and, casting a suspicious eye toward me, hoped out loud that the party wouldn't be spoiled.

I lay in bed that night with my sister curled asleep against my back and listened to the music from the Coogans' house flutter down the hill. I wondered whether Nell had been allowed to stay up, as she sometimes was. Maybe she had put on a party dress and was twisting with her mom in the living room. I thought about slipping past the baby-sitter downstairs and skipping up the hill, through the back door, filling my belly with perfumed rice, and dancing, dancing. When I awoke again, it was pitch dark and the music had stopped. I heard my parents on the stairs, their voices slippery, excited, and I knew the party had been a success. I was sure the rice Mrs. Coogan and I had made had contributed at least a little to the merriment. As the door closed softly behind my parents, and the night once more quieted, I lay awake hankering to cook up a party again and tickled by the strange taste still lightly simmering on my tongue.

—*Pat Willard*

"**Laugh** as much as possible, *always laugh.*"

—*Maya Angelou*

THERE ARE THREE BASIC WAYS to combine ingredients to yield a mean (or a sweet) cocktail: shake, stir on the rocks, or stir straight up. A cocktail shaker comes in handy for all those methods. We like the stainless steel varieties, which are easy to find, relatively inexpensive, and work like a charm every time. They also have a built-in strainer, which cuts down on spillage.

Shake it up, baby

Fill the shaker two-thirds of the way with ice, pour in your cocktail ingredients, fit on the strainer portion of the shaker, and cap tightly. And we do mean tightly—a good cocktail is a terrible thing to waste! Now, firmly grasp the top in your right hand, the bottom in your left, and shake, shake, shake, until a sweat or fine frost forms on the outside of the shaker. Break the seal by whacking it sharply with the heel of your hand at the frost line. Remove the cap and pour your perfectly chilled cocktail into a stemmed glass for your admirers. Garnish and serve.

Stirred cocktail "on the rocks"

"On the rocks" simply means over ice. For a stirred cocktail over ice, start again with your shaker filled about two-thirds of the way with ice. Pour in your ingredients and use the straight end of a long metal spoon to stir the drink. Securely affix the strainer portion of your shaker to keep the cubes from pouring into the drink. Outfit a short glass with fresh ice cubes, and pour your stirred cocktail through the strainer. Garnish and serve.

Stirred cocktail "straight up"

"Straight up" means without ice in the glass. Follow the same directions for a stirred cocktail on the rocks, but at the end, pour the cocktail into an ice-free glass. Garnish and serve.

"Give me a whiskey, *ginger ale on the side . . .* and don't be stingy, baby!" —*Greta Garbo*

WHETHER HOMEMADE OR PROFESSIONALLY RENDERED, these libations are strictly for the ladies—or for the very secure and endearing gentlemen who love chicktails!

Clementini

1 part Grey Goose vodka

1 part fresh clementine juice

½ part Cointreau

Splash of champagne

Shake first three lovely liquids well with ice, top with champagne, and pour into a martini glass. (This martini was created for Candace Bushnell.)

Blushing Laura

6 ounces cranberry juice

1 ounce Absolut Mandarin vodka

2 ounces lemon-lime soda

Stir with ice in a tall drink glass and garnish with a twisted sliver of lime.

Scarlett O'Hara

1½ ounces Southern Comfort

1½ ounces cranberry juice

A squeeze of lime juice

Pour the ingredients into a glass with ice, stir, and, frankly, my dear, you will give a damn.

Bahama Mama

1½ ounces rum

½ ounce Malibu rum

Splash of cream of coconut

1 ounce orange juice

1 ounce pineapple juice

Shake it all up with ice and strain into an ice-filled Collins glass garnished with a pineapple wedge and a maraschino cherry on a cocktail pick.

Classic Cosmopolitan

4 parts vodka

2 parts Triple Sec

2 parts cranberry juice

1 part fresh lime juice

Shake it all up with ice, strain into a martini glass, and garnish with a twisted sliver of lime or lemon peel.

Margarita on the Rocks

1 ounce Cointreau

2 ounces fresh lime juice

3 ounces tequila

Shake it all up with ice, strain into a salt-rimmed glass over ice, and garnish with a lime wedge. If a frozen margarita strikes your fancy, just add ice and blend in an electric blender until slushy. Pour into a margarita glass and garnish with a quarter of lime.

Jezebel

Layer equal parts Southern Comfort and Bailey's Irish Cream Liqueur in a short glass and serve.

Woo Woo

1 ounce peach Schnapps

1 ounce vodka

Splash of cranberry juice

Shake it all up with ice and strain into a highball glass.

Pure Cinderella

2 ounces orange juice

2 ounces pineapple juice

Dash of grenadine

Splash of sour mix

Club soda

Shake the juices, grenadine, and sour mix with ice, pour into a glass, and top off with club soda. Garnish with a cherry.

Virgin Margarita

2 ounces sour mix

Juice of 1 lime

Splash of orange juice

1 cup ice

In a blender, mix until slushy, pour into a margarita glass, and garnish with a lime wedge.

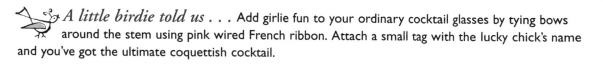

A little birdie told us . . . Add girlie fun to your ordinary cocktail glasses by tying bows around the stem using pink wired French ribbon. Attach a small tag with the lucky chick's name and you've got the ultimate coquettish cocktail.

EnTertain*ing* INc.

I'LL ALWAYS REMEMBER A CERTAIN PICNIC in D. H. Lawrence's novel *Women in Love,* because it had that magical feeling that one always hopes for in any party, large or small, formal or informal. Lawrence's characters stumble upon a quiet meadow, spread out a lacy coverlet, and share a simple meal of chicken, bread, and fresh figs. Somehow, because the company is warm and the trees are evocative, and the figs are indescribably plump, the small gathering becomes the kind of extraordinary, spontaneous, once-in-a-lifetime event that ultimately is the most gratifying to every host and guest.

Some events seem fortuitous, like Lawrence's picnic, without any planning or foresight. I recall one evening when a guest impulsively sat down at the piano and played a spectacular medley of 1950s ballads—"Wake Up, Little Susie" and "Heartbreak Hotel"—which we all sang with nostalgic passion; another when two Italian guests brought a whole crowd to life with funny and moving childhood tales; another when guests at a formal dinner filled up their Baccarat goblets with water to different levels and attempted, like children, to make music. These interesting developments, which eventually made the evenings, were unpredictable, and yet they had something to do with the way a hostess had organized each gathering, with sensitivity to the guest list, with an eye toward a convivial situation. She had, in each case, made everyone comfortable enough to be his own natural, impulsive, expressive, social self. Many occasions, however beautifully orchestrated, don't have that ease and end up, like the guests, polite, proper, polished, but dull.

One of the most important moments on which to expend extra effort is the beginning of the party, often an awkward time, when guests feel tentative and insecure. This is particularly true at a large buffet or cocktail party, when you will find guests fixing their eyes on the door in anticipation of other guests, or maybe an early escape. At this moment, some hostesses give a house tour; others might take a guest aside to show him a new book or record. It is a time for a gesture to make that person feel he is in a home and not a restaurant. I usually bring early arrivals into the kitchen with me, where I am often still chopping, arranging, or just meditating on what is to come. I give them a drink, and depending on their interests, I might ask them to lend a hand with the salad or the coffee grinding. The kitchen is a warm, easy place, and it breaks any ice. As the other guests arrive, the kitchen expands, and when it is full, we adjourn to the parlor.

—*Martha Stewart*

Let's face it, the standard place card can get a little tired. So next time you want to seat your guests, try one of these ploys. If finding your place at the table is entertaining, just think how fun the rest of the party can be!

And You Are?

At each place setting, put a little-known fact about each person. (Be sure to confirm the little-known fact before you go public with it!) Your guests will have fun figuring out who hiked Mt. Everest, was a homecoming queen, or is afraid to eat blue M&Ms.

Caught on Film

Take photos you have of the guests and make close-ups of one feature (an eye, a piece of jewelry, a nose, an eyebrow) and place one at each setting. People have to "find themselves" or help others find their seats. This is especially revealing at family gatherings where we think we "know everything" about each other. (Note: If Grandma doesn't already know you have a tattoo, this may not be the best way to break the news.)

Oh, Baby!

The advance prep for this one is worth the effort. Have guests send you a baby picture. Photocopy the pics so they are all the same size, mount them on card stock, and place one atop each plate. This really has a way of "leveling the playing field," so to speak, and is especially good with guests who don't know each other well.

Pick Your Alter Ego

Ever fantasize about being someone else? Well, dream on! Assemble a wild collection of famous people, historical figures, and celebrities and put their names or pictures at each place setting. Imagine the buzz at a party with King Louis XIV, Julia Child, Cary Grant, Mother Teresa, Bill Clinton, Britney Spears, William Shakespeare, and the great Garbo. Tell guests to gravitate to the person they feel most drawn to. On the back of the name cards or pictures add a little bio or fact about the person. This is a great icebreaker, and your guests' choices might make for surprising revelations and lively conversations.

> "We gave that famous, famous party. It was written up everywhere. It was my idea—all books. All the place cards at the dinner were books. In front of Irving Thalberg's place I put Dreiser's *Genius*. That's just before he married Norma Shearer. So in front of Norma's place I put Serena Blandish's *The Difficulty of Getting Married*—she'd been trying and trying, and Irving's mother wanted him to marry a nice Jewish girl. It was so funny because Irving walked right in and saw *Genius* and sat right down. But Norma kept walking around. She wouldn't sit down in front of *The Difficulty of Getting Married*. Not at all! And there was that writer at MGM who had lost a leg in the war, and I gave him *The Devil on Two Sticks*."
>
> —Louise Brooks, flapper, femme fatale, and silent-film star of the Roaring Twenties

at Gertrude & Alice's

SOME HOSTESSES GO TO GREAT LENGTHS for their guests, and the great ones attain immortality for their efforts. The Parisian salon of Gertrude Stein and Alice B. Toklas was one of the most distinguished social gatherings of the 1920s and 1930s. Gertrude Stein, a writer admired by authors and literary critics, was also a consummate host, and she and her partner, Alice, an extraordinary cook, entertained every Saturday evening. Being in the company of Gertrude and Alice meant vibrant conversation, delicious food, seamless hospitality, and a remarkable guest list—Ernest Hemingway, Pablo Picasso, Zelda and F. Scott Fitzgerald, Henry and Clare Boothe Luce, and Henri Matisse—to name just a few.

No effort was too great for this pair of hostesses to expend on behalf of their guests. For a lunch with Picasso, Alice decorated a striped bass to please the artist's palate as well as his palette. "I covered the fish with an ordinary mayonnaise and, using a pastry tube, decorated it with a red mayonnaise, not coloured catsup—horror of horrors—but with tomato paste. Then I made a design with sieved hard-boiled eggs, the whites and yolks apart, with truffles and with finely chopped *fines herbes*."

While Alice fussed over the food, Gertrude would set the stage for the salon. Once, after hanging some of their newly acquired paintings and installing special gas lights that showed them off to advantage, they planned a luncheon for the artists. "You know how painters are, I wanted to make them happy so I placed each one opposite his own picture," said Gertrude, "and they were happy, so happy that we had to send out twice for more bread." Only Matisse, upon his departure, noticed the contrived arrangement, saying later, "Yes, I know Mademoiselle Gertrude, the world is a theater for you."

It was only upon publication of *The Alice B. Toklas Cookbook* in 1954 that the world learned of the secret recipe that had perhaps enhanced the mood and enlivened the conversations at the salon. There Alice revealed her Hashish Fudge, described as "the food of Paradise. . . . Euphoria and brilliant storms of laughter; ecstatic reveries and extensions of one's personality on several simultaneous planes are to be complacently expected." No wonder they kept coming back for more!

"Give me new faces new faces." —*Gertrude Stein*

A little birdie told us . . . Changing your table linens, centerpiece, and water glasses will give your table a whole new look. They needn't be fancy or expensive—just colorful, nonpretentious, and lively.

BREAKING THE SET RULES

These days many chicks happily skip home ec in favor of woodworking, and a lot of dads set the table. We believe that once you know the set rules it's easier to break them, so here's a little refresher on the art of setting a table—to be taken with a great big fat grain of kosher salt.

Festiveness always takes preference over formality, so don't fret if you don't have complete, matched sets of dishes. On the contrary, the interest of mixing patterns, colors, and styles gives your table personality. Below is an individual place setting for an informal dinner. Moving from the outside in, place cutlery and glasses in the order in which they are to be used. And don't forget salt and pepper shakers, a water pitcher, and a bread basket. Some flowers, some wine, and you're set!

Chick Cheat Sheet

BUTTER KNIFE on rim of bread plate *(optional)*

WINEGLASS above dinner knife

BREAD PLATE

WATER GLASS right of wineglass

DINNER FORK left of dinner plate

SALAD FORK left of dinner fork

NAPKIN folded and placed left of salad fork

DINNER PLATE with **SALAD PLATE** on top

DINNER KNIFE right of dinner plate

DESSERT SPOON right of dinner knife

SOUP SPOON right of dessert spoon *(optional)*

the PArty To End *All* PaRties

O K. I'M THIRTY-SIX AND I STILL GIVE PAR-
TIES AS IF I'M IN COLLEGE. A lot of them.
And I keep telling myself that this one
will be the last one. But it never is.

For some unknown reason, I still think a keg of
beer, potato chips, and Jell-O shots are perfectly

Miranda was having such a wonderful time at her party that
she didn't get upset even when she realized she'd forgotten
to mail the invitations.

delightful treats to serve at one's party. How could
such a social disconnect have happened? I am not an
eternal graduate student or a high-school football
coach. I am well traveled, and well educated. I grew
up in a Connecticut home where we used cloth napkins and weren't allowed to leave the catsup bottle on
the dinner table. So far I believe my social, intellectual, and professional development has progressed
according to the "expected timetable/growth chart,"
but somehow my hosting style has yet to
evolve past Early Sorority.

As a student at Columbia, a borrowed keg and
some pretzels were all we could afford when we wanted
to "entertain." Once my mother asked what my girlfriends and I (a.k.a. "the Fun Bunch") were serving at
the monthly party in our dorm suite. I laughingly told
her we were providing a bottle of Jack Daniel's and
some grain alcohol. (Tee-hee.) Four years of tailgates,
fraternity parties, and semiweekly games of Quarters
later, we graduated looking like human kegs. The constant partying had to end, and we were glad of it.

But that didn't have to mean never again. We
were not only a fun, but a determined bunch.

I went on to graduate school in New York and
moved to Bleecker Street, into one of those rare New
York apartments that felt like a home. It had three
bedrooms, wood floors, brick walls, a big living room
with a fireplace . . . and a huge private deck in the
back. *The perfect place to throw a bash!* And my room-
mates and I did, all the time. After a long day at my

desk writing or running between the television studio and the editing room, a blowout bash offered the perfect opportunity to blow off steam. The first party coincided with the annual Greenwich Village Halloween Parade. I next decided that spring fever called for a yearly Cinco de Mayo celebration. That glorious apartment with its expansive deck was the venue for at least two huge parties a year for the eleven years I resided there.

The party preparation was honed down to a science: beer, Twizzlers, candles, vodka, and mixers. Delivered. The furniture was moved into the bedroom, the rug rolled, and a blanket thrown over the duvet (come on, I'm not a complete animal). Then my best pals would come early and I'd suffer the inevitable party anxiety. Who was going to come all the way downtown? Would anyone really come this time? But by 10 or 11 P.M., the place would be hopping, people would be spilling into the bedrooms and out on the deck. It would be fair to say that we'd get close to 100 revelers throughout the evening. A cross section of college pals, NYU friends, CBS page buddies, the Sally Jessy Raphael girls, relatives, and friends of friends could be found on the deck in back, all revved up and indulging in the festivities. As the years went by, the parties sometimes ended a bit earlier, and people were more inclined to bring a bottle of wine than a six-pack (maybe), but the point remained the same: to create, or re-create, a tight and casual community of like-minded people making a life for themselves in the Big Pond. I always tried to be a good hostess, making connections for my guests. Love connections, business connections, work connections; I just wanted to let networking happen in a carefree setting.

But by 3 A.M. I'd be done working it and would kick people out and attempt to clean up. I learned quickly to enlist professional help the day after such extravaganzas. Still, I hated waking up with a hangover and the floors sticky with beer, plastic cups half filled with magic punch, and cigarette butts. I vowed after every party that it had been the last one; it was too much of an effort, too messy, too annoying.

I had thrown my share of dinner parties, but they were too expensive. And I had tried a "sophisticated" cocktail party, but somehow things always got out of hand, the guest list expanded, and there I was, ready to roll out the keg all over again. Why did I insist on "entertaining" this way? What was wrong with having a quiet dinner party with a few friends and food requiring a fork and knife? Why did my parties refuse to mature?

▶

Two years ago, after 9/11, I moved from that one-of-a-kind apartment on Bleecker Street all the way to West Hollywood. I've heard it said you can move half a world away, but you can never escape your real self. How true that is. For my thirty-fifth birthday, I threw a party in my new backyard in sunny California. I considered cosmos and martinis, but then I confidently ordered a keg. My fancy friends kidded me about being déclassé, but to me it felt like an old school party. And who says thirty-five-year-olds can't enjoy a kegger?

Although I would never wish to be eighteen and in college again, throwing a fraternity-style blowout makes me feel like I am back to my carefree youth, and who needs a dose of lighthearted revelry more than a "worldly adult"? As my father yearns for the halcyon days of his childhood back in Brooklyn and the taste of a Nathan's egg cream, I love returning to the simpler days of hanging out with my best friends over a keg, with the taste of a cherry Jell-O shot.

—*Jill Pollack*

"Your taste in parties tells the world as much about you as your taste in hats."

—*Dorothy Draper*

A Lulu of a Party

Tallulah Bankhead, silent film star, performer, and nonstop party girl, did her part to put the roar into the roaring '20's. Her country estate in upstate New York was the scene of many famous fetes. At one party Tallulah offered her guests bathing suits, then declared in her signature drawl, "I never wear a suit," and promptly perched on the diving board wearing only her pearls. When asked why she staged the impromptu peep show, Tallulah remarked, "I just wanted to prove that I was a natural ash blonde."

Who's Your Party Persona?

Whether she's brash or bashful, every chick has an inner belle of the ball, a party persona who reigns on festive occasions. Read this to find yours.

BACKYARD BETTY. You put the *grrrr* in grill and your yard-party expertise makes even the most casual gathering a thrill ride. Pool party, barbecue, picnic—you are the original outdoorsy type who can banish mosquitoes, start a fire with sticks, whip up a rousing game of volleyball, and toast up the world's best s'mores without ruffling a feather.

HOBNOB HEDDY. You like your society high and your party prep low. What to make? Reservations with a caterer for five luscious courses. Your silver and china know no bounds. And cleanup? You leave that to the next day's crew. Spoiled, maybe, but everyone hankers to be on your guest list. Pinkie extended, raise a toast to effortless entertaining.

LAISSEZ-FAIRE LILLY. Come one, come all, at your nest it's family style or no style. You roll out an irresistible welcome mat, tempting folks with the smell of fresh-baked bread and oatmeal cookies. Both kids and adults love to party at your house, where nothing's off-limits. You don't own anything that can't be cleaned, replaced, or thrown out. Your brand of comfort and carefree entertaining keeps them beating a path to your door.

STYLING STELLA. You're known as the Cocktail Queen and you'd rather be caught in last year's couture than seen toasting with yesterday's drink. Your recipe for a great cocktail party is simple: one part pleasing appetizers, two parts dynamite drinks! Your guests include the hip, the haute, and the hilarious, but everyone knows that as long as they can hold a martini glass, you'll let them in the door.

TAKE-OUT TESS. You might have time to run a company, but cooking for eight has got to wait until your golden parachute opens. As an executive you know how to delegate, and you bring those skills home with just the right take-out food and a hired clean-up crew. Pshew—life's a party!

ROCKIN' RACHEL. Your reputation precedes you; your lively guests look forward to a guaranteed blowout. You never run out of beverages or munchies, and you handle those pesky interruptions by the police with savoir-faire. Though your events might be a little crowded for some, those with the stamina and the stomach to match find your bashes irresistible.

THELMA, THEME QUEEN. Whether it's Murder Mystery Night, a Seventies Smash, or a Mardi Gras Gathering—your parties have focus. From invites and decorations to costumes galore, you set the stage for frivolity and fantasy that keeps tongues wagging for months.

Adventure is worthwhile in itself."

—*Amelia Earhart*

THE GRAPE ESCAPE Hosting a Wine-Tasting Party

Next time you get the gang together, why not indulge in a bit of bacchanalian exploration, some gourmet games, an exercise in connoisseurship? We see it as a good excuse to drink some fine wine. Invite an adventurous group and let the games begin.

The easiest way to throw a wine-tasting party is to have everyone bring a bottle of wine to taste. If guests bring their favorite bottle, you'll have a wide variety of wines of which to partake. You can assign varieties to each guest or limit it to one vintage or even just "color." You can get specific and hold a tasting of just sparkling wines, chardonnays, cabernets, merlots, dessert wines, etc. Limiting choices to a region is fun as well: Italian, French, Australian, Californian, New York, you name it. Depending on your guest list, it might be a good idea to give a price limit for people to stay under or over.

KEEP THINGS INFORMAL. Tonight is not the time for a crisp white tablecloth. Trust us, by the end of the night it will be ruined (if your party goes well). Set out a wineglass and a water glass for each guest; a pitcher of room-temperature water (chilled water numbs taste buds); a tall, opaque vase or container for spitting into; some fun cocktail napkins; wine charms (see page 127 and make your own); a clean, lint-free dishcloth so that the tantalized tasters can dry their wineglasses between sips; some unsalted crackers or French bread; and an array of hors d'oeuvres. Load up the

CD player with good tunes, light a few candles, and get ready for action.

GIVE A BUBBLY WELCOME. When your guests arrive, serve them a glass of sparkling wine, like Prosecco, an inexpensive bubbly from Italy. Its light taste will not interfere with the tasting to come and it will get things loosened up. Set out some simple, bite-sized food—an antipasto platter of mild meats, cheeses, and bread is great. A pasta salad, vegetable and fruit trays, mini quiches, or cheese straws also work well.

DISGUISE THE BOTTLES. While you are waiting for everyone to arrive, begin disguising the bottles for the tasting. With a marker, assign each bottle a number and write it on the label. This is the best way to

Bubbly Boosters

Don't burst your bubble by improperly tasting sparkling wine. When tasting champagne or sparkling wine, use lint-free towels, paper towels, or coffee filters to dry the glass in between tastings. Pouring bubbly into a wet glass diminishes your "mousse," which is that lovely white froth that forms on the top of the wine, and the "perlage," which is the stream of tiny bubbles that makes champagne sparkle. Chicks love champagne mousse and perlage!

focus on the taste and not be influenced by the label art, the pedigree, the year, or the reputation of the vineyard. Wines are usually set out in groups of four. Make a little "cheat sheet" for your guests with criteria such as color, aroma, body, and finish (how long the wine's taste and feel stay in your mouth). Provide little notepads for guests to write their notes and rank the mystery vintages.

SEE, SNIFF, SIP. Basic tasting etiquette is to pour a small amount into each glass; swirl it a bit and hold it up to a white background such as a white napkin so you can see the color and consistency of the wine; inhale deeply to appreciate the bouquet; then take a small sip and roll it around in your mouth. Try to bring in a little air with your wine so you can get the fullness of the flavors. You can swallow it or spit it out—either is acceptable. Have a cracker and a sip of water to cleanse your palate, and move on to the next one.

Have everyone share their reviews and nominate their favorites over a dreamy dessert wine and chocolates. The hostess will announce the preferences by number and reveal what each bottle really is.

Note: You can have a tasting for anything you deem worthy of culinary comparison: chocolate, caviar, cheese, olives, balsamic vinegar, olive oil, ice cream, macaroni and cheese, etc. Pick an obsession and host a tasting.

Show-and-Take
Clothes Swap Party

We have our chick friend Kris King to thank for this party idea. A year ago she sent us this irresistible invitation: *Hey, Ladies! Clear your schedule and clean out your closet for our annual clothes exchange party. We'll pile up all those things we never wear anymore and dig through them for well-worn (or unworn!) treasures. It's the perfect excuse to pour on the girl bonding glue—you know, fashion, new nail polish, cocktails, chocolate, racy jokes, stain-removal hints, and gossip! Old books, shoes, jewelry, handbags, and other accessories are welcome additions to the pile. Facials, pedicures, dancing, and catwalking also encouraged.*

Talk about multitasking: You get a painful domestic chore out of the way, you add some groovy new finds to your closet, you get to hang out with your girlfriends over nibbles and drinks, and you won't have any shocking surprises lurking on your credit card statement.

Set the stage for this fashion show-and-take by getting the invitations out at least three weeks in advance, so your chicks will have time to gather all their goodies. You provide the cocktails and ask everyone to bring a snack or hors d'oeuvre so you can focus on "shopping" along with everyone else. Remind your guests to bring a couple of shopping bags for carting home their booty! Designate a few areas in your home as changing rooms, pick some fun music, and you've got a party that rivals fashion week in New York. Coordinate with a charity beforehand to pick up any leftover items or you can drop them off yourself.

THE BEAUTY OF HORS D'OEUVRES is the number of options they give a chick. They can be tailored to fit any crowd, from the pinkie-extending set to the finger-lickin' crew. In copious amounts and heartier variations they can take the place of a meal, and since most can be prepared ahead of time, you can actually party at your party.

PRESENTATION IS EVERYTHING: The difference between formal and casual hors d'oeuvres can hinge on the placement of a garnish or the tray you use to serve them on. Dress 'em up, dress 'em down, from cut crystal to paper plates, anything goes—as long as it suits your party. Great garnishes include herbs, sliced carrots and radishes, water chestnuts marinated in ginger soy sauce, sliced almonds, orange slices . . .

QUANTITY AND AMOUNTS: Three different hors d'oeuvres per party should suffice, and about two portions of each per guest (unless you aren't serving a main course).

VARIETY: Be sure to mix it up a bit. Serve something filling and something light. One hors d'oeuvre should be the "mainstay," or the generously portioned appetizer that is set out before your guests arrive. Prepare the spread for both nibblers and gobblers. For your sake, serve only one labor-intensive type (and try to get that one out of the way the day before).

Melon & Prosciutto

This slightly upscale appetizer can rest on silver or paper. It tastes marvelous either way.

1 fresh honeydew or cantaloupe melon
1 pound prosciutto, sliced

Slice melon into finger-sized rectangles and remove rind. Wrap each peachy morsel in prosciutto and secure with a toothpick.

Nancy's Twist & Shout Ring Bread

This gorgeous hot bread ring creates a delicious aroma for arriving guests.

2 loaves frozen commercial French bread dough
3 tablespoons cornmeal
Your favorite dip or extra-virgin olive oil

1. Defrost bread dough per package instructions and gently twist.

2. Join two ends together to make a ring.

3. Slash the top of the dough with a knife at 2-inch intervals, ½ inch deep. Sprinkle with cornmeal. Bake per package instructions.

4. Serve alone or with your favorite dip or olive oil.

BLTeenies

This is a great treat, delicious on melba toast or as a dip.

¼ cup mayonnaise

¾ cup sour cream

¼ teaspoon garlic powder

¼ teaspoon onion powder

9 slices of cooked bacon, cooled and crumbled

2 medium tomatoes, diced fine

1 cup chopped arugula with stems removed

1 package melba toast or thin baguette slices, toasted

1. Combine mayonnaise, sour cream, garlic powder, onion powder, and bacon in a medium-sized bowl. Cover and chill for at least 5 hours and up to 24 hours. Remove from refrigerator an hour before serving.

2. Before serving, mix in the arugula and half of the tomatoes. Spread onto melba toast or baguette slices and top with diced tomato.

Serves 10 to 12

Variation: To make this as a dip, double the recipe to yield 4 cups. Just before serving, mix in the arugula, tomatoes, and bacon. Serve with melba toast, breadsticks, crackers, or pretzels.

Chew on This

"What really frosts me is that a hostess will never reveal what she is serving on her hors d'oeuvres. 'What's this little brown thing on top?' I ask. 'What do you think it is?' she chirps.

"I then get twenty questions to come up with the answer. 'Is it living or dead? Is it American? Is it in politics or the arts? Would I be likely to find it in my house? Is it bigger than a breadbox? Is it considered to be a gourmet treat in this country but bait everywhere else? Does it run under a rock whenever there are bathers nearby? Did it look like this when it was young?'"

—Erma Bombeck

"Big, fat, greasy, lumpy things that require three or four bites, smear your lipstick, and get food caught in your teeth are the worst. I'm a fanatic about small, single-bite-sized hors d'oeuvres you can pop in your mouth and swallow in one gulp, then continue on with the conversation without having to juggle something in your hand along with your drink and everything else. If you want to serve large, unwieldy hors d'oeuvres, then put them on the buffet and have little plates so people can choose to deal with them if they're really hungry or if they don't mind the hassle. Also, try to skip really fishy-smelling hors d'oeuvres or big hunks of cheese, which don't do much for people's breath. My all-time most hated hors d'oeuvre is the cherry tomato stuffed with crabmeat. They're too big for one bite, they squirt and drip, they leave your breath smelling fishy, and they get stuck in your teeth."

—Sally Quinn

Shirley's Hot Mamas

These are delicious and not too spicy. (If you are serving younger children, put jalapeños on only one side of the dough.)

8 ounces cream cheese
Crescent roll dough
6-ounce jar chopped mild jalapeños

1. Soften cream cheese for 4 to 6 hours.

2. Preheat oven to 350°F.

3. Carefully unroll (but don't tear apart) the crescent dough on a cookie sheet so you have a rectangle of dough. Spread the cream cheese on the dough and sprinkle the jalapeños evenly on top of the cream cheese, then roll the dough up from the short end.

4. Slice the roll of dough at 1- to 2-inch intervals. Lay the slices on the cookie sheet, bake for 10 minutes, and serve immediately.

Serves 6 to 8

Herbed Goat Cheese on Baguette Toast

½ pound log mild goat cheese
1 teaspoon fresh rosemary or ⅓ teaspoon dried
2 tablespoons fresh thyme or 2 teaspoons dried
1 teaspoon freshly ground pepper
¼ cup extra-virgin olive oil
1 fresh baguette, cut into ½-inch slices

1. Cut the log of cheese into thin slices and place them flat in a dish. Sprinkle with herbs and pepper, then drizzle with half the olive oil. Cover and let stand at room temperature for about 45 minutes.

2. Toast the baguette slices on both sides under a broiler until golden brown. Place a slice of cheese on top of each piece of toast, drizzle with more olive oil, and broil again for 1 or 2 minutes, until soft and hot. Garnish with chopped fresh parsley or slices of black olive or a little salsa or pesto or . . .

Makes 15 pieces

Peggy's Hot Crab Dip

This yummy dip can be doubled for a larger crowd. (Do not microwave this recipe.)

8 ounces cream cheese
2 tablespoons milk
1 6-ounce can flaked crabmeat
2 tablespoons finely chopped green onion
1 teaspoon cream-style horseradish
¼ teaspoon salt
¼ teaspoon pepper
⅔ cup slivered raw almonds

1. Set the cream cheese out and let it soften for 4 to 6 hours. Preheat oven to 375°F.

2. Beat cream cheese and milk together in a mixing bowl. Add the crab, green onion, horseradish, salt, pepper and half of the almonds. Mix well and put into an ovenproof serving dish. Sprinkle the remaining almonds on top.

3. Bake until warmed through, about 20 minutes. Serve immediately with plain crackers or baguette toasts.

Serves 6 to 8

"The idea with food for cocktails is to give your guest something a little special but not to go to so much trouble that your guests feel like you went to too much trouble—**no one wants to have guilt served up with their martini."**

—*Candace Bushnell*

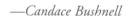

Ladies Who Lunch

BRENDA ABRAMS HAD AN ORANGE SHAG CARPET AND A THING FOR ELTON JOHN. My room was hot pink and my heart belonged to Cat Stevens. We both believed in Herbal Essence, Frye boots, and boys named Brad. We got our periods, our ears pierced, and our learner's permits—in exactly that order. All we knew of drugs was what we'd read in *Go Ask Alice*. All we knew of sex was what we saw in *The Way We Were*. We gorged on Twinkies and Fritos and red pop, never dreaming that cellulite could someday come between us and our Calvins. We were good girls. We were best friends.

Thirty years have come and gone. She's Brenda Josephs now, living with her husband, three kids, and nanny in a big suburban house outside Manhattan. I'm still me, living alone in a small prewar co-op inside Manhattan. She's on the board of trustees at her children's school, practicing law in her spare time. I'm on the computer writing this article, and my spare time is spent wondering how people find spare time. Most days I don't want her life. Most days she doesn't want mine—but we each have the occasional pang. We are still best friends.

There is an unspoken understanding that in case of emergency, we will always come early and stay late for each other, but our days of sharing a locker and nights of marathon phone sessions are behind us. We're down to meeting for lunch—it is an act of faith in faithless times.

On the first Monday of every other month, we take our latest assortment of absurdities, insights, outrages, and ironies to the little café on the fifth floor of Bergdorf Goodman and meet for the same meal we've been having forever. Brenda orders her standard, tuna salad on pumpernickel. She's a straightforward, no-nonsense eater. Her mother's desperate attempt to instill culinary diversity is still referred to as "the turkey tetrazzini incident of '74." I go with my usual open-faced-sandwich combo—three little toast discs topped with lobster in lemon mayonnaise, shrimp in brandy-chive dressing, and gravlax with dill. Though Brenda insists I've got a Lipton monkey on my back, I always order iced tea. Though I insist she's got a death wish, she always opts for New York City tap water. Between bites we catch up on Jan, Sue, Gina, Jacqui, and Alison—friends now scattered across the Midwest. Sometimes we find ourselves aching for a past we couldn't wait to finish. Sometimes we study the very chic shoppers for signs of a face-lift. Sometimes we study each other. Brenda wears a simple black twinset and a silver chain around her neck. I wear burgundy lipstick and my heart on my sleeve. "I want a baby," I tell my friend, who has heard it all before.

"I know you do—I'm saving Lily's crib for when you have one," my friend answers in a voice that never fails to soothe.

"Can I have one of yours?" I ask.

"No."

"Then can I have your pickle?"

"No problem."

When the waitress offers us dessert, we simultaneously answer, "Just the check, please," then quickly reverse our decision and request one raspberry crème brûlée with two spoons.

I crack through the burnt-sugar lid to the satiny custard below and complain that Brenda's half has all the berries. She wonders whether it's possible to actually feel one's arteries clogging, but I assure her that the egg yolks cancel out the heavy cream. "You'll see," I promise, "it'll be the raspberries that do us in."

The two women at the next table begin arguing over whose turn it is to pick up the check. They're eighty years old if they're a day. "Oh, for God's sake, Rosalie, I'm not calling you next time I'm in the city," says one as she grabs for the bill. "Joanne, your money's no good here," says the other as she snatches it right back.

And in a flash we taste our future memories.

—*Lisa Kogan*

The Red Hat Society

Most chicks don't need an excuse to behave extravagantly and paint the town red, but it never hurts to have one—and in 2000, Sue Ellen Cooper and her friends in southern California gave every bird over fifty a red-letter reason to dress up, behave royally, and turn some heads. They formed the Red Hat Society—something like an adult play group—that encourages women over fifty to "make up for the sobriety of their youth" and frolic with other kindred spirits. The idea spread like wildfire and now the group has more than 400,000 members nationwide. Inspired by the poem "When I get old, I shall wear purple," members wear purple dresses, red hats, and red feather boas when they flock together at monthly meetings.

The Red Hats have only one rule: no rules. And lots of "hattitude." Their splashy activities often involve riding in flashy red and purple vehicles usually reserved for men in midlife. The San Francisco chapter, the Redwood Rubies, rented an old fire engine to take them on a tour of their city, blowing bubbles all the way.

When they don't feel like cruising around like homecoming queens, the Red Hats have no problem planning other activities. Les Chapeaux Rouges of Connecticut schedule unbirthday parties to make up for all of the birthdays they missed during the years before they knew one another. The Soaring Sisters of Downey, California, once went to a photo studio where each member had a glamour shot taken in her fanciest red-and-purple ensemble, but not before hitting the makeup chair of a professional stylist. From potlucks and prom-theme slumber parties to high teas and Red Hat parades—these hens aren't afraid to strut their stuff. A big (red) hats-off to these feisty ladies! For more information, visit their official Web site at www.redhatsociety.com.

Holidays, Chick Style

Chicks never let the calendar limit their opportunities to congregate. *Au contraire*—we look to the seasons for excuses and irrefutable reasons to flock together year-round. Here's a seasonal guide to partying with the chicks.

NEW YEAR'S TLC. That's Toenail polish, Lip gloss, and Cocktails—to start the New Year off right. Invite all your favorite babes, recruit a massage therapist (or two), and dedicate an afternoon to post-holiday recovery and beautification. Serve some spa-inspired refreshments like fruit, cucumber sandwiches, and white wine spritzers. Have everyone write down one New Year's resolution and have friends comment/question/lend support to hold you to it.

PAINT THE TOWN PINK. Have a ro-tic (that's romantic without the man) Valentine evening. Don your sexiest attire and hit the town with freewheeling gals who will keep your mind off romance and on their witty repartee. Drop into one of the hottest bars in town and make it yours. Surprise your gal pals by bringing a valentine for each one.

ST. PAT'S DAY CRAWL. Invite all your Patties for a traditional pub crawl to the hippest joints in town. You'll need a St. Patty to map out four spots for spirits and a mother hen who will keep her beak out of the beverages and see that the flock gets home safely. The rest will be responsible for wearing garish green garb and creating a merry melee.

CHICKO DE MAYO. Chicks love the spring—and this spicy at-home gathering is the springtime "Hola" wagon. Mexican fare with margaritas or sangria is a must. Blast the mariachi music and hoist up a piñata filled with lipsticks, lotions, and makeup brushes (in durable packaging) and get the chicks swinging.

FOURTH OF JULY BARBIE-CUE. Invite all the dolls over to lounge in the sun while sipping daiquiris, lighting sparklers, and flipping burgers. A patriotic theme—from invitations and nibbles to drinks and music—will make the event a doodle-dandy.

CHICK OR TREAT. Host a haunting for your best ghoulfriends. Go all-out on spooky decor, serve orange cocktails, real-looking "finger food," and candied apples. Chicks must be costumed and the tunes must be terrifying.

A GIRLFRIEND'S GRATITUDE GATHERING. Invite your gaggle to cozy up to the table and count your blessings. Stroll down memory lane, reminiscing and reliving your year—the talking, laughing, eating, drinking, and sistership. Serve up plenty of comfort food (see page 159) and thank each gal for the inspiration, love, support, and day-to-day sanity you bestow on each other!

LADIES AND LATKES. Throw a holiday party on or around Hanukkah for friends of all faiths. Fry up some latkes, bake some dreidel-shaped cookies, and ask your divas to bring a wrapped gift within a preset price range. Before the gift exchange, count your guests, put that many numbers in a hat, and have each guest draw a number. Number one gets first pick of the wrapped goodies. Number two can choose a new gift or take number one's prize (if she takes number one's gift, number one gets to unwrap another present) and so on until the lucky last number gets to choose from all the previous gifts—or the one remaining mystery prize.

Cindy may have won the annual margarita drinking contest but she was definitely not the last chick standing.

"**Celebrate** the happiness that friends are always giving, make every day a holiday and celebrate just living!"

—*Amanda Bradley*

Cheep Dates: *Cinema Therapy*

We love to weave a little tinsel into our nests now and then, so next time you're craving a hit of Hollywood, save that movie ticket money for your nest egg. Rent a few DVDs or videos, invite the chicks over, put out a tasty spread, and light up the marquee with your own home film festival.

CHICK FLICK FILM FEST

Invite all your girlfriends over for an evening of femme-fabulous flicks. Bring out all your pillows and set the stage for lolling about, eating, drinking, and talking through the movie without anyone hissing "Shhhh!"

Feature presentations: *Legally Blonde, Steel Magnolias, Thelma and Louise, Bridget Jones's Diary, Shirley Valentine, Emma, How Stella Got Her Groove Back, Charlie's Angels, Muriel's Wedding, Dirty Dancing, Sex and the City* reruns

Fare: Buttered popcorn, chocolate-chip brownies, hot tamales, nachos, M&Ms, and cosmopolitans

CHICKS FLY SOUTH

Y'all turn the air conditioning off, chip some ice, and stroll about in your house dress. Don't forget the mosquito repellent.

Feature presentations: *Sweet Home Alabama, Gone with the Wind, Forrest Gump, Fried Green Tomatoes, A Streetcar Named Desire, Divine Secrets of the Ya-Ya Sisterhood, O Brother, Where Art Thou?, The Grass Harp, Down in the Delta, The Color Purple, Crazy in Alabama, Driving Miss Daisy*

Fare: Fried chicken, biscuits, deviled eggs, peanuts, Moon Pies, Scarlett O'Haras (see page 90), sweet tea, and lemonade

CHICKS IN LOVE

Shoo the baby chicks off to bed early while you curl up and play a little cluck-cluck with your favorite rooster.

Feature presentations: *The English Patient, A Room with a View, An Officer and a Gentleman, When Harry Met Sally,*

Say Anything, Amélie, Casablanca, Moonstruck, Chocolat, The Big Sleep, Titanic, Shakespeare in Love, The Way We Were, Roman Holiday, It Happened One Night

Fare: Cheese fondue with chunks of French bread, grapes, chocolate-covered strawberries, and champagne

NYC (NEW YORK CHICKS)
Go urban and take a bite out of the Big Apple with these Gotham City–based adventures.

Feature presentations: *Breakfast at Tiffany's, An Affair to Remember, New York Stories, King Kong, Kate and Leopold, The Age of Innocence, Escape from New York, Hannah and Her Sisters, Working Girl, West Side Story, The Apartment, Manhattan*

Fare: Pizza, bagels, knish, anything take-out, Manhattans, and cosmopolitans

SCREAMIN' CHICKS
Dim all the lights, lock the doors and windows, and DO NOT leave the room alone to investigate that mysterious thudding noise in the back room. . . .

Feature presentations: *The Exorcist, Fatal Attraction, Halloween, Psycho, Rosemary's Baby, Alien, The Sixth Sense, Carrie, The Silence of the Lambs, Panic Room, The Others, Signs*

Fare: Spaghetti with meatballs, garlic bread, and Chianti

ROOSTER ROUSERS
"This is testosterone, it is only testosterone, please don't attempt to adjust your television sets. . . ."

Feature presentations: *Gladiator, Rocky, The Godfather, Reservoir Dogs, Mission: Impossible, Braveheart,* any James Bond, *The Matrix, Ben-Hur, Goodfellas, Unforgiven, Field of Dreams, Star Wars, Lara Croft: Tomb Raider*

Fare: Steak, baked potatoes, apple pie, and scotch

"Need I tell you that being a party pooper is a cardinal sin in the Church of Vivi? It's the eleventh commandment, which Moses forgot to bring down the mountain: **Thou Shalt Not be a Party Pooper.**"

—*Vivi Abbott,
in* Divine Secrets of the Ya-Ya Sisterhood

Suck it UP *Getting Down and Clean*

CLEANING UP BEFORE A PARTY HAS TO BE THE WORLD'S WORST TASK. Without fail my husband and I would bicker nonstop while cleaning, then be forced to play nice-nice and put on happy smiles when the guests arrived at our spotless abode. Finally I found a solution to break this pattern: I send Bud off to do errands and I summon up my own Mr. Clean, Barry White.

I know this takes a bit of imagination, sisters, but "get down" music really can help you get down to business when cleaning your house. Viewed the right way, housework can be an especially sensual task. First, you've got to turn the music up loud. You want to hear Barry say, "That's it, baby," as you glide the Hoover back and forth, back and forth, *uh huh.* Barry will whisper encouragement as you rub a dust rag over the base of the lamp and slide it up the neck. Even washing windows takes on a whole new luster with Barry in the background. I find myself racing to catch the stream of Windex dripping down the window as I gyrate to the music.

There is only one problem—what to do when your husband comes home and finds you, flushed and sweaty, sitting on the washing machine, singing along.

—*Ellen Birkett Morris*

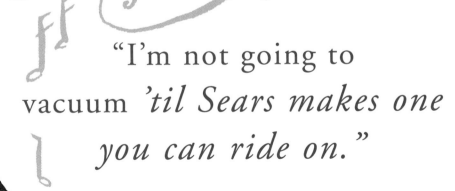

"I'm not going to vacuum *'til Sears makes one you can ride on.*"

—*Roseanne Barr*

for Better or Worse
AN ENTERTAINING PARTNERSHIP

When it comes to entertaining, some couples resemble the dynamic duo; others fall a bit short. Entertaining is all about strategy, and nothing is more important than the dynamics of your team. So get to know your rooster's party M.O., before the feathers fly. Here's how to diagnose and deal with your cohost:

THE RABBLE-ROUSER. He's been known to break the garbage disposal and spill margarita salt all over the kitchen floor as the first arrivals ring the doorbell. Or, while your twenty guests wait patiently for their lamb chops, he informs you that your mint jelly looked a little green and he tossed it yesterday. His talents are best exercised by running lengthy errands right up to dinnertime.

THE REFEREE. He calls it like he sees it, as if he's there to officiate and make sure you don't use appliances incorrectly. All is fair in love and cooking, and sometimes his fanaticism actually enhances your performance, so don't totally bench him. But do put him in charge of something—*anything*—to avoid his upstaging your meal with a lengthy lecture. (Make sure he thinks his assigned task is of extreme importance.)

THE REFUGEE. The ultimate introvert, this rooster rarely struts his stuff in public and typically disappears when the guests arrive. Though it might take a mighty nice filet mignon to coax him from his roost, his shy presence warms a seat nicely. Coo softly in his ear and, once the flock flies the coop, toss him the sponge and soap so he can clean up.

THE REGALER. Though he couldn't operate a Cuisinart if his life depended on it, this rooster's witty repartee is the life of the party and he entertains your guests effortlessly. A great distraction if the meal takes too long, he warms everyone's cockles with his cock tales. Assign him to greet your guests; he'll soon have them eating anything out of his hand.

A little birdie told us . . . Tell your partner that there will be no house tours given at the party—at least not of the master bedroom. You need one safe haven for all those baskets of laundry.

113

it's *an* UNPArty!

MY "GIRLS" HAVE BEEN MY "GIRLS" SINCE HIGH SCHOOL (and we did just celebrate our twentieth high school reunion), and we know that one of the greatest things about being a girl is being a Party Girl. Let's just say that through the years, we've celebrated a lot together.

In 1978, we had a big party in Jane's garage. That was the night Jane kissed Bill Dyrek and we were all so jealous. A year later, I had the slumber party where half the girls were late and I wouldn't let them in. As our high school years sped by, we added Kidnap Breakfasts, Super Bowl parties, and pre-prom parties to the list.

Then came college. We all ended up at different schools but managed to share good times together nonetheless. After college, the four of us lived together in a big house in Oakland Hills. As house-mates for three years, we had Bay-to-Breakers parties where we all looked cute in matching jogging outfits that we did not wear to jog in.

We had parties to celebrate master's degrees, and dress-up parties with our parents for Halloween. And we always had a lavish New Year's Eve party. The invitations were gorgeous and our clothes were even better.

Fast-forward seven years. Now there are husbands and a bunch of kids added to the mix. We try to keep up the New Year's Eve festivities, but frankly, after a few times squeezing into our cute little black dresses, choosing designated drivers, and ending up throwing confetti on someone's else's work colleague who we don't even know, we'd had enough. We said adios to our wild-child New Year's Eve parties and created a new tradition: the New Year's Eve Unparty.

Here's how you plan an unparty: You don't shower at all that day. (You stay in your pajamas, or grungy sweats.) You cook nothing, buy nothing, decorate nothing, and you do not hire a baby-sitter. You send no invitations and you have no beginning or ending time. You don't hire a D.J. And you definitely do NOT clean your house. Those are the rules. All you have to do to throw an unparty is tell everyone you love, whenever you see them, to come to your unparty on New Year's Eve. (Remember to give them the rules too.)

Since my first one, I've hosted a New Year's unparty almost every year, and we have more fun at it than at all of our other parties combined. What? Fun? With no planning and no money (OK, very little) spent? You bet! Because, the truth is, the fun is

"*Only those are unwise* who have

about being with my friends . . . not what we wear, eat, or drink, or where we go. We have everything we need at my house to entertain ourselves until the wee hours of the morning and beyond.

So, what goes on at my unparties? Nothing! Or as little as possible. But there are a few activities to help get the unparty rolling. First, we walk to a local convenience store and buy snacks, alcohol, and if we're really feeling naughty, some cigarettes or cigars. No brie or pâté is allowed. The snacks have to require no preparation—just pour them in a bowl or take the wrapper off and you're set. Chips, Ho-Hos, Dove bars, and M&Ms are big hits. Same thing with the drinks: No blending allowed. Mix it with soda or drink it straight.

Then we walk home with our goodies and tune into a station that is playing the Top 500 of the year, plug in the disco ball I got for $10 at a Halloween store sale, turn out the lights, turn the music up loud, open the doors and sit on the front porch, and have a good time. (It doesn't matter how cold it is— everyone can grab a coat or an old sweatshirt.) You'll be amazed how many people will just wander on over. Let the kids run wild (remember, you didn't clean up the house, so how much worse can it get?). They can fill up on chips and a few more videos won't hurt them. They're happy, you're happy.

When we're ready to turn the party up a notch, I have some good standby games in my closet. Twister is an old favorite—remember, this is the game where you have to put your right hand on red and your left foot on green. Trust me, there's nothing like having your best friend's husband's butt in your face to cause hysterical laughter. Then there's the old karaoke machine. We put in a little Shania Twain or Madonna, grab a broom or the vacuum cleaner for some musical accompaniment, and jump onto the furniture, singing our hearts out. If someone videotapes us, even better. Then watching the video becomes entertainment too.

The gals and I (and our families) swear by the New Year's Eve Unparty. After all, when is the last time any of us have had a chance to just hang out— no uncomfortable clothing, no worry about diets or money—and have fun? The unparty usually turns into an unsleepover (no assigned beds, no washing your makeup off) and we all get to be together on the first day of the new year, laughing at the craziness of the night before.

—*Katie Thompson*

A little birdie told us . . . You can host half parties too. You buy the basics, and invite your guests to bring the rest. And you attempt to clean up, but when your attempt fails, you let go and have fun anyway. You can adopt our friend Sally's mantra: "The messier the house, the more fun you must be having."

never dared to be fools." —*Elsie de Wolfe*

Putting on a Poker Face: *How to Host a Pink Poker Party*

We might not know when to walk away, or when to run, but we know chicks dig studs, chips, and jackpots. Time to get your core group of girlfriends together for a Pink Poker Party. Here's how to start shuffling:

1. Invite six savvy high-spirited gals. Emphasize that the first game is a "practice run."

2. Read through a book on poker, such as *The Rules of Neighborhood Poker According to Hoyle*, by Stewart Wolpin, and ask a poker enthusiast to "walk you through" the basics.

3. Create cheat sheets on the rules, showing different types of hands for yourself and the other players.

4. Encourage themed dress—cowboy boots, green visors, or even pink fuzzy slippers—anything goes!

5. Tell your buddies to raid their change drawers because you're playing for real money—pennies, nickels or quarters. Advise them that $5 should be enough to start. (Wink).

6. Create a "Diva Booty" by asking your friends to wear something special to bet on the last hand of the night—a piece of over-the-top costume jewelry, a tiara, a boa, long black evening gloves, etc. (The winner will be able to boast, "I won this playing poker with the chicks.")

7. Acquire a couple of fun card decks and a set of poker chips.

8. Create or ask a friend to mix up a fun selection of gambling music ("The Gambler" by Kenny Rogers, "Money Changes Everything" by Cyndi Lauper, "Whose Bed Have Your Boots Been Under?" by Shania Twain).

9. Serve finger food that allows you to eat while playing (deviled eggs, chicken fingers, carrot sticks, bridge mix, bite-size brownies).

10. Provide real or bubblegum cigars for each player.

Put on your best poker face and let the games begin!

"I always play cards on my wedding night." —*Lillian Russell*

FLYING THE COOP CHICK GETAWAYS

It's not easy to juggle all that life hands us and still be a girlfriend ringleader or active participant, but flocking away with the gals, if only for a brief retreat, is critical to mental health. Be it to a spa, a beach, or a golf course, make retreating with your gaggle of girls a regular part of your life. Here are a few ways to stage a getaway:

Set the date six to twelve months in advance to maximize attendance, then send reminders as it comes closer. Some chicks are superb at managing their schedules; others of us put our hen scratches on Post-its and hope they don't blow away. E-mail is the easiest way to communicate, but if you prefer regular mail, a festive "save the date" card always works wonders.

Send out a query to the group on how much they want to spend and whether they're willing to pay for airfare or prefer a destination within driving distance. Also determine how long people would like the retreat to last (weekend, long weekend, a year). Then set an approximate budget and length of the retreat.

Put your virtual heads together to decide whether you want to be having breakfast in bed before your scheduled pedicure or horseback riding before dawn. Some years your group might prefer a more mellow activity and other times they might be up for an exciting physical challenge. Here are just a few ideas for you and your gals:

Dude ranch
Surf camp
Spa retreat
Cruise
White-water rafting trip
Flea market/Antiquing/Auction expedition
Camping/Backpacking trip
Bed-and-breakfast scenic getaway
Wine tasting
Ski trip
Tennis or golf tournament
Yoga/Meditation retreat
Thelma & Louise road trip adventure
Cooking classes

Don't try to do it all yourself: If your trip requires multiple reservations or meal planning, get some volunteers from the gang to help with the planning.

When you are all together soaking up the sun with umbrella drinks or surging through white-water rapids, be sure to mention "next time" and get an idea from the group as to when, where, and what that might be! Also remember to pass on the torch of retreat-planner to another chick for next year.

A little birdie told us . . . Chicks from everywhere fly south to the Sweet Potato Queen's, a.k.a. Jill Connor Browne's, annual St. Patrick's Day march in Jackson, Mississippi. It is a hoot of a gals' gathering, with activities planned throughout the weekend. For more information go to: www.sweetpotatoqueens.com.

SEASON'S CHEATINGS Making Holiday Entertaining Easier

Don't let drudgery dampen your holiday revelry. With some smart planning and a revised perspective here and there, you can concentrate on the best part of any holiday—having fun.

1. Stock up on baking supplies and nonperishables two or three months before the holidays to cut down on last-minute trips to the store.

2. Keep party supplies organized by season and in clearly labeled boxes or plastic containers. That way, when you want those Halloween cocktail napkins or the holiday music you know exactly where to find them.

3. Host some parties that pull double duty—gatherings that are both fun and productive. Invite another family to make gingerbread houses with you; gather the girlfriends and make ornaments, bake cookies, write cards, or wrap gifts together; or organize a toy drive and have chili and spiced cider with your friends.

4. Make one-dish party foods (see Family-Style Meals, page 130) instead of five different hors d'oeuvres. For drinks, set out a bowl of punch or eggnog instead of serving mixed cocktails.

5. Stock up on some handy hostess gifts in advance of partygoing season (see page 136 for ideas).

6. Keep some stain busters—vinegar, carpet cleaner, club soda—in an easily accessible spot.

7. Instead of baking traditional pies, make crisps or cobblers.

8. Use canned cranberry sauce; just don't forget to stir and chill before serving.

9. If you have to buy many gifts, buy the same gift for as many people on your list as possible.

10. Opt for a relaxed open house instead of formal parties or sit-down meals. This sets a stress-free tone, and nobody is ever late—including the hosts!

from Bridget Jones's Diary

"Usually, week before Christmas, am hung over and hysterical, furious with self for not escaping to tiny woodman's cottage deep in forest to sit quietly by fire, instead of waking up in huge, throbbing, mountingly hysterical city with population gnawing off entire fists as thought of work/cards/present deadlines, getting trussed up like chickens in order to sit in gridlocked streets bellowing like bears at newly employed minicab drivers for trying to locate Soho Square using a map of central Addis Ababa, then arrive at parties to be greeted by same group of people have seen for last three nights only three times more drunk and hung over and want to shout, 'WILL YOU ALL JUST SOD OFF!' and go home. That attitude is both negative and wrong."

—Helen Field

fOil*ing* All *the* Fun

HERE IS A REEE-ALLY CHEAP THING TO DO AT PARTIES—your kids' or your own. Go to Sam's Club and buy some giant rolls of heavy-duty aluminum foil. Serve a couple rounds of drinks to the parents and then whip out the foil and instruct everyone to make outfits for themselves. See, the great thing about that heavy foil is that you can shape it into anything and it will stay put.

I take full credit for this discovery. Tammy Carol was moving to a new house and she invited a whole big lot of people over to eat and drink up everything in the old house so's she wouldn't have to haul it to the new one. As will so often happen when you have a whole big lot of people, a separation occurred— not by anyone's design, it just happened, and suddenly we found there was a group of *us* and a group of *them*. *Us* went inside to root around and see what hadn't been consumed yet, while *them* sat out in the shade by the pool. Malcolm White and I were the bosses of *us*. Malcolm was plundering the liquor cabinet and I was in the pantry when I saw it—a very large, unopened box of heavy-duty aluminum foil, literally thousands of yards of the stuff—and it just came to me, as the best ideas will do, and I hollered at Malcolm to come see, which he did. "Let's make outfits!" I said, and he never even gave it a thought—just snatched the box and yanked off a big sheet of foil and commenced designing.

That's when we discovered that you can make a thong out of aluminum foil. You can also make a preternaturally large codpiece. In no time at all, all of *us*, Tammy Carol included, had fashioned what we thought were extremely fetching outfits, and we decided that all of *them* would probably like to play, too, so out we pranced for what we considered their viewing pleasure and creative inspiration but turned out instead to be their ultimate befuddlement. Not only did they not want to join in; they didn't understand why we were so completely carried away over it.

So you will have to judge for yourself the nature and quality of the crowd at your party. Kids will love making aluminum foil outfits, of course, but make sure they're old enough that you don't have to be making their outfits for them, which definitely cuts into your own enjoyment. If the parents are a bunch of *us*, by all means, whip out the foil. If you've got a bunch of *them* for parents, don't bother. But if you're planning your own birthday (or other) party, you might want to examine your guest list closely. A group of *them* will require a whole lot more money and effort on your part, while a group of *us* is way more fun and it just doesn't take booshitdiddly to entertain *us*.

We might as well face the truth: The only kids worth having a birthday party for are us.

—*Jill Conner Browne, THE Sweet Potato Queen*

"The Queens are always searching for **new entertainment**." —*Jill Conner Browne*

TLC *turkey-loathing chick*

THIS IS THE STORY OF A TURKEY, and the things she cooked for Thanksgiving dinner. It is not an easy story to tell. It includes a bulb baster, those useless little metal rods Julia Child uses for trussing, and quantities of cheesecloth heretofore undreamed of. And butter—my God, the butter. Even now, a full year later, I can see my hands stretched before me, gleaming horribly like that cranberry jelly you get in a can.

It's hard to know where to begin. My husband says that I was conscious and not on drugs, alcohol, or cold medication when I decided to invite both my family and his family to our home for Thanksgiving dinner last year. Only eighteen people could make it. Some had other commitments. Perhaps they had heard that it would be my first turkey.

I bought the bird from the butcher. "I need the biggest fresh turkey you can manage to trot out," I said, struggling into my competent person's air like a pair of 501 Levi's two sizes too small. The butcher wrote on a piece of brown paper. I went home and read cookbooks. One said that in cooking turkey, allow fifteen minutes a pound. Another said allow twenty-five minutes a pound. One said to cook the turkey five hours. Another said to cook the turkey eight hours. "It depends," said my mother-in-law. "On what?" "On how accurate your oven temperature is," she said.

I was doomed.

"I make a mean duck with orange-cranberry relish," I said hopefully to my husband at breakfast.

"Not on Thanksgiving you don't," he said without looking up from his newspaper.

I knew that there were turkeys available shot full of some stuff that made them all plump and juicy, turkeys that came with little slimy instruction booklets packed in with the giblets, turkeys that had those plastic daggers that pop up to tell you when they're done. I couldn't buy one of those turkeys because I had long ago sworn off that kind of prepared foodstuff (although on nights when my husband had to work late and the kids were safely tucked away in bed, I would sometimes make myself a big portion of Kraft macaroni and cheese, for old time's sake). I needed a fresh turkey, with no additives, no preservatives, no chemicals, nothing to protect me from the possibility that I would pull something from the oven with white meat resembling wallboard.

It's important to note here what I think of as Quindlen's dictum: It is impossible to cook badly something you love. I am constitutionally incapable of making bad fudge or bad fettuccine Alfredo. But I do not love turkey; I don't even like turkey. The only part I eat is the big triangular piece of skin covering the stuffing at the back. My brother-in-law and I

"Flops are part of life's menu, and I've never been a girl

have for years bickered over it, although now that we both have children we've gotten pretty adult about the whole thing. We split it and then bicker over who gets the bigger piece. As far as I'm concerned, the rest of the turkey is a testimonial to what boring people we've turned the Pilgrims into. Calvin Trillin is leading a nationwide campaign to have spaghetti carbonara declared the official Thanksgiving food. I say, "Hear, hear!"

That said, the turkey was delivered on Wednesday afternoon. "I hope it fits in your oven," said the butcher, with what I can only describe as a smile. The turkey was enormous. It was as ugly as a baby just after birth and looked about the same: wrinkled, misshapen, with odd bumps and bruises and a weird white-pink color. Luckily, it fit in my oven. It did not, however, fit in my refrigerator.

I was doomed.

"Put it on the fire escape," a friend of mine said, "it's colder out there today than it is in your refrigerator."

"Stray cats," I said.

"Wrap it in foil and put it in a box."

"Rain."

"Put a tarp over it."

"You think of everything," I said. "You come over here and cook this thing."

Well, I did put it on the fire escape, at least until I could farm out all the other food in the refrigerator to my friends. In the morning I put it in the oven.

First I stuffed it, rubbed two sticks of soft butter into its pathetic skin, and shrouded it in cheesecloth. I worked out a roasting time between five hours and eight hours, basted it every half hour, and hoped for the best.

Inevitably, my mind kept turning to the time I first made a chicken, which sounds soothing but wasn't. I was seventeen. My mother talked me through it: season, truss, roast, let rest, carve. The only thing she left out was thaw. Even today, when family members have had a little eggnog and want a good laugh, someone says, "Anna's chicken!" and they all roar and roll around while I have another drink.

I was doomed.

Or so I thought. It was a good turkey; not a great turkey, but not a "family joke" turkey either. It was pretty juicy, and it wasn't raw, and it looks good in the photographs, which is more than you can say for me. The only complaint I have about the whole episode is that I was so busy worrying about the turkey that my brother-in-law got a much bigger piece of the skin than I did, which I can assure you will not happen this year. Oh, yes, I'm doing it again this Thanksgiving, making my second turkey for only eleven people. A lot of the others say that since they were here last year, they have to go to the in-laws' this year. None of them know about the fire escape, so maybe they are telling the truth.

—*Anna Quindlen*

to miss out on any of the courses." —*Rosalind Russell*

Need some new serving containers to brighten up your buffet table? Try the grocery store or farmers' market. (Note: Though these natural bowls are typically watertight, they may be unpredictable, so we recommend that you set them on a plate or protected surface in case they leak.)

BELL PEPPERS

With red, yellow, orange, and green to choose from, you're sure to pick a pepper that looks good with your party spread. Find the biggest, roundest ones you can, slice the tops off, and clean them out. Fill them with dips, condiments, or salad dressings.

MELONS

We've all seen the watermelon basket at least once. If that's too tired an idea, take it down a notch and create a rustic bowl for fruit salad, punch, or an ice bucket to chill wine. Halved cantaloupes and honeydew melons are the perfect size for single servings of fruit salad or cold soup. They also make a great presentation for yogurt or sweet sauces.

CITRUS FRUITS

Use hollowed-out grapefruits, lemons, or oranges to serve bar garnishes like cherries, lemon slices, and mint sprigs. Or make an unusual dessert presentation: Slice the top off and clean out the pulp of a lemon or orange, squirt in some juice, and fill it with the same-flavored sorbet and freeze. (You might need to shave the bottom a bit so it's stable.)

PUMPKIN

Remove the top and clean it out for the perfect savory soup tureen.

APPLES, MINI PUMPKINS, AND SQUASH

Use a paring knife to carve out a little recess for a tea light. Slice a bit off the bottom to stabilize it, set a few on the table, and get ready for the compliments.

❋ A trademark party-girl accessory that gets you in the mood and sets the tone for your party—a tiara, a boa, or fiery red cowgirl boots!

❋ A collection of party music for a variety of moods: romantic, rowdy, mellow, or refined

❋ Ingredients for whipping up a deliciously strong drink

❋ A platter full of frozen hors d'oeuvres in the freezer

❋ A set of nice table linens

❋ A set of well-worn table linens and/or some bright, funky vinyl tablecloths

❋ Stationery for scratching down stylish greetings and thank-you notes

❋ A calendar with all the red-letter days marked—birthdays, anniversaries, holidays, girls' night out

❋ A friend from whom you can borrow that very item (creamer, extra salt and pepper, gravy boat) you need at the last minute

❋ A welcoming adornment on the front door—a wreath, a sign, a beribboned tag

❋ Countless holidays to celebrate with friends (see Holidays, Chick Style, page 108)

❋ A gang of gals who will always be at your soiree, come hell, high water, or hunky new boyfriends

❋ A list of "day-after" damage-control service providers: a reliable carpet and upholstery cleaning service, a florist (for soothing neighbors' ruffled feathers), a handyman, and a massage therapist who makes house calls

uNleasHed *at* HYannispOrt

ONE FALL MY HUSBAND AND I WERE INVITED TO ETHEL KENNEDY'S Hyannisport home for a fund-raiser for the RFK Foundation. Since we did not party with the Kennedys on a regular basis (OK, never), this was a highly anticipated event for our extended family, friends, neighbors, and former neighbors. I was instructed to take copious notes on the evening, knowing that our family would probably eat out on the story for months to come. As parents of very young children, our typical evening outings were to places that had self-serve soda. I was out of practice at pulling myself together for anything more than a kiddie "play-date" and had no idea what my postchildbirth size was (nor was I ready to know). But, in a stroke of good fortune, I found a long-forgotten black cocktail dress in the back of my closet, which, with the appropriate steel-lined under-garments and a few breathing exercises, fit. My husband wore his preppy blue blazer and a favorite Brooks Brothers tie.

Ethel's home was an elegant mix of formality and beachy ease, with striking contemporary art in gilded frames and countless family photographs. It was unsettling to find my glance at an unassuming black-and-white photograph being met by the gaze of someone famous, and I couldn't help but stare a little too long. The warmly lit living room had whitewashed floors, over-stuffed blue and white chairs, and round side tables covered with pictures in silver frames and porcelain knickknacks. When Ethel turned to greet me in the receiving line I had a brief, but horrible, amnesiac moment. I was so entranced by the surreality of wandering through her home that I temporarily forgot who I was and why I was there. While I struggled for the right words to introduce myself, she patiently waited and her unhurried, reassuring handshake helped me relax and recover. As I moved on down the receiving line, she gave me a smile and a small pat on the back. Later, I couldn't help but notice that she didn't give small pats to everyone in the line.

The party was on the lawn under a monstrous tent facing the beachfront. It felt almost like a small town with its own tunnels, kitchen, and bathrooms. Before dinner, as we enjoyed our cocktails and appetizers, I hissed loudly to Dave, "That's KEVIN COSTNER!" When he did not respond with a raised eyebrow, or even a nod, I hissed it again—louder. Kevin and his date looked at me coolly as they walked over to the bar.

I barely had time to recover from that social gaffe when the next opportunity for embarrassment hit; there was a gift bag. People like me should be warned about goodie bags beforehand—especially when they are really, really, really great. This wasn't just a "bag." It was a very sleek, sophisticated black bag, and to someone who'd been lugging around a diaper bag for two years, this was a big deal. Yet I might have feigned calm, if the bag hadn't been stuffed with goodies like Kiehl's beauty products, a Tiffany key chain, an RFK Foundation silver pen, and a watch. Then the goodie-bag hander-outer told me I could have two! (That's when I started jumping up and down.) And that's the moment when I became aware of the animals. There was a squeal after I jumped—for an instant I thought it might have been emitted by me (a sort of subconscious vocal discharge brought on by my goodie bag excitement)—but then I looked down, and realized I had landed on a dog's paw. Another guest looked and muttered disapprovingly, "I hope that wasn't Ethel's dog" as the dog scurried away through one of the long tunnels. Well, Ethel's dog or not, I was not going to chase after some canine; clearly I needed to compose myself and concentrate on salvaging my social graces.

Dave and I hustled off to our table and as we ate I noticed there were several other dogs, of different breeds and sizes, roaming freely inside the tent, indulging in doggy things like sniffing and scratching.

We had been deliciously seated next to a table of younger Kennedys, one or two of whom were patting dogs beside them. I couldn't resist taking another peek into my goodie bag, which was under the table. As I leaned down, I noticed that the scruffy terrier I had maimed earlier was under my table poking and prodding for food. Our eyes met and he came over to lick my hand and beg for food. This was the last thing I needed—I was at an adults-only event for the first time in months, if not

years, and I was not going to socialize with a dog. But I did feel a little guilty, so, in an attempt at an apology, I took a scrap of uneaten meat from my plate, gave the terrier a whiff, then lobbed it delicately near the younger, dog-loving Kennedys' table.

My head was deeply in my goodie bag when I heard fierce growling and barking coming from the table where I had thrown the meat. Suddenly the lovely rose and wildflower centerpiece lurched and the entire table crashed over as a pack of rowdy dogs waged combat underneath. The young Kennedys' meals went flying as they struggled to separate the dogs and shield themselves from soaring china and silverware. I was shocked. I was also terrified: I was not ready to go home, and surely instigating a canine feeding frenzy would be grounds for a swift and embarrassing dismissal. My husband and I stood frozen, awkwardly staring at the upside-down table, fleeing dogs, and food-splattered Kennedys. Then the laughter started and rolled through the tent like a wave. We relaxed and noticed that the loudest chuckle came from Ethel, who hadn't missed a beat in her energetic dancing—as if things like this happened all the time.

—*Emily Miles Terry*

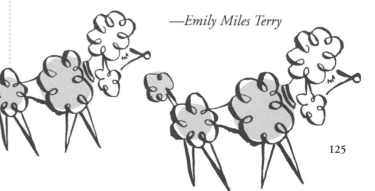

NOTHING GETS A PARTY OFF TO A GOOD START like greeting your guests with a little treat as they arrive; or sending them home with a thoughtful parting gift. Here are a few offerings that can pull double duty.

nestwarmers

Buy inexpensive glass votives and get crafty. Create a paper template for a "sleeve" to wrap around the holder. (Be sure to keep it at least ⅛ of an inch from the top lip of the holder.) Using your template, cut some pretty tissue, handmade paper, fabric, or wrapping paper (anything sheer ought to allow the light to shine through). Now get creative—inscribe a name, a message, or a quote with a gold paint pen; rubber-stamp a design; or punch holes to make a pattern. Then secure the sleeve to the votive holder with permanent double-stick tape and "belt it" with a ribbon or piece of raffia. Pop in a scented tea light, and your guest will glow with gratitude.

picture perfect

Tiny picture frames are easy to find at discount stores and they make unique place card holders. You can keep it simple and fill the frame with a piece of pretty paper with the guest's name written on it, or you can funk it up with designs. Photocopy a quirky close-up of the guest of honor, and frame it. Or clip "art" from magazines and create little collages, choosing images or symbols that fit the theme of your party. Or frame a fortune from a fortune cookie at each setting. Artistic expression is unlimited.

Betty's homemade cheese ball always whipped the party into a frenzy.

magnetic mementos

You can find cut-to-size magnetic sheets at all craft supply stores. Photocopy a fun picture or piece of art, stick it to the magnet, and you've created a useful and unique party favor that will hang around with your guest for years.

sweet partings

Fill miniature Chinese take-out boxes (found at party supply stores and ethnic markets) with fun candies. You could do a retro theme, with Tootsie Rolls, gum drops, and Necco wafers. A garden party might feature gummy worms and flower-embellished truffles. Or simply choose gourmet jelly beans in a fitting color scheme. Toss in a kitschy plastic toy or type up a whimsical fortune or horoscope. Tie with a ribbon, top with a silk flower, and add a key tag.

party animals

At large pet supply stores they have machines that will engrave pet ID tags while you wait: The designs range from simple circles to hearts. (Avoid the fire hydrant or bone tag.) Have one engraved for each of your guests and, using thin ribbon, tie it to the wine glass at each place setting. It's a great way to keep drinks with their rightful owners, and they can take the dog tags home.

a charming wine

Wine charms are easy to make and you can personalize them any way you want. Use your guests' real names, or make up a collection of fun pseudonyms: Diva, Queen, Tipsy, Kitten, Buzzed, Foxy, etc. If you are creating charms for a special event, personalizing the wine charms is a great way to celebrate the guest of honor, pair guests up, or initiate conversation-starting games.

Supplies*

Eight ¾-inch wire hoops
Eight 2-inch head pins
Eight crystal beads in different colors
Alphabet beads
Small round-nose pliers
Small wire-cutting pliers

Start out with a colored crystal bead on the head pin, then spell out the names of your guests in alphabet beads. Clip the excess wire from the top of the head pin with wire cutters, being sure to leave enough to create a small loop using the round-nose pliers. Use the pliers to attach the name to the wire hoop and close the loop to secure.

* All found at a craft or jewelry supply store.

plastic PeTunias *(how to give a garden party with no garden)*

IN THE EARLY 1960S, PLASTIC FLOWERS WERE A NOVELTY and were considered exotic. One day, with a bare garden, and the ladies of her social club on their way to a luncheon at our house, my mother began to experiment with plastic posies. My father and I stared amazed as stunted, bare bushes of the box hedge variety began sporting roses. Sad yellow azaleas sprouted white daisies, and wilted pale geraniums burst forth with trumpet lilies. As my mother pinned and tied each flower on, she explained her entertaining philosophy to her small audience: "When you are entertaining in your home, you must paint a sensory picture for your arriving guests," she said. "A whiff of delicious food cooking, candlelight, music, and flowers. With a little creativity you can achieve quite a lovely scene."

Years after the successful plastic-petunia ladies luncheon (my mother's guests never even noticed), as I walked breezily through our garden one day, I was brought to an abrupt halt as I saw that my mother was once again preparing for guests. "Mom, did you wrap plastic flowers into all the outdoor plants?" I asked. With a slow turn of her head, and an enigmatic smile, she replied, "Well, there was a drought this year. And Karen, when you are entertaining, you must paint a picture." And she went back to her plants singing softly, "Take my hand. I'm a stranger in paradise . . ."

Whether it was a bare garden, drought, fire, or pestilence, nothing prevented my mother from entertaining with grace and style, nor from painting that beautiful picture for her guests. Here are a few of the lessons I learned from her about rising to *any* occasion when entertaining:

1. When the tediousness of chopping and mixing get to you: *Choose a hostess theme song and sing it throughout your preparations. Hers is* "Stranger in Paradise."

2. When the water has been turned off right before a dinner party: *Replace the water in any recipes with wine and serve aperitifs instead of coffee.*

3. When an inebriated guest has fallen asleep on the dining-room table, threatening to take the tablecloth and everything on it with him: *Hang on to the corner of the tablecloth and tell one of your best stories—as if nothing has happened.*

4. When the chef gets drunk and begins to chase the female caterers around your kitchen: *Confiscate the brandy.*

5. When your husband brings home a skinned possum for a family reunion dinner in your cabin in the woods: *Refuse, on the grounds that you have already cooked squirrel, duck, and venison on a wood-burning stove.*

6. When you're giving a party and the hillside in back of your home catches fire: *Turn on the sprinklers, and politely ask the firemen to lower their voices.*

—*Karen Miles*

Tongue flappers

When it comes to delivering the perfect bons mots, party girls can use a little inspiration. Take your cues from some chicks who weren't afraid to open up in a crowd. Here are some famous witty utterances to use in certain situations to enliven the party. Just begin your sentence with "Didn't someone once say . . ."

WHEN SOMEONE ACTS SILLY

"The secret of eternal youth is arrested development." —Alice Roosevelt Longworth

ON NOT BEING RECOGNIZED

"What's the matter, dahling, don't you recognize me with my clothes on?" —Tallulah Bankhead

TO A MAN WHOSE SHIRT IS UNBUTTONED TOO LOW

"I see your fly is open higher than usual today." —Dorothy Parker

WHEN SEATED NEXT TO SOMEONE WITH A TESTOSTERONE IMBALANCE

"The roosters may crow, but the hens deliver the goods." —Ann Richards

WHEN PRESSED FOR DETAILS ABOUT A DELICATE MATTER

"That ain't the half of it, honey, but that's all I'm telling." —Alice Coachman

IF YOUR GLASS RUNS DRY

"Fill what's empty, empty what's full and scratch where it itches." —Alice Roosevelt Longworth

DUCKING OUT OF A GOSSIPY CONVERSATION

"Gossip is news running ahead of itself in a red satin dress." —Liz Smith

ON RELATIONSHIPS

"A woman has got to love a bad man once or twice in her life, to be thankful for a good one." —Marjorie Kinnan Rawlings

WHEN CAUGHT BEHAVING BADLY

"I know I've been a perfect bitch. But I couldn't help myself." —Bette Davis

WHEN OFFERED YOUR CHOICE OF DESSERT

"When caught between two evils, I generally like to take the one I never tried." —Mae West

EVERY CHICK NEEDS TO BE ABLE TO WHIP UP ONE BIG DISH IN A PINCH. Here are a couple of fantastic family-style meals for all types of crowds.

Phony macaroni

Okay, we confess that this is not as fabulous as a totally-from-scratch recipe, but it is delicious, and it sure hits the spot when you are short on time and longing for comfort food. (This dish is all about instant gratification, so buy the cheeses already grated and shredded.)

1 family-size box (14.5 oz) white cheddar macaroni and cheese mix

¼ cup milk (this is in addition to the amount called for on the box)

⅓ cup grated romano cheese

1 cup shredded cheddar cheese

3 tablespoons butter

1½ cups white bread cut into ¼-inch cubes

1. In a large saucepan, boil the macaroni according to the directions on the box. When it is cooked, drain the pasta in a colander and set aside.

2. In the saucepan, over medium heat, melt the amount of butter called for on the box. To the melted butter, add the amount of milk called for on the box directions plus the additional ¼ cup milk. Stir in the cheese sauce packet from the box.

3. Add the grated romano and ½ cup shredded cheddar and stir until melted.

4. Stir the macaroni into the cheese mixture. Pour into a 9 x 9 baking dish.

5. For the topping, melt the butter in the microwave, in a medium-sized glass bowl. Add the bread cubes to the bowl and toss to coat. Cover the top of the macaroni and cheese with the bread cubes; then sprinkle with ½ cup cheddar cheese.

6. Broil for 5 minutes, or until golden brown.

Serves 8

Turkey Tetrazzini

Great for leftover turkey or chicken, this dish can be modified to fit family preferences, or taken to potluck suppers. A connoisseur's casserole.

4 cups shredded or cubed cooked turkey

12 ounces green fettuccine

¼ pound butter, plus 2 tablespoons to grease pan

1 cup cream

1¼ cups grated parmesan cheese

3 tablespoons chopped parsley

8 ounces sliced fresh mushrooms

3 shallots diced

3 cups low-sodium chicken stock

¼ teaspoon white pepper

1. Preheat oven to 375°F. Cook, drain, rinse, and cool the fettuccine.

2. Heat butter in a medium frying pan, add mushrooms, and sauté for 3 minutes.

3. Add shallots and cook for 2 minutes. Stir in cream, pepper, and parsley.

4. Cook over low heat for about 5 minutes, until mixture begins to thicken, stirring frequently.

5. Slowly add in the chicken stock. Stir until blended over low heat for 2 minutes.

6. Add 1 cup parmesan cheese, reserving ¼ cup to top the dish. Cook over low heat, stirring constantly until cheese melts.

7. Remove immediately from heat and stir in turkey. Let sit while preparing the casserole dish.

8. Butter a large casserole dish. Line the bottom of the dish evenly with cooked noodles. Pour sauce mixture over the noodles. Top with remaining parmesan cheese.

9. Bake until bubbly and heated through, about 35 to 40 minutes. (Freezes nicely if prepared ahead of time.)

Serves 6 to 8

"I finally figured out that the only reason to be alive is to enjoy it."

—*Rita Mae Brown*

Dear Morgana,

I JUST WANTED TO DROP YOU A QUICK NOTE to thank you for inviting me to your party last week. I'm not very good at parties. But I guess you know that by now. I feel awkward at them and tend to overcompensate by acting in a way that others who don't know me well might consider a tad weird. However, you know me well and besides, you're a very perceptive and, I might add, very forgiving person.

I guess what I'm trying to say is I'm really really really sorry for what happened. Maybe it was good, though. Maybe this will be one of those things that a little while from now you'll look back on and laugh at. Okay, maybe it will be longer than a little while. Eventually, though, after at most a few decades, there's bound to be some laughter. Isn't there? Oh God, I'm so sorry.

I know that we're good enough friends that I could just call you on the phone, but I thought a letter would be preferable for two reasons. One, often it's easier to say things in a letter than it is to say them in person. And two, you don't seem to be answering my phone calls anymore.

Sometimes nobody answers the phone—even if I let it ring over five hundred times (I've counted). At other times, somebody who sounds like you (but I'm sure isn't)

TO DO:
1. call
2. apologize
3. write Letter
4. send flowers
5. grovel

answers and asks who it is. When I say "Ellen," that person (who, as I said before, I'm sure isn't you, because you are much too compassionate) immediately develops an obviously fake Russian accent and says, "She not home. She move far away to place with no phone. I begging you, please leave alone."

All that being said, let me begin my apology.

I think a lot of what happened can be traced back to the rum cake I brought over. I just looked over the recipe, and I see now that it called for two tablespoons of rum. For some reason, maybe because I was nervous because I don't cook that much, I misread that as two bottles of rum. It's an honest mistake, and your little nephews were eventually going to find out what a hangover is anyway.

I had at least two slices of the rum cake, and I believe that's why I blurted out that your real name is Marge. I thought everybody already knew! I also thought that everybody would find your old nickname, "Large Marge," funny. I understand now that it isn't funny. Anyway, it shouldn't bother you because you're not heavy anymore. Oh yes, I'm also sorry that I told people about your liposuction. But at least I didn't tell anybody about your breast enlargement surgery. Oh, that's right, I did. Sorry.

As for what I call "the charades incident," for some reason I get a little competitive (okay, way too competitive) playing party games—once again, to make up for my own insecurities. That's why when Reverend Green couldn't figure out I was doing *Fried Green Tomatoes* and kept on guessing *Two Mules for Sister Sarah* (which, you have to admit, isn't even close—it doesn't even have the same number of words!) I got mad.

That in no way excuses my calling him a rat @4%^#$%, *%$@-eating moron. Isn't it cute when you write your curses out that way? It's too bad I didn't say it like that. Also, when I jokingly implied that he was a child molester, I had no idea about the recent trial (though I am happy to hear that all the charges have been dropped).

Now, the gift. I was under the mistaken impression (boy, hindsight is twenty-twenty, isn't it?) that the party was for your wedding shower. That's why I got what I considered to be a gag gift. I didn't know it was a party for your grandmother's ninetieth birthday. Otherwise, I never would

have gotten her the crotchless underwear and the coupon for the free nipple piercing. . . .

—*Ellen DeGeneres*

A little birdie told us . . . If you forget a name, don't try to avoid the person or awkwardly skirt the issue. Unless the person is your next-door neighbor, face up to your lapse with a simple "Please tell me your name again." Or "I remember we met at . . . , but I'm terrible with names."

"If three people say you are an ass, put on a bridle."

—*Spanish proverb*

Being a gracious partygoer is more or less an intuitive skill, but there are some tried-and-true tricks to staying on the best-guest list. Take the guesswork out of guest etiquette with this handy guide for the Party Girl on the go.

RSVP MEANS "RÉPONDEZ, S'IL VOUS PLAÎT." (Or, in plain English, "Please respond.") Nothing boils a person more than an unacknowledged invitation. Unless the invitation specifies regrets only, reply promptly and graciously, whether or not you can attend the party.

PREPARE TO PARTY. Don't wait until the day of the party to get directions, buy a hostess gift (see "Present and Accounted For," page 136), or plan your outfit. Last-minute snags can seriously put the kibosh on your party-girl mojo.

EARLY BIRDS ANNOY CHICKS. Typically you should plan to arrive "fashionably on time," which means a good ten to fifteen minutes after the party is set to begin—unless it's a surprise party, in which case you should arrive precisely on time.

DON'T BRING UNINVITED COMPANY—EVER. If you have a dire circumstance, and know the host very well, give her a courtesy call as far in advance as you can, explain your dilemma, beg her forgiveness, and leave her a gracious out.

BEAR NO-HASSLE GIFTS. Your present shouldn't require attention from your hostess. Fresh flowers should be arranged in a vase and foods should be ready to serve.

LET YOUR PARTY PERSONA ROCK. Leave your grudges at the door (bad directions, inconvenient time, mud that ruined your shoes) and set your sights on breathing a breath of fresh air into the event. Listen to the rhythm of the room and show off your best guest moves.

DON'T HOG THE HOSTESS. Of course you probably know her well, but you aren't the only one in the room, so don't keep her from circulating among her guests or attending to other duties.

STAY OUT OF THE KITCHEN'S CLUTCHES. Unless your hosts specifically request your help or your presence, avoid congregating in the kitchen.

OBSERVE THE RULES OF ENGAGEMENT. Introduce yourself to other guests and stoke the fires of conversation. A friendly compliment ("I love your shoes!") or a "How do you know each other?" are easy ways to spark a conversation with another guest.

ENJOY THE FOOD. And don't be afraid to ask for more. It's the ultimate form of flattery.

CHICKS KNOW HOW TO SAY CIAO. Don't feel you have to say good-bye to everyone present, but always find and thank your hosts before you take off. Don't indulge in long good-byes: just pay your dues and be on your way.

duLy noted

I DON'T LIKE TO THINK OF MYSELF AS THE KIND OF PERSON WHO BRINGS WINE OR FLOWERS to a dinner party just to get credit with the hostess. But when you've spent an entire evening stressing about whether the hostess knows the Rabbit Ridge merlot is from you, as I did the other night, you have to face certain truths about yourself.

A lot has been written about partygoing strategies—how to mingle and network and dress and not overeat—but the literature on gift-giving tactics is surprisingly slim, especially for something so crucial.

"What's really scary," a friend said, "is when you're greeted at the door by the spouse who doesn't care about such things, or, even worse, by a guest who has deputized himself as a para-host. He—it's usually a guy—takes your wine, or whatever you've brought, and puts it down on some remote table, and you know the hostess will never see it or hear about it. She'll go to her grave thinking you came empty-handed."

Should this horrible situation arise, what should you do?

"You can't let it happen in the first place," a frequent partygoer advised. "No matter what happens, you don't let go of that wine bottle until you've shown it to the hostess yourself—even if you have to duke it out with the person taking your coat."

"What I do," a friend explained, "is bring something in Tupperware that has to be transferred to a serving plate, or which needs to have a fancy glaze added at the last minute. That way, I'm right there in the kitchen, so there's no way the hostess won't notice me and my 'gift.'"

A variation on this theme involves bringing cut flowers and then conducting a very obvious search for a vase, or arriving with a dessert that needs to be flambéed.

But there's a problem with those maneuvers. If the annoyance factor of accepting your offering becomes too high (or if you set the living room on fire), it may actually outweigh the gift itself, thereby canceling the credit. And then your hostess will remember, but for all the wrong reasons.

"I like to have a bouquet delivered to the hostess the afternoon of the party," a professional guest revealed. "It's very elegant." Yeah, maybe, but pricey, too. In which case, why not take your chances that your present will be noticed, and if it's not, simply do what George Costanza did in one of my favorite *Seinfeld* episodes: Steal it back. The self-regifting maneuver is not without its appeal, but getting caught stuffing a dripping bouquet into your clutch is even worse than being busted scoping out the medicine cabinet, and besides, it still leaves you in a no-credit situation. You've got your flowers back, but your reputation's gone.

So, S., if you're reading this, that great merlot was from me.

—Beth Teitell

Present and Accounted For

ood guests never show up empty-handed, but sometimes you want to arrive bearing something beyond the usual bottle of wine or bouquet of flowers. Something you know the hostess is particularly fond of is best. Here are some fun, easy alternatives to consider:

- An elegant wine stopper, an insulated wine tote, or a fun corkscrew are unexpected add-ons to the typical bottle of wine

- A bottle of high-quality extra-virgin olive oil or balsamic vinegar

- A plant for her new garden

- A recipe book of cocktails or appetizers

- A scented pillar candle or set of aromatherapy votives

- Cheese spreaders

- Homemade Herbes de Provence in a pretty jar or antique sugar shaker (see recipe)

- An I-Zone camera and film for taking party pictures

- Nuts or chocolates on an attractive serving dish for her to keep

- A cocktail accessory kit that includes colorful paper napkins, decorative picks, a jar of cherries, and a jar of olives

- A set of pretty boxed notecards

- Mulling spices for wine or cider with a side of cinnamon sticks

HOMEMADE HERBES DE PROVENCE

Of course, if this recipe is made with your own home-grown and dried herbs, it will be even more appreciated.

  3 tablespoons dried thyme
  3 tablespoons dried marjoram
  3 tablespoons dried savory
  1 teaspoon dried basil
  1 teaspoon dried rosemary
  ½ teaspoon dried sage
  ½ teaspoon fennel seeds

Combine all ingredients and mix well. Pour into a tightly lidded jar. When stored in a cool, dark place, the spices will keep up to 4 months.

A little birdie told us . . . Gifts are sometimes separated from their givers in the heat of the meet and greet, so ensure that your gift gets credit by attaching a small note or decorative tag.

tHe "*Guest*" Bed

A SECRET DOOR, A DIMLY LIT FLAGSTONE PASSAGE, echoing footsteps where no feet ought to be, a hollow murmur, a gust of wind, an extinguished candle . . .

In these days when "helpless heroine" is an oxymoron and no deeds are nameless, it's hard to take those old Gothic novels seriously. If you'd ever spent a night in our house, however, with my old mother and me, you might feel differently.

In those books the interest eventually settles on a piece of furniture or a fantastical element of architecture—a heavy-lidded chest, a locked drawer in an ormolu cabinet, a ruined chapel, or a sliding panel behind a gloomy tapestry. In our house it is a bed—a huge bed, dark oak, with some swampy-looking vegetation dimly depicted in bas relief on the headboard. An old aunt of mine temporarily took leave of her senses and went out and bought it. Her sanity returned soon afterward, but by then it was too late. Forty-five strong men had delivered the bed and had set it up in the guest room.

And it is not only a bed: by means of a series of hair triggers and precisely balanced weights and counterweights it can be made to swing up and fold itself into its headboard to reveal on the underside, now nearly vertical, an enormous beveled mirror. The two little iron legs at what was the foot of the bed can then be folded into neat grooves

specially made for them and there, through the dust and cobwebs on the glass your own reflection peers dimly out at you.

However, as you might imagine, in neither position is the thing satisfactory as a piece of furniture. In the mirror position the top leans out slightly, as if it were yearning to unfold itself and become a bed again, so that your image appears as a monster with a huge watermelon-sized head and dwindles down to a pair of tiny, remote feet almost hidden in the shadows. And as a bed it seems always to be on the verge of becoming a mirror, with the weights and counterweights groaning and the two iron legs at the foot lifting themselves ever so slightly off the floor. There's no room for springs, so the wafer-thin mattress lies on a steel net of something that looks like chain mail stretched across the frame. Over the years sprongs of steel have popped loose and snagged the mattress ticking to reveal the horse-hair stuffing. I've noticed that the hair is all the same color. This, combined with the extreme thinness of the mattress, has led me to conclude that the hair all came from just one horse. The oppressive size, the dark color of the oak, and the steel sprongs have made bedtime a dreaded moment for guests in my family for nearly one hundred years.

But the worst part is the tendency the bed has in the ▶

dead of night when all is quiet in the house, to transmogrify itself into a mirror. Some mysterious atmospheric change will release a catch somewhere, and slowly and majestically the foot of the bed will begin to rise. The weights and counterweights mutter to each other, the old oak joints creak and groan, and the mirror reveals its phantasmagoric images to the night as it lifts itself upright. The poor guest wakes out of a strange dream to find the covers bunched on his chest, all his blood settling at his head, and his bare, drained, ice-cold feet pointing to the ceiling. It's hard to recover from this position in the dark of night in a strange house, and usually the guest falls into a trancelike swoon that lasts until morning, when Mama discovers his predicament, snatches the foot of the bed down again, briskly clicks the latch back into position, and says, "We should have warned you about the bed."

Half an hour later the poor fellow will stagger out, hollow-eyed and grim, suitcase packed, and catch an early train home, never to return.

Over the years the word must have spread. No one comes to visit us now. We just live here all alone, my mother and I, like Briar Rose behind her hedge of thorns.

This evening, though, we got a telephone call. A distant cousin from Philadelphia whom we've never met is passing through on her way to Florida. "I want to stay with my old relations," she tells Mama on the telephone.

It is dusk. I hear the wind soughing through the pine trees as I take clean sheets into the guest room. The light from the twenty-watt bulb dangling on its cord from the vaulted ceiling barely reaches the edges of the room. The dark draperies sway against the windows.

"I've heard so much about Southern hospitality," the cousin chirps on the telephone. "Now I will be able to experience it for myself."

From far way I hear the rumble of thunder. Or is it the lead weights in the bed beginning their groaning chorus of the night? "We will expect you in a half hour," Mama says confidently. "You are welcome to stay as long as you like."

—*Bailey White*

"I'm obsessed with having *the perfect linens*. I sleep a lot. My bed's like a big hug."

—*Reese Witherspoon*

Most of us can rise to the challenge of entertaining guests for an evening, but some guests feel like they're fleeing the Bates Motel after an overnight stay. Much as we might enjoy our overnight guests, there's a trick to making them feel at home when they're at your home. We've quizzed those rare birds who have a great knack for making a guest's overnight stay both luxurious and fun.

Creature Comforts

BEDS & BEDDING. A comfortable bed is a must for a high-minded hostess, and if your sofa-bed is more than a few eons old, try it out for a night. If you're too scared to do that, ask a (brutally) honest relative who has spent some time on it to describe the experience. You don't always have to replace a mattress—you can just top the bed off with a featherbed or new foam padding to make it more comfortable; or sometimes a board placed underneath can give a saggy mattress much-needed support. If twin beds are all you have for guests, consider investing in a converter kit that fuses twin beds into a king. It might also be worth purchasing a special set of guest sheets, towels, and blankets so you're always prepared. And speaking of blankets, let your guests know where they can find extras in case they get cold during the night. (Remember to ask if a guest has any type of allergy—down is a common one.)

BATHROOM. Nothing is more tiresome for both the host family and the guest than the guest's need to keep requesting bathroom items; and let's face it, some people need an entire pharmacy. Stock your bathroom as if your guest is the queen of England, and she has lost her overnight bag. That is, include items for all the basic (extra toothbrushes), emergency (Mylanta, Tylenol, etc.), and even decadent (perfumed lotion) bathroom needs. Also, be sure to provide extras of items that tend to run out—toilet and tissue paper, soap, etc. And place a nightlight in the bathroom. If you share a bathroom with your guests, make sure their towels are a different color than yours, and have them on their bed when they arrive.

WELCOMING SPACE. Besides a comfortable bed, guests need space for their things. Clear a closet, drawer, and counter space in the guest room and find a place for them to put their luggage.

FLOURISHES AND CARING TOUCHES. If you want to create a very special visit for your guests, here is a list of little extras for their room that will make even the most weary traveler feel like she's in a posh bed-and-breakfast. *Warning: Use of these tips encourages repeat visits.*

- Small guest-room bouquet (with flowers that aren't too fragrant or messy)
- Guest-room library filled with good reads, as well as information and guidebooks about your area
- Reading light
- Guest basket filled with tasty snack items, lotions, a throwaway camera
- Fuzzy bathrobe
- A new toy or book for a visiting child
- "Welcome" cards/signs created by host-children
- Photographs of your guests placed in a noticeable spot in your home

ANNE AND CURT LARGE ARE THE KING AND QUEEN of weekend hosting friends and family in the Washington, D.C., area. They've kindly shared a version of their kid-friendly menu and a couple of their easy and delicious recipes.

The beauty of this menu is the variety and the way most of the meals allow for advance preparation, which frees you up to visit with your guests. Additional meals can be filled in with local take-out; pizzas for a family or more exotic cuisine for adult guests.

THE FAMILY WEEKEND MENU

FIRST DAY

Breakfast: Baked Banana-Stuffed French Toast (see recipe) • Fruit salad • Bagels and cream cheese • Bacon • Coffee and orange juice

Lunch: Pesto Chicken Salad (see recipe) • Sandwich buffet (variety of breads, meats, mustards, and sandwich toppings) • Chips • Lemonade

Dinner: Turkey burgers with diced red onion on rolls • Grilled marinated vegetables • Couscous • Make-your-own ice-cream sundaes

SECOND DAY

Breakfast: Cheesy scrambled eggs • Fruit salad • Remaining Banana-Stuffed French Toast • Bagels and cream cheese • Coffee and orange juice

Lunch: Cheddar sourdough melts with fresh basil • Green salad with blue cheese and cranberries • Chips • Lemonade

Baked Banana-Stuffed French Toast

2 tablespoons unsalted butter

2 tablespoons sugar

2 tablespoons water

3 large ripe bananas, peeled, cut into ½-inch-thick slices

5 large eggs

1 loaf bread (challah, Italian, or French), cut into 1-inch-thick slices

1½ cups half-and-half

1 teaspoon vanilla

¼ teaspoon salt

1. Melt butter in heavy large skillet over medium heat. Add sugar and water and stir until sugar dissolves. Continue stirring until mixture is foamy, about 2 minutes.

2. Add bananas; cook until tender, stirring occasionally, about 5 minutes.

3. Transfer to small bowl; cool. (Can be prepared 4 hours ahead. Cover and chill.)

4. Using small sharp knife, cut 2-inch-long slit in one side of each bread slice, cutting ¾ of way through bread and creating a pocket that leaves three sides of bread intact.

5. Divide banana mixture equally among pockets in bread. Butter a baking dish just large enough to hold the bread in one layer, and arrange bread slices, squeezing them slightly to fit.

6. Whisk together eggs, half-and-half, vanilla, and salt until well combined and pour evenly over bread.

7. Chill, covered, at least 8 hours and up to 1 day.

8. Preheat oven to 350°F and bring bread to room temperature.

9. Bake bread mixture, uncovered, in middle of oven until puffed and edges are pale golden, 35 to 40 minutes. Dust with confectioners' sugar, and serve with maple syrup.

Serves 6

Pesto Chicken Salad

1½ pounds penne, cooked

Walnut pesto (below)

3 cups cooked, shredded chicken

1 pint cherry or grape tomatoes

½ cup pitted kalamata olives

½ cup walnut pieces (optional)

Combine pasta with the pesto, then add chicken, tomatoes, and olives. Sprinkle walnut pieces on top.

Walnut Pesto

½ cup walnut pieces

1 clove garlic, chopped

2 cups packed basil leaves

¼ teaspoon salt

1 cup Italian parsley

½ cup olive oil

⅓ cup grated parmesan cheese

1. Chop walnut and garlic in food processor. Add half of basil and salt and process. Add remaining basil and parsley and process. Add olive oil and process.

2. Place in a small bowl and fold in parmesan cheese.

Serves 8

LuXury

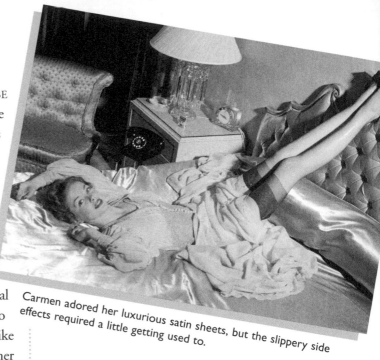

Carmen adored her luxurious satin sheets, but the slippery side effects required a little getting used to.

THE WORD "LUXURY" SEEMS TO BE BANDIED ABOUT in a curious way these days. People's ideas of what it means vary enormously. I'm never quite sure what a "luxury flat" is, though I believe it should have running water and a radiator or two. Better than not having them, I admit, but what is real luxury?

For me, a winter weekend sticks in the memory. I was staying with an artist and his wife in Dorset. I can't remember if there was central heating, but I do remember my hostess coming into my room before breakfast, her head tied in a duster like Miss Moppet, laying and lighting a coal fire for her guest to dress by. If you've never dressed in front of a coal fire, you don't know what luxury is. They also had half a cow—the farmer had the other half—which meant they had not only proper cream but real butter, a rare commodity indeed.

I can't help comparing that house with many bigger, richer, electric-fired households, some of which are at the center of hundreds of acres of their own farms, milking big herds of cows. But no one can be bothered to skim and churn, and thereby profit from what they own by producing what is described in old-fashioned cookery books as "best butter." My Dorset friends win the luxury stakes hands down. A coal fire, half an acre, and half a cow, that's the thing.

—*Deborah Vivien Freeman-Mitford Cavendish Devonshire, the Duchess of Devonshire*

Pampering by Pauline

"If you fall asleep with your arm hanging over the bed, you wake up with a manicure," one of Pauline de Rothschild's pampered guests is quoted as saying. Nothing but the best would do for Pauline's parties—her drawing room boasted gold leaf moldings, and guests reclined on museum-quality Louis XVI chairs. Necessities for a guest room included new books carefully chosen for each guest, an array of daily newspapers delivered to the room, gilt scissors for clipping articles, sharpened pencils, lilac-scented baths drawn by servants, and a twenty-four-hour laundry service.

Meeting *the* neigHbors

ONE POSITIVE THING YOU CAN SAY FOR DISASTERS is that they are frequently a good way to get to know the neighbors. Ralph and I first learned this when we bought our first house (in Colorado) and, one week later, accidentally set it on fire.

Actually, "we" didn't set it on fire; Ralph did. As he admitted later, "you put three quarts of French-fry oil on a burner and forget about it."

It fortunately wasn't a serious fire, thanks, of course, to the fire department. It scorched one wall and left the back door rather on the charred side.

Of course, before the fire, we'd been meaning to go out and meet the neighbors, particularly the ones next door. But our evenings had always been occupied with unpacking boxes and building bookcases —which was exactly what Ralph was doing when he forgot about the oil.

Frankly, I've never quite forgiven Ralph for his timing. At the moment the kitchen ignited, I happened to be off . . . in the shower, trying to recover from a very hard day at work. Just as I was getting into some very pleasant . . . memories, Ralph comes charging in, yelling, "Fire!"

Heart in mouth, I grabbed my pink quilted bathrobe—the ratty one with only one button left and the fallen hem—that I'd gotten when I was twelve, and while Ralph rounded up the cat and dog, I went dashing over to the next-door neighbors' and began pounding on their door.

Did I mention it was twenty-two degrees and snowing?

I don't need to say that the expression on the face of the neighbor's teenage son when he opened the door and saw a dripping-wet stranger standing barefoot in the snow clutching a ratty pink bathrobe around her was one of surprise.

"I'm-your-neighbor-Quick!-Call-the-fire-depart-ment-our-house-is-on-fire!" I blurted breathlessly.

"Oh, sure! Right away!" Before I could say another word, he had slammed the front door shut and rushed toward the phone, where I could hear him urgently talking to the operator as I stood on the porch, freezing to death.

For dramatic quality, there's nothing like four fire engines screeching to a halt in front of your house to bring the neighbors out in droves. Quickly, the firemen extinguished the blaze and began to disperse the thick smoke in the house with huge fans. ▶

There we are standing in the snow and dark, the cat and dog and I (in the ratty bathrobe) and Ralph (who later turns out to be in partial shock, having suffered second-degree burns from mid-thigh to ankle after initially having tried to put out the fire himself), and we're thanking God we're safe, and watching smoke billow out our front door, and wondering how serious the damage will be, and suddenly someone is tapping me on the shoulder.

"Hi! You must be the new neighbors. Name's Tom Hammond. My wife, Jean. Looks like you folks are having a little trouble here." (As we're blinded by flashing lights from the four fire trucks and the police car that has since arrived.)

"Nothing serious, I hope?"

Well, next thing we know, there are all these people milling around our front yard chatting with each other and introducing themselves to us.

After that incident, we just seemed to be part of the neighborhood. There is something about sharing a disaster, or even a potential one, with your neighbors that instantly puts you on a first-name basis.

Next time we bought a house, however, we just had a cocktail party.

—*Louise DeGrave*

"Love thy neighbor as thyself, *but choose your neighborhood.*"

—*Louise Beal*

Even if you aren't the "Hidy-ho, neighbor" type, the sight of a moving van pulling up next door strikes a chord. Whether it's curiosity, sympathy, or civic responsibility, it's always a smart idea to give the new folks on the block a warm reception. So make your grandma proud and exercise some good old-fashioned hospitality. It doesn't have to be over the top; in fact, exerting too much effort might make your new neighbors suspicious. ("Doesn't this chick have any friends?")

Here are some simple ways to extend a warm "welcome to the 'hood." But remember not to linger at the doorstep—they have a nest to put together!

DELIVER A SMALL GIFT. A bouquet of flowers from your yard, a scented candle, a gourmet gift from a local shop. Introduce yourself, say a few words of welcome, and leave a card with your name, address, and telephone number so they know you mean it when you offer help.

CREATE A PACKET OF LOCAL INFORMATION. Help them keep up with the Joneses by telling them who lives where on the street. Also include a "best of" list with recommendations for take-out restaurants, cleaners, the nearest or best grocery store, bakery, library, pharmacy, deli, hardware store, parks, places to hike, baby-sitters, etc.

BESTOW THE CLASSIC WELCOME GIFT. A homemade dessert such as a berry pie, coffee cake, or bread.

GIVE A GIFT CERTIFICATE to the best pizza parlor in town.

OFFER A LITTLE ELBOW GREASE. Perhaps you have a strong back, a green thumb, or some other helpful house know-how that can help lighten their load. If you've ever moved or unpacked, you will appreciate the sweetness of this offer.

INVITE THEM TO JOIN YOU FOR A LOCAL OUTING. It could be a minor league baseball game, a street fair, or some other community activity.

GIVE THE PROVERBIAL WELCOME WAGON. If your neighborhood boasts a special event—a concert in the park or movie night—give your new neighbors a red wagon (tied with a ribbon) to cart their food, blankets, or small children to and from the event.

AND FOR THE BEST WELCOME GIFT OF ALL. Throw a party in their honor so they can meet all their new neighbors!

A little birdie told us . . . Don't forget the outgoing neighbors—write them a note or prepare a care package to send them on their way.

THE TIES THAT BIND

With a little initiative and some planning, you too can have one of those coveted close-knit 'hoods. The best neighborhoods have one or two ringleaders who usually orchestrate get-togethers. Participation is not mandatory, yet everyone is invited. If your neighborhood doesn't already have a party planner, appoint yourself to the position and plan something. Having neighborhood traditions and annual gatherings help things gel, and you may be surprised at the enthusiasm you meet with once you get the ball rolling. Though the onus might be on you the first time, keep your eye out for a successor, someone who can help you plan the next event. While the name of the game is inclusion (yes, even *them*), here are some specific ideas for get-togethers.

NEIGHBORHOOD MOVIE NIGHT. Rent a simple projector, screen, and movie from your local camera or video store and set it up in someone's yard or a nearby park that can accommodate everyone. Movie choices should be confined to family-friendly G-rated movies. Pass around a sign-up sheet asking for volunteers to bring popcorn, soda, cotton candy, and other fun movie snacks. Tell everyone to bring their own blankets, lawn chairs, and pillows.

FRIDAY NIGHT OPEN HOUSE. Nothing like a casual neighborhood get-together to help unwind after a long week and usher in the weekend. Rotating from house to house is a nice way to share the responsibilities.

You'll need:

Plenty to drink—nonalcoholic sodas and juice and divine cocktails.

Heavy appetizers—enough to serve as dinner for those too weary to cook their own (see pages 102–103 for ideas).

CHILI COOK-OFF BLOCK PARTY. After school starts and the neighbors are back from vacation is a perfect time for a block party. Call or visit your neighbors to get input on setting a date and post a sign-up sheet in a convenient location (on a porch or back door) so that attendees can commit to bringing whatever suits their fancy. You'll need a few families to make chili (make sure there is a meatless version) and others to provide rice, hot dogs, condiments, corn bread, salad, drinks, utensils and paper products. Depending on your street or town, you might also need to obtain permission from the police to block the traffic for a few hours and get some traffic cones to place at the entrance/exit to your street.

HALLOWEEN CELEBRATIONS. Plan an outdoor party for the weekend before Halloween in a large yard, a nearby park, or on your block. Activities such as a kiddie costume parade, jack-o'-lantern competition, candy hunt, and hayrides (in a hay-filled dump wagon hitched to a minivan) make for a great time. Many neighborhoods have started the tradition of being "ghosted" or "booed" in the week leading up to Halloween. It works a little bit like "Ring and Run." Stick a white paper ghost on your neighbor's front door with a note to pass it on and leave a little bag of treats. Then ring, and run. The neighbor who receives a treat should then leave one for someone else, and so on.

CAROLING. Look around; you might have some aspiring, or real, neighborhood divas just waiting in the wings for an opportunity to crow and croon. This holiday season, organize a caroling group and let the neighbors know when to expect you. Depending on your neighborhood and the preference of your singers, you can choose either religious or secular songs. With a little encouragement, even elderly neighbors and young children might partake. Everyone can be invited to dress up (or disguise themselves) in Victorian attire. One house should be chosen as the final stop, where carolers will be welcomed in for hot cocoa and dessert.

EASTER EGG HUNT. Pick a neighbor with a yard big enough to "host" an Easter egg hunt the Saturday before Easter Sunday. During the week before, each participating family should drop off candy-filled plastic eggs (one dozen per child) with the host. The morning of the hunt, the host family hides the eggs and sets up a table in their driveway. Others bring coffee, doughnuts, juice, and baskets for the children. Then stand back and watch the fun!

> "We can do no great things, *only small things* with great love."
>
> —*Mother Theresa*

A little birdie told us . . . Don't rely on word of mouth to get the word out to neighbors. Someone should take on the job of creating a flyer to place in each mailbox. It's also a good idea to compile your neighbors' e-mail addresses so that you can reach each other efficiently.

CHICK tips ... *for flocking together*

Start a ritual. Be it a traditional holiday party or a Mardi Gras masquerade ball, find an occasion to celebrate annually.

Invite an interesting mix of people. Different ages, different occupations, and different parts of your life make for a "when worlds collide" approach and a unique experience.

Make every guest feel special. When planning your party and creating your guest list, take some time to think about each guest or guest-family and what they like.

Be a delegating diva! If your friend has a recipe she's dying to try, give her your blessing and tell her to bring it along.

Strive for a good time, not a perfect time. Guests won't remember that your napkin rings didn't match, but they will recall how you remembered they loved Italian sodas and chocolate cake.

Keep it between the lines but don't be afraid to mix it up. Every gathering can't be a blow-out bash but when it's easy and doable, interject the unexpected.

Party with a passion. If you are in a soiree slump, look to themes for inspiration. Whatever it is—old movies, gardening, the color pink, Paris—use it to freshen up your next gathering.

Go with the flow. If a party takes a different turn, don't fight it. If people are having a good time talking, don't insist they sit down for dinner at the time you had anticipated.

part three

"Never eat more than you can carry." —*Miss Piggy*

Chicks
and Chow

Sweet Dishes and Hot Tamales . . .

my BEst friend's wedding cAke

CYNTHIA, MY BEST FRIEND, WAS NOT TOUCHED OR OVERJOYED or even grateful when I told her I wanted to make her wedding cake. Her e-mail did not mince words:

Ahem. Have you ever made a cake for 120 to 150? I don't mean to sound like I lack faith, but this is what I fear: The caterer's assistants will have to be working around you as you ice the cake, the kitchen will be in an uproar, icing everywhere, the layers of the cake not adhering, and the assistants will have to pitch in to help. Besides, I really love our caterer, Gracie. . . .

Some people might have found this reply discouraging, but it only piqued my resolve. Was I going to allow her to place more faith in the hired help than in me? A privilege of best friendship is to never take no for an answer, in the certainty that the person will thank you later. I was determined: I would make a cake she would forever thank me for. Although my baking history is checkered, each cake's problems were unique, and, as I reminded Cynthia, only the initial experience was a half disaster. A decade ago, my first college friends, Annie and Mark, decided to become prematurely grown-up and got engaged. They had no money, and when the caterers informed them the cake would cost $500 (the standard fee), they were shocked. I told them I could make them a free cake in a jiffy.

Modern friendship sometimes strikes me as a sadly attenuated affair, more talk than action. I like a friendship with a lot of tangibles—and what is more tangible than a five-layer English fruitcake blanketed in marzipan? I was in graduate school then, with work to avoid, which I did for weeks by drying and candying cherries and apricots and pineapples, piping marzipan roses, and converting the British recipe's measurements from pounds to cups. I was a tad anxious as I increased the baking powder tenfold. What if it rose a hundredfold? Would it explode? The layers did emerge from the oven as round as bombs, so they didn't balance on top of one another. (I didn't then know the trick of lopping off the curved tops with a dental-floss guillotine.) Far from stabilizing the layers, the glossy icing that went over the marzipan was slippery.

On the day of the wedding, although I got the cake assembled on a table in the reception tent, it soon began to resemble the Matterhorn, the top layers sloping precariously to one side. When we got back from the church, it looked like an earthquake had struck: A deep fissure had formed, revealing the dark fruit-and-nut innards of a slab that appeared to be minutes away from toppling to the floor.

Panic. I downed a tall glass of champagne, and the giddiness of catastrophe began to set in. The great thing about a baking disaster, I realized, is that it is, after all, just that. Just because the cake is unsound doesn't mean the marriage will be. I repeated this to myself as I jury-rigged the cake with barbecue skewers and frosted over them. The skewers held the layers together long enough for the pictures although the ceremonial first cut couldn't be too deep.

I didn't do any event baking for a long stretch after that. But when, five years later, my old boyfriend, Bob, decided to get married, I saw an opportunity to redeem my previous maladroitness by making the groom's cake—a Southern tradition of having a second smaller cake of a different variety. I settled on a Lady Baltimore, an almond-flavored cake iced with nerve-wracking candied frosting. (Why had I volunteered, I wondered as I tried to fold boiling caramelized sugar into masses of egg whites. To demonstrate I was happy about this wedding?) Luckily, I *was* happy, and the cake was flawless. I was the only one who thought so, though, because the hotel staff forgot to serve it! I didn't want to trouble the bride and groom with such a trifle. But two hundred and fifty dessert plates went out to the guests with the hotel's lame Sanka-colored slices while my beautiful creation, dressed in white roses and ribbons, sat forsaken on a banquet table. I like to think the kitchen staff tasted it before they discarded it.

That might have been my finale if the experience hadn't been so maddeningly purposeless—but I had a last chance to make the perfect wedding cake. Cynthia apprehensively agreed. She and her fiancé Jim were planning an outdoor Wiccan ceremony in their 1740 farmhouse in rural Pennsylvania. I wanted to make a version of an old English fruitcake—the traditional wedding cakes before the advent of refrigeration. I

decided to make the fool-proof bourbon-pecan cake that I had been making for my father's birthdays since I was ten. It has three main ingredients: pecans, raisins (or prunes or dried cherries), and decent bourbon (Southern Comfort won't do.) The cake bears the same relation to fruitcake that mock turtle soup does to real turtle soup: people prefer it.

What makes a wedding cake riskier than others is that it has to feed so many but that it's one cake. If a single cake is supposed to represent the unity of the couple, I decided, a multiplicity of cakes could represent richness, heterogeneity, or even a subversion of genre (as Cynthia and I might have said when we met in English graduate school). So I made six cakes, each of which I decorated with a miniature bride-and-groom-figurine topper—that I bought on eBay—and surrounded with garlands from Cynthia's garden.

A few days after the wedding, I received an e-mail with the heading "Apologia":

I apologize from the bottom of my heart for all my fears. Your flock of cakes was gorgeous beyond belief—like a Mardi Gras parade on the table. To have friend-made cakes gave the wedding a sweet, old-fashioned touch, as if we lived in the same small village instead of different cities. The cake toppers, a century's worth of happy couples, are now awaiting their next duties—as attendants at your wedding? I wonder who will make those cakes (she says, glancing around nervously). I know you said it was easy, but—really—how easy?

—*Melanie Thernstrom*

Chocolate or Vanilla?

Whether you dream about swimming through the chocolate river in Willy Wonka's chocolate factory or swoon at the memory of your first bite of velvety vanilla buttercream candy, one thing is certain, chicks love these two tantalizing treats. While most of us fall firmly into one camp or the other, for some of us the decision is not simply a black or white issue—we can't decide until the urge strikes. Whether you choose chocolate or vanilla, or a little or a lot of both, some tasty reflections and mouthwatering recipes might help you decide which one you are in the mood for (today).

JILL CONNER BROWNE ON CHOCOLATE. The Sweet Potato Queen's drug of choice is clearly my famous Chocolate Stuff. I got the recipe from my mother, who called it something like "fudge pudding." None of my friends could remember the name, however; they'd simply beg me to make them "some of that chocolate stuff." The biggest problem with the recipe is that it doesn't make very much. I'd recommend that you automatically double the ingredients. Doubled, it will make three pans. This has proven to be just enough.

Unfortunately it has to bake 40 to 50 minutes, which is a helluva long time when you're suffering. Good news: It's really just as fine—some factions argue better—eaten raw as fully cooked! We've been known to eat entire batches of it right out of the mixing bowl, skipping the baking altogether. Usually we're content with leaving copious amounts of the precious goo in the bowl and sticking our faces into the bowl while the oven works its magic on the major portion. When you make your personal judgment call, keep in mind that the recipe contains eggs, at this point raw, and you may be risking your very life in pursuit of instant gratification.

The Sweet Potato Queen's Chocolate Stuff

2 eggs
1 cup sugar
½ cup flour
¼ teaspoon salt
1 stick of salted butter
2 heaping tablespoons Hershey's cocoa
1 running over teaspoon vanilla
1½ cups pecans chopped fine (optional)

Preheat oven to 300°F.

Beat eggs, sugar, flour and salt together.

In microwave, melt together the butter and cocoa. Dump the butter and cocoa mixture in with the eggs, sugar, and flour mixture and stir well. Add the vanilla.

Pour the mixture into a greased loaf pan, set the loaf pan into a pan of water, and cook at 300 degrees for about 40 to 50 minutes or until the top feels crunchy to the touch. You do not want to overcook it.

— J. C. B.

DIANE ACKERMAN ON VANILLA. Craving vanilla, I start the bathwater gushing, and unscrew the lid of a heavy glass jar of Ann Steeger of Paris's Bain Crème, senteur vanille. A wallop of potent vanilla hits my nose as I reach into the lotion, let it seep through my fingers, and carry a handful to the faucet. Fragrant bubbles fill the tub. A large bar of vanilla bath soap, sitting in an antique porcelain dish, acts as an aromatic beacon. While I steep in waves of vanilla, a friend brings me a vanilla cream seltzer, followed by a custard made with vanilla beans that have come all the way from Madagascar. Brown flecks float through the creamy yellow curds. . . . When I finally emerge from the tub . . . I apply Ann Steeger's vanilla body veil, which smells edible and thick as smoke. Then Jean Laporte's Vanilla perfume, vanilla with a bitter sting. The inside of a vanilla bean contains a figlike marrow, and if I were to scrape some out, I could prepare spicy vanilla bisque for dinner, followed by chicken in a vanilla glaze, salad with vanilla vinaigrette, vanilla ice cream with a sauce of chestnuts in vanilla marinade, followed by warm brandy flavored with chopped vanilla pod, and then, in a divine vanilla stupor, step into bed and fall into a heavy, orchidlike sleep.

Velvety Vanilla Custard

5 egg yolks, beaten

1½ cups milk

¼ cup sugar

1½ tsp. pure vanilla extract

Fresh berries of choice: raspberries, strawberries, or blueberries

1. In a heavy medium saucepan use a wooden spoon to combine yolks, milk, and sugar. Cook, stirring continuously over medium heat until the custard just coats the back of a clean metal spoon. Remove from heat, stir in vanilla.

2. Place saucepan in a large bowl of ice water for about 2 minutes to cool. Keep stirring.

3. Pour custard into a bowl and cover surface with plastic wrap to keep a skin from forming on the surface. Chill for 2 to 3 hours at least. Serve a dollop, sprinkled with fresh berries, to 8 of your friends or to 4 of your very best friends.

"All I really need is love, but *a little chocolate now and then* doesn't hurt."

—*Lucy, in* Peanuts

The Black-and-White Shake

(when you can't decide)

1 pint high-quality vanilla ice cream, softened

¼ cup chocolate syrup

¼ cup whole milk

Whipped cream, for topping

Maraschino cherry

Blend first three ingredients until smooth. Serve in a tall glass, with whipped cream and a cherry on top.

the Bubbly Widows

WHAT IS IT ABOUT A DEAD HUS-BAND that can make a woman want to break out the bubbly? Over the last two centuries several prominent champagne houses in France lost their founding fathers, but instead of crying over spilt sparkly, their wives took charge and shook things up with explosive success. Veuve Clicquot, Pommery, Bollinger, Roederer, and Perrier were all successfully run by the queens, or *veuves* ("widows"), of the châteaux, after the deaths of their husbands.

The grande dame of them all was Barbe-Nicole Clicquot-Ponsardin, known as Veuve Clicquot. After she was widowed in 1805, at the age of twenty-seven, she led her company for several decades. As a young woman, Madame Clicquot knew little about the business of sparkling wine, but once she acquired savoir faire she began to aggressively and creatively spread her influence. When the unbecoming sediment that clouded sparkling wine began to offend her, she cut holes in her kitchen table and invented a system that clarified the champagne—a technique that is still used today. When she wanted her bottles to be more distinctive, she stamped her corks with an anchor and the letters VCP. A few years later, she went further and engraved the same monogram on the glass of the bottles and then designed the famous yellow label that still decorates bottles of Veuve Clicquot today. Never one to let anyone get in the way of a sale, Madame Clicquot even defied Napoléon (a Moët drinker) by shipping champagne to Russia in 1814 through one of his wartime blockades. Betting that the Russians, though wartime enemies of the French, couldn't resist her champagne, Madame's cargo was accepted, and the sales coup led to brisk business with Russia. Lending credence to the belief that champagne increases longevity, Madame Clicquot lived until her eighty-ninth year, and Veuve Clicquot is still one of the world's premier champagnes.

So next time you pop a cork, raise your glass to the effervescent widows who spread their joyous, bubbly wine throughout the world.

"Champagne is the only wine that *leaves a woman beautiful* after drinking it."

—*Madame de Pompadour*

Lily's Law

"I only drink champagne when I'm happy, and when I'm sad. Sometimes I drink it when I'm alone. When I have company, I consider it obligatory. I trifle with it if I am not hungry and drink it when I am. Otherwise I never touch it—unless I'm thirsty." —Lily Bollinger

PoOr fooD

I AM THINKING NOW OF SOME OF THE BEST MEALS in my life, and almost without exception they have been so because of the superlative honesty of "poor food," rather than sophistication. I admire and often even *like* what is now called the classical cuisine—the intricate sauces of great chefs, and the complexities of their entremets and their pastries. But for strength, both of the body and of the spirit, I turn without hesitation to the simplest cooks.

I remember the best sauce I ever ate.

It was not at Foyot's, in the old days in Paris. It was in a cabin with tar-paper walls on a rain-swept hillside in southern California. The air was heavy with the scent of wet sage from outside and the fumes of a cheap kerosene stove within. Three or four children piped for more, more, from the big bowl of steaming gravy in the center of the heavy old round table crowded between the family's cots. We ate it from soup plates, the kind you used to get free with labels from cereal packages. It was made from a couple of young cottontails, and a few pulls of fresh herbs from the underbrush, and spring water and some Red Ink from the bottom of Uncle Johnnie's birthday jug—and a great deal of love. It was all we had, with cold flapjacks left from breakfast to scoop it up. It was *good*, and I knew that I was indeed fortunate, to have driven up the hill that night in the rain and to have friends who would share with me.

I remember the best stew I ever ate, too.

It was not a bouillabaisse at Isnard's in Marseille. It was made further east on the Mediterranean at Cassis, by a very old small woman for a great lusty batch of relatives and other people she loved. Little grandnephews dove for equally young octopuses and delicate sea eggs, and older sons sent their rowboats silently up the dark *calanques* for rockfish lurking among the sunken German U-boats from the First War, and grizzling cousins brought in from the deep sea a fine catch of rays and other curious scaly monsters. Little girls and their mothers and great-aunts went up into the bone-dry hills for aromatic leaves and blossoms, and on the way home picked up a few bottles of herby wine from the tiny vineyards where they worked in the right seasons.

The very old small woman cooked and pounded and skinned and ruminated, and about noon, two days later, we met in her one-room house and spent some twenty more hours, as I remember, eating and eating . . . and talking and singing and then eating again, from seemingly bottomless pots of the most delicious stew in my whole life. It again, had been made with love. . . .   ▶

And out of a beautiful odorous collection of good breads in my life I still taste, in my memory, the *best*.

There have been others that smelled better, or looked better, or cut better, but this one, made by a desolately lonesome Spanish-Greek Jewess for me when I was about five, was the best. Perhaps it was the shape. It was baked in pans just like the big ones we used every Saturday, but tiny, perhaps one by three inches. And it rose just the way ours did, but tinily. (Many years later, when I read *Memoirs of a Midget* and suffered for the difficulties of such a small person's meals, I wished I could have taken to her, from time to time and wrapped in a doll's linen napkin, a fresh loaf from my friend's oven).

Yes, that was and still is the best bread. It came from the kitchen of a very simple woman, who knew instinctively that she could solace her loneliness through the ritual of honest cooking. It taught me, although I did not understand it then, a prime lesson in survival. I must eat well. And in these days of spurious and distorted values, the best way to eat is simply, without affectation or adulteration. Given honest flour, pure water, and a good fire, there is really only one more thing needed to make the best bread in the world, fit for the greatest gourmet ever born: and that is honest love.

—M. F. K. Fisher

Cooking the Books

While it's sometimes said that good cooking relies more on intuition and natural flair than textbook technique, the truth is, most cooks are backed by a library that aids and inspires their culinary adventures. A tried-and-true stack of cookbooks will help you whip up everything from the mundane to the extraordinary. Our chicks swear by these stalwarts. Toss in your local women's club or community collection and you'll be cooking with class.

The Barefoot Contessa by Ina Garten

The Best Recipes by the editors of *Cook's Illustrated* magazine

Chez Panisse Vegetables by Alice Waters

The Essential Cuisines of Mexico by Diana Kennedy

The Good Fat Cookbook by Fran McCullough

How to Be a Domestic Goddess by Nigella Lawson

How to Cook Everything by Mark Bittman

Lidia's Italian Table by Lidia Bastianich

Mediterranean Cooking by Paula Wolfert

Moosewood Cookbook by Mollie Katzen

The New Joy of Cooking by Irma Rombauer

The New York Cookbook by Molly O'Neill

Romancing the Stove by Margie Lapanja

The Silver Palate Cookbook by Julee Rosso and Sheila Lukins

Comfy CoZy

REGARDLESS OF HOW SOPHISTI-CATED OUR PALATES may have become, we all need a little feel-good food from time to time. Most comfort foods have a strong association with foods we loved as little chicks—and a high level of carbohydrates (a mood elevator). So every self-comforting chick needs to know how to make at least one delicious home-cooked meal that warms the belly and reminds you there's no place like home. From extensive polling of chicks who love to eat (which is about every woman we've ever met), we've come up with the ultimate comfort food menu.

"Ask any good soulfood cook: including **a pinch of love** is the secret to doin' it right."

—*Deborah Kesten*

the ULTIMATE COMFORT FOOD MENU

ROAST CHICKEN
Rubbed with olive oil, salt, pepper, and fresh rosemary with a quartered lemon and onion inside.

BISCUITS AND GRAVY (*Southern comfort*)
Use Grandma's recipe.

MACARONI & CHEESE (*Yankee fix*)
Try the "Phony Macaroni" recipe on page 130.

MASHED POTATOES
Boil 'em up and mash 'em up to your chosen consistency, using whole milk. Don't be stingy with the butter, salt, and pepper. Mix in some fresh garlic or chives if you want a little kick.

SLICED TOMATOES
Hit the farmer's market or your garden for homegrown tomatoes. Slice 'em thick and sprinkle on some sea salt and pepper. Dress with olive oil and balsamic vinegar only if you must.

CHOCOLATE CHIP COOKIES & MILK
Your secret's safe with us if you use that roll of dough found in the refrigerated section of the grocery store. (For therapy that rates as high as any you'd get in the $200-an-hour range, make Margie Lapanja's Cowboy Cookies on page 185.)

A Love Affair with food

THE ORIGINAL HOT TAMALE, Julia McWilliams Child, proved that a bold and opinionated woman in the kitchen is very seductive. Armed with Irma Rombauer's *The Joy of Cooking*, young Julia aimed for her man's heart via the express route—his stomach. Her soon-to-be husband, Paul Child, was a cultured, artful, and sensuous man. "Paul's mother was a good cook and he had lived in France. If I was going to catch him, I would have to learn to cook," Julia later commented. Julia's recipes worked, of course, and the two simmered slowly for a while before their love affair hit the boiling point and they married.

Together, Julia and Paul confronted the culinary trends of the time. Campbell's soup was affecting pop culture in myriad ways, merchants hawking convenience and speed as opposed to flavor and technique. When it came to entertaining, they were a dynamic duo—she whipping up a fancy recipe and wreaking her eccentric brand of havoc in the kitchen, he setting the table with military precision and an artist's flair. In 1948 Paul's work landed the lovebirds in Paris, where Julia fell passionately and permanently in love with food. She flung herself into the culinary delights of France, taking cooking lessons, savoring the cuisine, celebrating with Paul the gastronomic joys of food, glorious, food! A year later she enrolled in the celebrated Cordon Bleu cooking school, and her life was never the same again.

With her diploma in hand, Julia and two gourmet girlfriends, Louisette Bertholle and Simone "Simca" Beck, formed *L' Ecole des Trois Gourmandes,* a cooking school that emphasized the pleasure of cooking as well as techniques, and they began to percolate a plan to compile a revolutionary cookbook that would demystify classic French cuisine. With the instinct of a secret agent, Julia insisted they keep their work under wraps. French chefs had never incorporated modern appliances, such as blenders, in the preparation of classic recipes, nor did they believe in doing part of the cooking ahead of time. Julia, Simca, and Louisette began testing, tasting, researching, and writing. In a letter to Simca in 1954, Julia wrote prophetically, "Always pretend we are cooking in front of an audience. That will help us to discipline ourselves."

Ten years later, after more than one helping of rejection from American publishers, numerous title changes, and tireless work, *Mastering the Art of French Cooking* was published by Alfred A. Knopf. Weighing in at three pounds, the 734-page book wowed critics and consumers alike. To promote the book, Julia toured with her own pots, pans, utensils, blenders, ingredients—everything but the kitchen sink—whipping audiences into a frenzy with her unique brand of solid instruction, delivered with her trademark wit and aplomb.

After a hugely enthusiastic response to one such appearance on WGBH, the station manager decided to back three pilot cooking programs hosted by Julia. Although the shows were produced on a shoestring budget, Julia was about to bid bon voyage to obscurity. Audiences adored her natural delivery, her endearing blunders, and her ever-present humor. Her down-to-earth teaching style and her understanding of the intimidating mysteries of classic French cooking proved to be an irresistible combination. And that voice! To one viewer who wrote in asking if she had asthma or emphysema, because she always seemed "out of breath," Julia responded that her lungs were healthy and that "the art of cooking is a labor of love and involves a lot of manual labor. Try whipping a soufflé sometime."

Julia has starred in eight television series and has authored or contributed to more than twenty-nine books. She founded the American Institute of Wine and Food and has won countless awards. In 2001, when Julia left Massachusetts to return home to California, she donated her studio kitchen, which was designed by Paul, to the Smithsonian Institution. At a time when a woman's place was in the kitchen yet, ironically, men dominated the professional field of cooking, Julia burst through the kitchen door, turned up the heat, and made room for everyone at the table. *Merci, Madame, et bon appétit.*

Paul on Julia

"The sight of Julia in front of her stove—full of boiling, frying, and simmering foods—has the same fascination for me as watching a kettle drummer at the symphony. Imagine this in y[ou]r mind's eye: Julie, with a blue denim apron on, a dish towel stuck under her belt, a spoon in each hand, stirring two pots at the same time. Warning bells are sounding-off like signals from the podium, and a garlic-flavored steam fills the air with an odoriferous leit-motif. The oven door opens and shuts so fast you hardly notice the deft thrust of a spoon as she dips into a casserole and up to her mouth for a taste-check like a perfectly timed double-beat on the drums. She stands there surrounded by a battery of instruments with an air of authority and confidence. Now and again a flash of the non-cooking Julie lights up the scene briefly, as it did the day before yesterday when with her bare fingers, she snatched a set of cannelloni out of the pot of boiling water with the cry, 'Wow! These damn things are as hot as a stiff cock.'"

—Paul Child

Bless your Cuisinart: *A Gal and Her Gadgets*

Just as the clotheshorse must have all the right accoutrements, so must the kitchen goddess have the proper accessories to get the job done. Here are some gizmos worth stocking—and some that aren't.

THE MUSTS

Salad spinner

Steel ice-cream scoop

Rotary cheese grater

Electric knife

Set of high-quality chef's knives

Spring-loaded kitchen shears

Pepper grinder

Powerful electric blender

Hand blender

Food processor and mini-processor

Juicer

Oxo fat-handled potato peeler

Oxo grater

2 spring-loaded tongs (1 short, 1 long)

Garlic peeler

Crock-Pot

A set of nice spatulas (small, medium, large)

GOOD IN THEORY BUT NOT IN PRACTICE

Pizza stone

Electric wok

Fondue pot

Pasta maker

Cappuccino maker

Popcorn popper

Bagel slicer

Sno-cone maker

Pressure cooker

Waffle cone maker

Culinary acetyline torch

"The French got it right when they christened the kitchen arsenal the *batterie de cuisine.* Hunger, like lust in action, is savage, extreme, rude, cruel. To satisfy it is to do battle, deploying a full range of artillery—crushers, scrapers, beaters, roasters, gougers, grinders, to name but a few of the thousand and two implements that line my walls and cram my drawers—in the daily struggle to turn ingredients into edibles for devouring mouths." —Betty Fussell

The Queen of Leftovers *(or the Nightly Dine-One-One)*

I DON'T KNOW HOW IT HAPPENED, BUT I'M MASSIVELY OVEREMPLOYED. One day I was thrust to the helm of our home—as chief lunch-maker, sergeant of chores, executive hostess, grocery battalion leader, and the search-and-rescue commando for lost toys.

My other career was supposed to protect me from this. In real life I'm one of those women who burst into spastic laughter over those magnets with women quipping, "I dreamed my whole house was clean." But of all my beloved duties, the one that really gets me is dinner. Even though it happens each night (HELLO!), dinner almost always sneaks up on me. I can bring home the bacon and fry it up in a pan—but just what I'll be frying is a mystery to me until five minutes before I light the stove. Around 5:30 is when it usually hits me—all the meat in the house is still frozen, the veggies are soggy, and we're completely out of bread. A little cocktail usually puts me in the necessary "creative mindset" to ponder the dinnerless situation properly and come up with a strategy for how to disguise my complete unpreparedness. That's where my knight in shining leftovers comes in.

Be it bruschetta, pulled pork, sesame noodles, Caesar salad, or pizza—I'm the queen of refreshing, reusing, and rebaking. I can bring a half-dead meal back to its former glory in thirty seconds. The primary tools of my trade as a master food restorer are my microwave and my skillet. Many long years of experience with leftovers have allowed me to develop some great techniques. (And you won't find these ever-so-useful tips in the pages of *Gourmet,* trust me.)

1. Don't just warm leftovers—revive the taste somehow. Refrying in olive oil with garlic, or reheating with a little butter or cooked bacon seriously enhances flavor.

2. Mix 'n' match—you didn't think that Chinese went with spaghetti? Or Indian with sushi? You'll never know till you try.

3. It's all in the presentation—take them out of the plastic cartons and put them on nice plates, light some candles, and add a sprig of parsley, cilantro, or anything fresh and green, and *voilà!* New life!

4. Shelf lives: Pizza keeps for only three days. On the fourth day it tastes old (but technically is still edible and seems to taste good to picky toddlers and men who watch football). I've also studied the refrigerator shelf ▶

life of Chinese/Thai food (three days); Krispy Kreme doughnuts (twelve hours, but six seconds in the microwave can give you another five hours); an opened bottle of wine (four days with the cork in).

5. Extracting wilted greens and isolating other soggy ingredients from salads or pasta is difficult but not impossible. Arm yourself with some "kitchen tweezers" for just such emergencies.

6. Remember: Anything slightly green or teal, or even celadon *GOES!*

And if all else fails . . .

7. Order take-out from the fastest place in town; tomorrow it'll make great leftovers.

—Emily Miles Terry

Sweet justice! Zelda finally had proof that Lorraine's signature bundt cakes were not homemade.

"You can fool all of the people some of the time *and some of the people all of the time.* And that's sufficient." *—Rose King*

It's Faux Good

Faking Your Way Around the Kitchen

Let's face it, elaborate home-cooked meals have gone the way of bread machines and Baked Alaska. What's "in" in haute cuisine is faux cuisine, and savvy chicks know just the right recipes for dishing up their phony baloney. Here's a primer for faux cooking that can be used when preparing elaborate faux dinners for two, or for twenty. Like Meg Ryan in *When Harry Met Sally*, a good faker is never stingy with her dramatic flair; she knows that all five senses of her "audience" must be equal parts distracted and satisfied. Keep these tips close to your breast—trust no one with them! Accomplices, if you need them, must always be sworn to secrecy.

Aromatherapy. First impressions are everything. A delicious fragrance greets your family or guests at the door and whispers "Come hither." Though every speck of food you are serving may be store-bought and store-baked, you can still concoct a luscious aroma.

1. Place a few drops of vanilla on tinfoil and bake for a few minutes.

2. Simmer sliced apples and cinnamon sticks in apple juice or cider on your stove top.

3. Fry up some garlic in olive oil and brush it on baguette slices.

4. Bake bread dough (the premade kind)

5. Light "foody" scented candles like vanilla, pumpkin, sugar cookie, rosemary, melon, etc.

Dress it up. Your dining or buffet table is the visual focal point of the meal: Don't forget, an attractive centerpiece can help keep up the ruse. Add plentiful serving dishes, table linens, and, if you're having a sit-down meal, place cards (see page 93). Your guests will be thinking "Boy, this chick went to a lot of trouble."

Tune in. Having background music implies that you were organized and Zen enough to fiddle with your stereo (hah!). If it's loud enough, your guests might not notice the empty food cartons in your trash can.

Illegitimate entrées and salads. In order to join the ranks of range-free chicks, you need some main dishes and salads that you can scratch together. Here are some of our favorite store-bought dishes to serve up, doctor up a bit, and call your own. If you have a sensational gourmet market or take-out caterer, feel free to expand your repertoire. Otherwise, if you have a standard supermarket deli, these are probably safe enough for your sham. Make sure to transfer into your own dish for reheating and serving, and top with fresh garnishes—ground pepper, grated parmesan, fresh herbs, etc.

ROAST CHICKEN • FRIED CHICKEN

• RIBS • EGGPLANT PARMESAN

• LASAGNA • SOUP

• SPAGHETTI & MEATBALLS • PASTA SALAD

• MOZZARELLA, TOMATOES, AND BASIL

• COLE SLAW

CHICK CHEATS

Getting caught without key ingredients at critical moments is so yesterday! With this little chick cheat list, you'll never be caught with your apron strings untied.

DON'T HAVE	DON'T SWEAT IT • USE THIS INSTEAD
1 cup cake flour	1 cup all-purpose flour minus 2 tablespoons
1 egg (for cake batter)	2 tablespoons mayonnaise
1 tablespoon cornstarch	2 tablespoons all-purpose flour
1 cup granulated sugar	1 cup packed brown sugar or 2 cups sifted powdered sugar
1 cup powdered sugar	1 cup sugar plus 1 tablespoon cornstarch processed in food processor
1 cup honey	1 cup granulated sugar plus ¼ cup water
1 cup whole milk	½ cup evaporated milk plus ½ cup water
1 teaspoon dry mustard	1 tablespoon prepared mustard
1 teaspoon lemon zest	½ teaspoon lemon extract
1 clove garlic	⅛ teaspoon garlic powder
1 cup oil (in baking)	1 cup applesauce
1 teaspoon cream of tartar	3 teaspoons lemon juice
1 teaspoon baking powder	¼ teaspoon baking soda plus ½ teaspoon cream of tartar
Baking soda	There is no substitute for baking soda
1 cup mayonnaise	1 cup pureed cottage cheese
1 cup buttermilk	1 tablespoon lemon juice or vinegar with enough regular milk added to make 1 cup; let stand 5 minutes
1 tablespoon fresh herbs	1 teaspoon dried herbs
1 ounce semisweet chocolate	½ ounce unsweetened chocolate plus 1 tablespoon sugar
1 ounce unsweetened chocolate	3 tablespoons unsweetened cocoa powder plus 1 tablespoon butter or margarine plus 2 tablespoons water
1 cup sour cream	1 cup plain yogurt or ¾ cup buttermilk plus ⅓ cup butter or margarine
1 cup butter	⅞ cup vegetable oil, lard, or shortening

What Kind of Dish Are You?

If you find yourself beating your head against the refrigerator door more often than you're beating a happy path to the stove, it might be time for a culinary identity check. Gourmet gal or fast-food flirt, it helps to embrace a specialty, a signature dish, a *pièce de résistance*. While we prefer to define ourselves by what comes out of our mouths as opposed to what goes in, maybe there is something to the adage "you are what you eat"—so start with what you love and go from there. We hope these classic "dishes" will provide you with some inspiration.

CHILI CHIQUITA. You are the original Spice Girl. Flavor is your game and you're hot for anything that simmers on the tongue. Your well-stocked kitchen sports jalapeños, chorizo, Tabasco, flaming mustards, and fire-breathing horseradish. You find that red high heels give you just enough boost to reach into your spice cabinet. Your menu reads like something from south of the border: fajitas, refried beans, Mexican rice, chili cornbread, guacamole, and salsa.

BRUNCH BABE. Not to be bothered with traditional "lunch" menus, you've been known to fix scrambled eggs for dinner on more than one occasion. Dress for dinner? Pajamas and fuzzy slippers are always appropriate. You snuggle down to scrambled eggs with lox and onions, Belgian waffles, sourdough toast, fruit salad, and bacon.

LETTUCE LADY OR SALAD BITCH. You've got a lovely head for crafting the tastiest of salads. Roaming the produce aisle and specialty food sections, you can combine tantalizing tidbits with tender leaves to create a delectable dish. Whether it's frisée, arugula, iceberg, or romaine, you dress it to the nines. Not since Adam and Eve have a few leaves caused such a stir.

THE BARBIE-CUE. Hand over that skewer, grillfriend, and light it up. From shish kebab to swordfish, your food is well done, and washing dishes is for people who can't stand the heat. A main course without black charcoal marks leaves you chilly, and you feel positively naked without your elbow-length oven mitt. Where there's smoke, there's fire . . . along with tuna with wasabi mayonnaise, marinated vegetables, and grilled pineapple sundaes.

APPETIZING ANGEL. As a kid you never could move beyond pigs in a blanket, and as an adult—why should you? Your chicken wings, baked brie, and filo pies leave them fat and happy. Besides, a little bit of this and a little bit of that are the perfect ways to accessorize your little black cocktail dress. Your buffet table sports small plates, cocktail picks, and an array of irresistible bite-size treats.

DESSERT DILETTANTE. You like to cut to the chase. Your fare is just desserts and leaves them sweet on you. You know the power of a come-hither look, a comfy couch, and a plate of homemade peanut butter cookies. Your wardrobe is rife with chocolate browns, vanilla creams, and that delicious strawberry pink sweater. Any way you slice it, it's *la dolce vita,* with chocolate cake, fruit crisp, cookies, strawberry mousse, and homemade ice cream.

Betty Is a Crock

BETTY CROCKER WAS "BORN" IN 1921 in Minneapolis, Minnesota, though it took about fifteen years before anyone knew what she looked like. The suits at the Washburn Crosby Company, a division of General Mills, needed a front woman to field the deluge of baking questions they received each year. So they borrowed the surname of a retired director, William Crocker, tossed "Betty," a popular name at the time, in front, and soon Betty Crocker was reporting to work.

At first she kept a low profile, just signing letters, but Betty, like all ambitious women, was destined for bigger things. In 1924, at the tender age of three, she hosted one of the nation's first radio cooking shows and finally got her big break in 1936, when an artist took all the women from the Home Service Department and blended their features to create a matronly portrait of the All-American white woman.

Later, Betty got her own television show and went on to author more than two hundred cookbooks and develop her own line of food products. She's rolling in dough these days as the front woman for a multimillion-dollar multimedia empire.

But then again, "virtual" chicks get a lot of breaks. Betty speaks with the utmost authority, is recognized everywhere, has the unwavering support of an enormous corporation, never has to shave her legs, and—the icing on the cake—she has an infinite shelf life, thanks to extensive makeovers every few years. And, unlike real women, she is immune to scandal. You'll never find Betty's mug on the cover of a tabloid, involved in a love triangle with the Marlboro Man or a clown like Ronald McDonald. And her closest friends, Aunt Jemima and the Pillsbury Doughboy? Something tells us they won't be spreading any rumors either.

> "At my age, *I enjoy every day.* When I'm really smart, I enjoy every moment."
>
> —*Dorismarie Welcher*

A little birdie told us . . . Instead of relying on premade baking mixes, make your own, and save yourself from those preservatives. All you need is flour, baking powder, vegetable oil, and salt. Per 1 cup flour, add 2 teaspoons baking powder, 2 tablespoons vegetable oil, and 1 teaspoon salt. And in no time you've got BisChick!

kitcHen COnfidential

YOU SHOULDN'T LEAVE A WOMAN ALONE IN THE KITCHEN TOO LONG. Things happen. She begins to hum Edith Piaf songs. Her women friends come over for strong coffee and stronger cheese. For a while they talk about schools for their children, presidential politics, the demoralization of our culture, good swing sets; then, with the first taste of bread and cheese together, there is some silent sharing of pleasure in the compatibility of the pale colors—bread the color of a Jersey cow, cheese a sheep's wool white—and the mixing of textures, one porous and gently resistant, and the other opaque and melting. Finally, after a pause, the conversation surges into the delta of mankind and womankind, creeps first into the larger waterways of habit, flows slowly between the trees of marriage, nudges softly but persistently against the small islands of children, and gradually fills in over the topography of daily history, flooding the whole land at last until it takes the form of a lake, still and broad, although it is really a delta, fingerlike, branching, a place in between river and sea.

It demands a lifetime, this conversation of women about men, because the connections and abrasions between them are so vast, wide, beautiful, unknown, concealing, murky, procreative, strangling, forever refreshed, and forever bogged down. The talk of women is like the hum of a distant universe that men know exists although they can't see it, and it surrounds them, becomes part of the white noise, or blue noise or red noise, depending upon the threat it poses or the pleasure it accords. We bend over our coffees, letting the soft steam warm our cheeks, and talk about the way women stack up into a column of shared experiences, and men orbit in a million different trajectories.

When I am in my kitchen, life seems to run like rapids between the banks of my countertops, and I feel like a pylon in the stream, sunk for a pier that will never be built. Here is my mind's life. The shared words of women friends drench me and the stretching limbs of children bed themselves like oysters all around me. I tie on an apron, remove myself from the world outside, and I lay myself bare to the world inside.

—Nora Seton

LOve me TeNder

THERE'S AN OLD SOUTHERN BELIEF that holds that a woman goes into a marriage thinking she can change her man, while a man wants his woman to stay the same as when he married her. I didn't want to change Elvis, but I did have the romantic delusion that once we were married, I could change our life-style.

For the first few days after the wedding, I thought my dream had come true. We divided our time between Graceland and the ranch, where Elvis and I had taken up residence in a large, three-bedroom trailer.

It was typical of Elvis to choose the trailer over the quaint little house. He had never lived in a trailer before and it intrigued him. The place was completely furnished, including a washer, a dryer, and a modern kitchen. It turned out to be very romantic.

I loved playing house. I personally washed all his clothes, along with the towels and sheets, and took pride in ironing his shirts and rolling up his socks the way my mother had taught me. Here was an opportunity to take care of him myself. No maids or housekeepers to pamper us. No large rooms to embrace the regular entourage.

I got up early, put on a pot of coffee, and started his breakfast with a pound of bacon and three eggs, proudly presented it to him the moment he woke up.

"You see, if we were ever stranded somewhere alone, you know I can take care of you."

It must have been difficult for him to eat the instant he opened his eyes—but he wasn't going to disappoint his new bride.

Although the rest of the group traveled with us, they respected our privacy as newlyweds and, for the most part, left us alone.

I understood Elvis's need for the camaraderie the entourage provided, and I didn't want to take him away from the people he loved, especially now that we were married. He had always criticized wives who tried to change the status quo. He told me about one wife, saying, "She doesn't like him to be around the boys so much. She's going to cause problems in the group." The last thing I wanted was for Elvis to think I'd be the kind of wife who'd come between her man and his friends.

I decided one evening to show off my cooking skills for everyone by making one of Elvis's favorite dishes, lasagna. I invited the regulars, bragging to one and all about how well I prepared this Italian specialty. Despite my outward confidence, I must have made ten long-distance calls to my mother in New Jersey, checking and rechecking on quantities and measurements. It was important for me to prove myself a success. Joe Esposito, our only Italian and a "gourmet chef," kidded me all week about how he bet that my lasagna wouldn't be as good as his. All that ribbing only made me more nervous. I kept thinking, What do I know about pasta? I'm not even Italian.

Finally, the night of the dinner came. Everyone was seated at the table, watching me expectantly. I tried to appear cool and confident as I brought out the fancily prepared platter and started cutting individual squares for my guests. I did notice that when I started slicing the lasagna, it felt a little tough, but thinking I was holding a dull knife, I continued dishing it out.

I sat down, smiled anxiously, and said, "Please start." We all took a bite and—crunch. There was a look of shock on everyone's face. I looked at my plate and was mortified when I realized I had forgotten to boil the pasta.

Elvis began laughing, but when he saw I was about to cry he turned to his plate and began eating, uncooked noodles and all. Taking their lead from him, everyone followed suit.

Joe Esposito still laughs about it, frequently saying, "Cilla? How about some lasagna?"

—*Priscilla Beaulieu Presley*

Priscilla-Proof Lasagna

Add a Caesar salad and garlic bread for a feast that's fit for a king (or a queen).

1 pound ground beef or ground turkey

2 jars (26 ounces each) tomato sauce

15 oz ricotta

¼ cup grated parmesan

½ cup frozen chopped spinach, thawed

9 no-boil lasagna noodles

3 cups shredded mozzarella (or Italian cheese blend)

1. Preheat the oven to 375°F. In a large skillet over medium-high heat, brown the beef until cooked through, about 5 minutes. Drain the meat and return it to the pan. Pour the pasta sauce into the meat.

2. In a bowl, combine the ricotta, parmesan, and spinach.

3. Cover the bottom of a 9-by-13-inch baking dish with a thin layer of the sauce and meat mixture. Top with 3 lasagna noodles, then top the noodles with one third of the ricotta mixture and 1 cup of the mozzarella. Repeat the layers two more times. Cover the dish with aluminum foil.

4. Bake until bubbly, about 40 minutes. Remove from the oven and let the lasagna sit for about 10 minutes before serving.

Serves 8

A little birdie told us . . . If you are in the mood for some inspirational new recipes, try www.epicurious.com. The Web site features free recipes from *Bon Appétit* and *Gourmet* magazines and you can even set up your own virtual "recipe box."

HOW TO BOIL WATER—SERIOUSLY

Yes, any birdbrain can throw water into a pot and put it on a stove—we're just letting you know how to do it better, faster, and smarter than before. Think of this as Bionic Boiling 101.

FOR EGGS

Place eggs in an uncovered saucepan and barely cover with room-temperature water. Bring water to a rolling boil over high heat. Remove the saucepan from heat immediately and cover. If you want soft-boiled eggs let them sit, covered, for 3 to 5 minutes. If you want hard-boiled eggs, let them stand for 10 to 12 minutes.

FOR PASTA

The key to well-cooked pasta is a lot of water. Fill a large pot full of cold water (about a gallon). Bring water to a rolling boil over high heat. Add 1 tablespoon sea salt or table salt. Boil the pasta until it turns a lighter color and is "al dente" (tender on the outside, firm on the inside—usually about 8 minutes). Drain pasta in a colander. If you plan to serve the pasta warm, don't rinse with water.

A little birdie told us . . . A watched pot never boils, but water will boil faster if placed in a lighter-weight pot with the lid on.

"Where are the eggs I asked you to separate?" said Mrs. Rogers.

"Here's one, one is behind the clock, and the other is over there. *Did I separate them far enough apart?*" asked Amelia Bedelia.

—*Peggy Parish, from* Amelia Bedelia

The Test Kitchen, Amelia Bedelia Style

To err is human, and the kitchen is fertile ground for mishaps. With all the heat, the wine, the conversation, the deadlines, it's a wonder a chick ever gets anything from paper to pan to plate without major incident. If professionals have test kitchens, why shouldn't the average chick proudly embrace her own share of laboratory mishaps? Take your lead from Peggy Parish's plucky heroine, Amelia Bedelia, who "dresses" the chicken in style and "trims" the steak in lace and ribbons. We polled our friends for their favorite stories in the spirit of Amelia Bedelia. Here are a few of our favorites:

I had a friend who once . . .

. . . served a pink turkey for Thanksgiving dinner. She used a wine basting recipe but in a flurry of innovation used red wine instead of the white wine that was called for.

. . . could not figure out why her dish wasn't done. It called for 360 degrees and she kept rotating it in a circle.

. . . cut the ends off of every ham she baked. When a friend asked why, she said that's the way her mother had taught her. The cook asked her mother next time they spoke why they did that, to which Mom replied, "Honey, I never had a pan big enough until last year."

. . . in an attempt at unique presentation, nestled cherry tomato appetizers in a platter of uncooked rice to hold them upright and steady. She thought it was a great idea until she repeatedly heard "ouch" and yikes of pain from her guests. The dried rice was sticking to the tomatoes and wreaking havoc on their teeth.

. . . baked fifteen homemade lemon pies for a bake sale using salt instead of sugar. Fortunately, in the spirit of philanthropy, no one demanded a refund.

. . . could hardly boil water. In an effort to impress her newlywed husband, she stuck an onion in the oven just before he came home. He'd rave, "That smells wonderful, sweetie," as she covertly dished the take-out from the local Italian restaurant onto their wedding china.

Isabel cursed her curiosity. The kitchen was dangerous—indeed, no place for a woman.

"No matter what happens in the kitchen, *never apologize.*"

—*Julia Child*

the BEst bite *Alice Waters*

ALICE WATERS LIES IN BED AT NIGHT WORRYING about what to feed you. She knows that she can make you happy. She also knows, in her hidden heart, that if she can find the perfect dish to feed each person who comes to her door, she can change the world.

Every great cook secretly believes in the power of food. Alice Waters just believes this more than anybody else. She is certain that we are what we eat, and she has made it her mission in life to make sure that people eat beautifully. Waters is creating a food revolution, even if she has to do it one meal at a time.

Alice didn't set out to change the way America eats. She just wanted to feed her friends. Having been to France, she had seen the way a good bistro could become the heart of a neighborhood, a place where people went for comfort and sustenance. She was not a professional cook, but she enjoyed feeding people, and she envisioned a cozy little café, which would be open every day for breakfast, lunch, and dinner, a place where everyone from the dishwashers to the cooks would be well-paid, a sort of endless party where everyone would have fun. Reality soon set in. Faced with financial ruin, Chez Panisse was forced to become a real business. Still, the dream did not die. It just changed.

"I was more obsessed," Alice explains. If she was going to have a restaurant, it was going to be the very best one she could possibly manage. Even if that meant rethinking the whole concept of what a restaurant might be.

She began with the ingredients. Every chef dreams of great produce, but most make do with what is available in the market. Not Alice. Disgusted with the fish that was sold in stores, she bought a truck and sent someone down to the port to find fishermen as they docked their boats. When she could not find the baby lettuces she had loved in France, she tore up her backyard and grew her own. She found foragers to hunt for mushrooms. She persuaded farmers to let their lambs run wild through the hills. She demanded better bread. Before long, she had developed an entire network of people producing food just for her.

The results were electric. Chez Panisse served only one meal a day, but people reserved months ahead of time and took their chances. You would find them shaking their heads over the menu, wailing, "Chicken? I've come all the way from Maine for chicken?" Then the dish would arrive, and they'd look down with dismay and say, "It's just a piece of chicken," as if they had somehow expected the poor bird to turn into a swan as it cooked. But they'd waited months for the reservation, so they would take a bite of the chicken and a sort of wonder would come over their faces. "It's the best chicken I have ever tasted," they'd whisper reverently. "I never knew that food could taste so good."

And Alice, walking by, would smile her secret little smile. Because, once again, she had done it. She had given them food that they would remember, a taste that would linger long beyond that night. And they would know, ever after, how a chicken raised in the open air, fed on corn, and cooked with care, could taste. She knew that they would carry that flavor away with them, and that every time they ate a chicken, no matter where it might be, they would remember. And if Alice had her way, they would go looking for that chicken—or that tomato, or that strawberry—until they found it. Because she had given them more than a meal—she had given them a memory.

—*Ruth Reichl*

Like a Virgin?

Whether we're dipping our bread in it or frying up sausages with it, we know that "virgin" olive oil is best; but need it also be refined, pure, and extra? Sandra Dee, where are you when we need you?!

Apparently, the answer lies in the processing—the less those little olives are handled, the better. Look for "extra virgin" and "cold process" or "first cold pressed" on the label—this means that the oil has been extracted using a chemical-free method. There are a lot of wannabe virgins out there, so another tip is that highest-quality olive oils will have an acidity level on their labels (an acidity level lower than 1 percent is one great olive oil) and the region where the olives were grown. Color and price are not good indicators of quality, and labels indicating "pure" and "light" are for lesser-quality oils. Once you have sampled a few olive oils, let your taste buds be the ultimate arbiters. And remember, olive oil is like wine: It needs to be stored in a cool, dark place. Once opened, it will be at its best for only about a year.

"You *have* to throw feeling into cooking." —*Rosa Lewis*

 *A little birdie told us . . .* Keep a bottle of less expensive olive oil for frying, baking, and sautéing and save your higher-quality, flavorful bottles for dressings, marinades, appetizers, and just plain dipping.

SPICE, SPICE BABY

Whether you desire sweet or sour, zesty or savory, pungent or pleasant, a girl's gotta have a great rack!

THE ESSENTIALS. The spices every cook needs: all-spice, bay leaves, chili powder, cayenne pepper, cloves, coriander, cream of tartar, cumin, curry powder, cinnamon, dill weed, garlic salt, ginger, nutmeg, lemon pepper, onion powder, paprika, pepper, red pepper flakes, white pepper, oregano, rosemary, sage, iodized salt, sea or kosher salt, tarragon, thyme, vanilla bean.

THE EXOTICS. Some spices to help you walk on the wild side:

WILD FENNEL POLLEN (POWDER) is popular for its versatility, enhancing everything from veggies to meat. It makes a great rub for fish, poultry, or pork (just mix with a little olive oil). Especially appealing to chicks who liked black jelly beans.

ANCHO CHILI POWDER is like a great fig—sweet and hot, rich and plummy. The sweetest of the dried chilis, bring it on when you want to liven up a sauce (particularly a Mexican one) or marinade.

SAFFRON (POWDER) still reigns as the most expensive spice in the world, but its intensity is fierce, so you don't need a lot. Fragrant and slightly bitter, saffron is unforgettable in soups and rice and a must in special recipes like bouillabaisse and paella.

> "If spices qualified as antiques, Sotheby's would be camping at my kitchen door."
>
> —*Erma Bombeck*

JUNIPER BERRIES (WHOLE) add a bittersweet, piney flavor to ordinary meat, stuffings, sausages, stews, and soups. Try crushing the berries to make marinades for game, fish, or chicken dishes.

VERBENA (LEAVES) Some of us need a little tartness to go along with our sugar, and we just can't get enough lemony flavors. Verbena is more intense than many other lemon-scented herbs and delicious on fruit and ice cream, in cakes, and with fish.

CARDAMOM SEEDS can be purchased at a good health-food or specialty-foods store, and can be ground or crushed until powdery. Used extensively in Scandinavian cooking, cardamom subtly flavors baked goods, pancakes, and waffles. A teaspoon or two creates a "I just can't name it, but it's scrumptious!" reaction.

NUTMEG (WHOLE) adds a delicate, lacy flavor to cream dishes, soups, chocolate mocha, confections, and eggnog. Use sparingly and grind with a special nutmeg grinder.

RAISING THE SALAD BAR SNAP OUT OF THE SALAD DAZE

Now and then a chick needs to turn over a new leaf, and there's no easier place to start than the salad bowl. The faithful green salad is like a little black dress—perfect for any occasion, given the right accessories and attitude. Next time you are feeling a little blue over your greens, toss in a few unexpected tidbits to mix things up. Break the iceberg habit and go really green with combinations that include mâche, frisée, Bibb or Boston lettuce, endive, radicchio, arugula, spinach, red leaf, or romaine. And don't forget fresh herbs to spice things up.

TO A BOWL OF MIXED GREENS, ADD:

1. Toasted pine nuts (spread them on tinfoil and broil until golden brown)
Crumbled feta cheese
Artichoke hearts
Dried cranberries

2. Crumbled chèvre
Unsalted macadamia nuts
Chopped dried apricots
Chopped dried pineapple

3. Red onion
Crumbled Saga blue cheese
Thinly sliced pears
Walnuts

4. Lemon cucumber
Yellow tomatoes
Orange tomatoes
Red bell pepper
Mint leaves

5. Pitted calamata olives
Strips of salami
Sliced green bell pepper
Roma tomatoes

6. Capers
Blanched green beans
Chunks of albacore tuna
Thin slices of blanched baby potatoes

7. Fresh mozzarella
Fresh basil
Cherry or grape tomatoes
Mint leaves

8. Crumbled Gorgonzola
Granny Smith apple slices
Golden raisins
Pecans

Dressed to Thrill

A Killer Vinaigrette

This tried-and-true basic tastes good on just about any green salad combination.

¼ cup good red or white wine vinegar (or balsamic vinegar)
1–2 cloves garlic, minced
1 teaspoon Dijon mustard
salt and freshly ground pepper
¾ cup extra-virgin olive oil

Mix first four ingredients in a bowl. Slowly whisk in olive oil.

Makes 1 cup

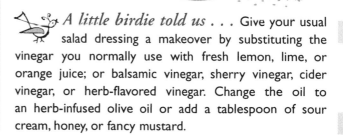

A little birdie told us . . . Give your usual salad dressing a makeover by substituting the vinegar you normally use with fresh lemon, lime, or orange juice; or balsamic vinegar, sherry vinegar, cider vinegar, or herb-flavored vinegar. Change the oil to an herb-infused olive oil or add a tablespoon of sour cream, honey, or fancy mustard.

Cock Tales
How Does Your Rooster Strut His Stuff?

Though men have reveled in the role of Iron Chef for decades, it's only recently that lucky chicks have found some guys who appreciate the joys of *home*cooking and aren't afraid to stir things up. Here's a Rooster Rorschach to help you identify your man's KQ (kitchen quotient).

THE LORD OF THE STOVE. On a good day your man could put Emeril to shame. He's inspired, he's skilled—from mixing to poaching—and he understands the difference between béchamel and cream sauce. His messes might make you long for Madge and a Palmolive soak, but dream of the leftovers and keep scrubbing.

THE SAMUEL ADAMS. Though even the grill can throw him for a loop, your chap is a wonder with any appliance or gadget that begets a beverage. As your drink-meister, he's a personal bartender, sommelier, and microbrewer all rolled into one. He never forgets the correct proportions or garnishes, and his concoctions are cheered and cherished.

THE ONE-HIT WONDER. At first taste, this guy is often mistaken for a Lord of the Stove. He's amazingly adept at preparing one entrée or side—be it lobster, lasagna, or leg of lamb, this specialty is beyond belief. But the amazing foreplay yields a surprisingly small menu, so you'll have to be satisfied with repeat performances of a hit single.

What does your cock-a-doodle Do?

THE HUNGRY MAN. This guy doesn't understand why you'd ever want to cook up a meal when you can order in or nuke a TV dinner. His preferred position is feet up, with beverage in one hand, remote in the other. He can be coaxed from his chair by some delicious-smelling fare, but he'll be back in his cozy perch before a chick has a chance to get her feathers ruffled.

THE RED-HOT ROMANCER. This rooster knows that the way to his chick's heart is through her belly and he appreciates the sensuality of food. His tool of choice—a hot grill and some long tongs. From shish kebabs to salmon, this razzmatazzer titillates your taste buds and knows how to keep things at a slow burn. For a grande finale, he'll take the fire inside to the fondue pot and feed you strawberries dipped in chocolate. Take it all in and worry about the dishes later.

"Cooking is like love. It should be entered into with abandon *or not at all.*" —*Harriet Van Horne*

LET'S FACE IT, DISH DUTY IS FOR THE BIRDS. Amuse yourself or a friend and put some dry humor into cleanup with personalized dish towels that have a smart-talkin' attitude.

You'll need:

100% cotton, lint-free dish towels or tea towels (the "flour sack" kind works great)

A snappy quote

A computer and printer

Ready-to-print iron-on transfer paper for your type of printer

Scissors

Iron

Choose or make up a quote for your dish towel and type it into your computer in the font and size you want. (Print a test on a piece of plain paper to make sure you like the way it looks.) Follow directions for your transfer paper and print out the quote. Use scissors to trim around the letters, and iron on according to directions. (Photos and other artwork can also be scanned in to create unique designs.)

Quotes to Dish Out

Emily was a little tired, but far from washed up.

Do I look domestic?

Our favorite recipes include the words "and shake over ice."

Yes, honey, that's right, Mommy forgot to make dinner.

I'm not feeling very domestic right now. Try again later.

It's five o'clock somewhere.

Exactly when does the "happily ever after" part begin?

You wash and I'll let you dry.

You're just in time for dinner! Where are we going?

The dishwasher isn't working—it's girl's night out.

I'd rather be reading.

This was not what I meant when I said, "I want to watch my soaps."

A little birdie told us . . . A sinkful of suds looks like work to us, but to little tykes it can be fun. Let them "wash" a few unbreakable dishes and help you clean up. Keep a cabinet or drawer where they can explore. Stock it with plastic bowls and gadgets, kid-scale tools, an apron just their size, and some oven mitts and they'll always enjoy being in the kitchen with you.

One biTe WoN't *Kill* You

MY KIDS WERE GOING TO BE GOOD EATERS. That was the plan.

After all, I'm a great eater myself. Too great an eater, to judge by my girth. The only foods I don't like are eggplant and boiled eggs. Oh, and also celery and olive oil and margarine and skim milk, but who needs those? Every other kind of food, I love.

I also love to cook. My children, I figured, would be exposed to fine cooking at such an early age that they wouldn't be able to *help* becoming little gourmets.

I'd gradually make their food spicier and spicier; by three, they'd be eating raw habañeros for breakfast. As soon as they could wield a fork, I'd introduce them to chopsticks; as soon as they could heft their own bottles, I'd start teaching them about wine. Garlic and onions? No problem! Mushrooms? They'd *beg* for them! They would leap onto each new food trend as avidly as I do myself. And they'd love all kinds of exotic takeout as well, so that on nights I didn't feel like cooking, I could still be proud of what a great job I was doing.

There wouldn't be any fights about food in my house, either. None of these just-one-bite debates and no-dessert-until-your-plate-is-empty remonstrances. Nothing like what I remember from my own childhood, when my brother wept about eating even one pea and my sister threw up whenever she looked at a tomato and I learned how to hide unwanted food in my cheek pouches for hours at a time. In *my* house, mealtimes would be simultaneously peaceful and adventurous. I would never need to coax *my* kids to eat. Or to bribe them. After all, they'd love main courses and vegetables as much as desserts—maybe even more!

But why am I even bothering to set this up? You already know the punch line. For a long time my children were the worst eaters I've ever seen (always with the exception of my vomit-at-will sister, now an adult who still won't eat tomatoes). They didn't like *anything*—or at least not anything interesting or healthful. Candy, ice cream, and fast food, they could handle. True, there were a dreadful couple of years when my son didn't like French fries and my daughter didn't like hamburgers, so even McDonald's became a minefield. True, there were years when the only soup the kids would eat was canned Campbell's Chicken Alphabet, poured into a strainer and rinsed repeatedly until all that poisonous broth was gone. True, they used to eat only the frosting on their cake and leave what they call "the breading" on the plate. But we're over that now.

We're not over the food fights, though. Every night I flinch when one of the kids walks into the kitchen and asks what's for dinner. (My friend Nora, who has five children, has solved this problem by always replying, "We're having Yuck, I Hate It.") Sometimes they don't even bother asking what I'm making; they just say, "What stinks?" I know that at least one of the items on the menu, and probably more than one, will be greeted with howls of disgust. I know that if I pick a food one of the kids likes, the other will hate it, that most vegetables will have to be either disguised or force-fed, and that the no-dessert threat is the only way to get through the main course.

The kids will undoubtedly leap to correct me as soon as they read this. My daughter, Laura, now fifteen, is finally developing a palate; my son, John, now eleven, hasn't quite reached the point of eating anything with green flecks in it, but at least he doesn't retch quite as loudly when I make him try something new. So I'm here to tell you there's hope.

On the other hand, there are also new complications. The kids go to a school where lunch is served to them—no bringing things from home—and I've never dared ask, "So what did you have for lunch?" since the day one of them answered, "A roll and some water. I hated everything else they were serving." Laura now eats no red meat, which pretty much limits its "acceptable" animal protein to poultry; she doesn't really like legumes, salad, or fish (and it goes without saying that John hates all these things), and she would prefer that all our food contain less than one gram of fat. She loves most vegetables, a taste John still hasn't caught up to, but it's not as easy as it used to be to force her to drink a daily quart of milk—and as every single goddamn newspaper points out every single goddamn day, the teen years are the time girls are

Barbie-cups

¾ pound lean ground beef, cooked and drained

½ cup barbecue sauce

2 tablespoons grated onion (optional)

1 tablespoon packed brown sugar

3 ounces cheddar, grated (about ¾ cup), plus more for topping

One 8-ounce tube Pillsbury refrigerated biscuits

Preheat the oven to 400°F. Stir together the beef, barbecue sauce, onion if desired, brown sugar, and cheddar. Separate the biscuits and press each one into a muffin tin cup, making sure that the dough reaches all the way to the top of the cup.

Fill each Barbie-cup with the beef mixture, and sprinkle on some more grated cheddar. Bake for 10 to 12 minutes, and serve right away.

Serves 2 or 3

—Ann Hodgman

supposed to be laying in the best supply of calcium to prevent osteoporosis later. . . .

Fortunately, though, I'm not alone. Practically everyone else I know also has kids who are the worst eaters in the world.

There's something else I have to tell you. At least five nights out of seven, we either read or watch *The Simpsons* while we eat. There. Now you know you're a better parent than I am. So cheer up and start cooking.

—*Ann Hodgman*

Playing with Your Food

In our neck of the woods, picky eating and childhood go hand in hand, so we are always on the lookout for new ways to seduce our little hunger strikers into taking in some form of nourishment that's not sugar-coated or sodium-packed. We are not beyond subterfuge in our quest—if they think they are doing a craft or playing a game, so be it, as long as they eat it. And, as we all know, *we* outgrew *our* picky tendencies—well, *most* of them.

THE ARTS AND CRAFTS APPROACH. Food preparation that mimics creative expression can inspire kids to eat. Dipping foods fall into this category, and if they do a little finger painting on the plate, that adds to the fun. Cut up fresh veggies and serve with ranch dressing. Slice apples, strawberries, pears, etc., and accompany with vanilla yogurt. Chicken and meats seem to go down easier with a side of ketchup. Or give them little cocktail picks (supervise this closely) and let them spear and dip with them. Make edible portraits using cream cheese on a bagel as the artist's canvas. Give it personality with faces made of sliced olives, shredded carrots, red bell pepper, lox, parsley, and tomatoes.

AN EVERYDAY SUNDAE. A fruity frozen yogurt sundae is the perfect way to get fruit and dairy into the little ones. All you need is a couple of scoops of frozen yogurt, and the world is your fruit basket: blueberries, strawberries, raspberries, peaches, nectarines, etc. Top with whipped cream.

THE ART OF DISGUISE. Kids love surprises, so "what-you-see-is-not-necessarily-what-you-get" food options really tickle them. Try toasting a slice of cheese on a slice of bread, then cutting it out with a cookie cutter into a fun shape. Or how about a "pizza" that's really a whole wheat pita topped with peanut butter, bananas, and raisins? Make corn muffins in colorful cupcake baking cups and frost them with veggie cream cheese. A circle of vanilla yogurt topped with half an apricot looks like a fried egg. Or spread cream cheese onto a piece of turkey, add some diced tomato, roll it up, and slice into pinwheel "cookies."

CRUNCHY CRITTERS. Kids go buggy for anything insect- or animal-inspired. Make edible "caterpillars" by alternating bite-size pieces of chicken with cherry tomatoes on a skewer. End with a cherry tomato "head" and add carrot slivers for antennae and olive pieces for eyes. (You can make a sweet version of the caterpillar by alternating fruit chunks, a strawberry head, lemon rind antennae, and currant eyes.)

Take the dough from canned biscuit and shape it into a turtle by pulling the biscuit into an oval shape; cut another biscuit into shapes to form the feet, head, and tail. Bake 'em, butter 'em up, and add raisins for eyes.

Make "dirt" and "ants" by crushing up graham crackers and adding a few chocolate sprinkles to top yogurt or ice cream.

every chick should have...

✳ Luxurious hand lotion next to her kitchen sink

✳ A stereo in the kitchen to play tunes that inspire, calm, and cheer

✳ At least one delicious frozen entrée in the freezer—for afternoons or evenings too fun to stand in front of the stove

✳ A well-worn recipe card with a favorite family dish from a grandmother or other cherished relative

✳ Pictures of family and friends on the refrigerator door

✳ Someone to call if you get into a culinary fix

✳ A hidden box or bag of some wonderful junk food

✳ A signature specialty that you can whip up with one arm tied behind your back

✳ Something distinctly "you" in your kitchen— a frilly apron, an oven mitt, or a trivet from a memorable trip.

✳ A beautiful bottle or tin of something deliciously refined and gourmet—like a limited-run, estate-bottled olive oil or balsamic vinegar, or English tea biscuits in a vintage tin

✳ A neighbor who will lend you an emergency cup of sugar or an egg

"Three be the things I shall never attain: Envy, content, *and sufficient champagne.*" —*Dorothy Parker*

One Smart Cookie

SOMETIMES YOU MEET A PERSON of such great humor, insight, integrity, and flair, you feel that he or she was sent into your life with a purpose and a gift. Such was my sensation upon meeting Dorismarie. We met in the middle of nowhere out in a remote range of the Rocky Mountains in an area called Old Snowmass Valley, about twenty miles from Aspen, Colorado.

With guidance and zeal she has brightened my life, made me laugh until I couldn't stand up, coached me through heartthrob and heartbreak, and inspired me to reach unabashedly for the stars. Her way of seeing the world has taught me to observe life and laugh often, open my heart to the will of the universe, and expect miracles. . . .

The first time I visited her home in Aspen, she was managing a household of four tenants, all twenty-something young, unattached men whose sole purpose in life was to ski and party. (Imagine trying to get this bunch to clean the house!) To me she would lament, "Margie, you can offer them sexual favors and hundred-dollar bills, but you still can't get them to clean." So she devised a plan.

One Saturday morning, knowing they'd return ravenous at lunchtime after catching first tracks, she fried up a bunch of her famous chicken wings while I helped bake a humongous batch of her Cowboy Cookies. She displayed the bounty on pretty plates, accompanied by fancy napkins and beer glasses. Energized riffs of jazz wafted through the house along with the cooking aromas of the meal. Then she calmly took a seat at the table and waited.

When the guys came in, they immediately made a dash for the wings and cookies. She stared at them with an eagle eye and in a deadpan voice said, "No, honey, not until you pick up your rooms, take out the garbage, and wash the windows."

I've yet to see such a comical sight: four men who didn't know a dust bunny from a Playboy bunny, whirring around at the speed of sound, panting in anticipation of chicken wings, beer, and Cowboy Cookies.

Years later, on the day Dorismarie decided to leave Aspen and take up residence in New York City, she handed me a piece of paper with her renowned cookie recipe on it. "Here Margie," she said. "Take this. With your ingenious Aquarian mind, you'll discover a way to make a lot of money with this someday." And millions I made . . . cookies, however, not dollars—and some of the best friends and fondest memories of my life.

During my rookie season managing bakeries at the Squaw Valley USA ski area in the Sierra Nevada, it rained on Christmas. Then a drought year ensued, and with it a desperate lack of skiers. The livelihoods of my bakers were at stake. Faced with the inevitable—having to lay off my workers—I headed for a beach on Lake Tahoe and hoped for an epiphany. The next day it hit me: I'd dig out that Cowboy Cookie recipe from Dorismarie and begin baking and selling them at the mountain.

It was lust at first bite. When word got around about the Cowboy Cookies, sales exploded; all of my bakers started working overtime to fill the cookie orders. That spring, I talked my boss into leasing the kitchen to me after hours so I could moonlight to retailers and other bakeries. The following year, I opened my own retail cookie bakery in Tahoe City, California—with a plate of hot cookies, I had persuaded a friend and cookie fan to finance the dream. Margie's Cowboy Cookies were in the chips!

The Cowboy Cookies were my entree to a charmed life. With a tin of cookies in hand, I developed enduring friendships; I traded cookies for skis, for backstage concert passes, for hotel accommodations, for fun. I convinced a car dealer to let me drive away in a new car with no money down and no credit history. I baked them for my husband-to-be on one of our first dates, and they were undoubtedly a catalyst in sealing our fate. . . .

With a batch of these gems in hand, you can expect serendipitous, magic-carpet Cowboy Cookie adventures to fly into your life. So, don your best aprons, wave your magic spatula, tip your hat to Dorismarie—and ride 'em, cowgirls!

—*Margie Lapanja*

Margie's Cowboy Cookies

1½ cups margarine, room temperature
2 cups brown sugar
2 cups white sugar
4 eggs
2 teaspoons vanilla
1 teaspoon salt
1 teaspoon baking powder
2 teaspoons baking soda
4 cups unbleached flour
4 cups old-fashioned oats
2 cups Hershey's chocolate chips
1 cup shredded coconut
1 cup chopped nuts

1. Preheat oven to 350°F. With an electric mixer, whip up the margarine and sugars in a large mixing bowl until fluffy. Add the eggs, vanilla, and salt and beat well.

2. In a large bowl, whisk the baking powder and baking soda into the flour. Tap this mixture into the creamed ingredients, mixing slowly with a sturdy wooden spoon, and stir in the oats until the dough comes together. Finally, add in the chocolate chips, coconut, and nuts.

3. Line a cookie sheet with parchment paper (the secret to perfectly baked cookies!) and scoop out the dough with a 2-ounce ice cream scoop. Press the top of the cookie dough mound down oh-so-slightly with a spoon. Cast your spell over the Cowboy Cookies and bake for 7 to 12 minutes, until light golden in color with tiny cracks on top.

Makes 4 dozen

ContraBaNd cAndy

ONCE MAMA AND DADDY HAD GONE TO TOWN and left Willadeene in charge. We looked all over the house for something to get into, and finally discovered that we had cocoa, sugar, butter, and milk—all the makings of chocolate candy. A committee was formed to pester Willadeene into making the candy. It did its job well. After about thirty minutes of "Please, Deene, please," she gave in on the condition that nobody tell Mama and Daddy. Of course we agreed to this. This was one sweet-starved group of young'uns that would have agreed to have some of their less favorite body parts amputated tomorrow for the promise of chocolate candy today. Personally, I never cared that much for my left foot anyway.

I watched every step of the way as my sister made the candy, made twice as delicious by the illegal nature of it. The chocolate smelled so good as it was brought to a boil and then poured onto a plate that eager if none too sanitary fingers had helped to butter. Of course we never really let it set properly. Mama and Daddy would be coming home, but that was just an excuse for the fact that we just couldn't wait. First, the chocolate that remained in the pan had to be spooned and licked up and fought over until no trace remained. Then there was that glorious plate full of goo. It was spooned and fingered and slid off the plate with the aid of the butter into one urchin mouth after another. Willadeene, all the while, was nervous about the whole operation. She knew she would be the one held responsible if our sweet secret was discovered. She carefully washed the pot and spoons and the other implements of illegal confectionery. She even smelled them for chocolate "giveaways" after they had been dried.

The cleanup had just been finished when Mama and Daddy pulled into the yard. Willadeene surveyed the house for any signs of candy-making and was in the process of fanning the smell out the back door with her apron when she was shocked to hear me in the front yard. I had rushed to the car as soon as the doors opened and offered loudly in my most confident voice, "Mama, Deene didn't make no chocolate candy." Mama would not have even needed the traces of chocolate in the corners of my mouth to know exactly what had gone on. We were punished, but they couldn't remove the satisfying swell of chocolate candy from our stomachs, and all in all, it was easier than an amputation.

I can remember what a wonderful thing candy was then, or any kind of sweets. I used to think that when I became a star, I would have candy and cakes and pies any time I felt like it. One need only look at the width of my butt in *The Best Little Whorehouse in Texas* to know that I kept that promise to myself, at least for a while. Wouldn't it be something if we could have things we love in abundance without their losing that special attraction the want of them held for us?

—*Dolly Parton*

> "If I tried to haul ass, *I would have to make two trips.*"
>
> *—Dolly Parton*

Quick Chick Toffee Fix

¾ cup butter, melted

1 box chocolate chip Teddy Graham cookies, finely crushed

1¼ cups English toffee bits (in the baking section)

1 cup semisweet choc chips

1 cup pecans

1 cup walnuts, chopped

1 can (14 ounces) sweetened condensed milk

1. Preheat oven to 325°F. Line a 13-by-9-inch pan with nonstick foil, allowing foil to extend over ends of pan. Pour melted butter into pan. Sprinkle cookie crumbs in bottom of pan; press firmly and bake for 5 minutes.

2. Layer toffee bits and next 3 ingredients over crust in pan, pressing each layer down firmly. Pour condensed milk over top. Bake for 30 minutes, or until edges are lightly browned. Cool completely in pan (better yet, put in the fridge for a couple of hours) before trying to remove them from the pan.

3. Lift foil out of pan. Cut into bars. Enjoy!

Makes about 20

Feastworthy Films

Be sure you have some satisfying snacks on hand before you press play on these delicious movies. A growling stomach is the *worst* distraction.

Babette's Feast
Big Night
Chocolat
Dinner Rush
Eat Drink Man Woman
Fried Green Tomatoes
Like Water for Chocolate
My Big Fat Greek Wedding
Mystic Pizza
Simply Irresistible
Soul Food
Tea with Mussolini
Tortilla Soup
Tampopo
Under the Tuscan Sun

ReCipes *for* DisAster

SINCE MY MOTHER'S DEATH several years ago, I've gathered a pile of hundreds of recipes from the derangement of papers every death leaves behind. I added a few hundred more when my grandmother—her mother-in-law—died a few years ago. This last cache of papers surprised me; I don't remember my grandmother ever cooking a meal for anyone. She lived next door to my mother and father for the last twenty years of her life, a perpetual ghost in my mother's living room, subsisting mainly on cigarettes and beer and the hot dishes cooked by other women and brought to her like peace offerings.

Still, here they are: recipes, hundreds of recipes, cut out of newspapers and magazines, from the bottom of advertisements and off can labels and on index cards and notepaper. Some are in my grandmother's meticulous schoolteacher's penmanship. A few are in mysterious hands, gifts from long-gone friends and neighbors scribbled on the backs of envelopes, bits of stationery, handed on, copied again and again.

These aren't lost classics or great secrets. Most of them share a single quality—speed. Here is Vegetable A La Supreme, requiring cream of mushroom soup, frozen broccoli, Minute rice, and an entire bottle of Cheez Whiz. Here is Tomato Soup Salad, with canned soup, Knox gelatin, cottage cheese, mayonnaise, and stuffed olives. Here is Easy Deviled Ham 'n Cheesewich, Saccharin Pickles, Chicken Spaghetti. There are a great many recipes using zucchini; zucchini with tomato juice, with

fried onion rings, with cream cheese, with whipped cream, with cream of mushroom soup, with nuts and crushed pineapple. These dishes are based on convenience, the ingenuity of making do with a few odd cans and boxes, combining anything and everything you can put your hands on so as to avoid yet another trip to the store. Here are the endless reinventions of fusion cuisine, the creativity of limited ethnic poverty, the surprise of nouvelle, the patent simplicity of country people, all wrapped into a Jet Age suburban gift box. Weird and wonderful, this criminal's urge to avoid work, this wily feminine conspiracy of 3 x 5 cards. My mother worked a lot. At the end of the day, what my mother wanted wasn't food but time—time out of her labor, time to goof off in her armchair reading romances and drinking coffee, smoking while she watched Mike Douglas watch someone else cook something.

In this whole pile are only a few familiar items, like Porcupine Meatballs—hamburger and rice rolled into balls and baked in a sauce of canned tomato soup—and Pigs in Blankets. I don't know if I loved the name, evocative of luxury and comfort, or the doughy combination of Vienna sausages and Bisquick, but they were one of my favorite treats, rarely had. The fact is that she cooked the same few things over and over. After a few swings at Porcupine Meatballs or Scalloped-Potatoes-and-Spam, you don't need a recipe. You don't even need a shopping list, and so you don't need to plan too much or think too far ahead. She kept a pantry stocked well enough for cataclysmic natural disasters, but the hundreds of boxes and cans were simply variations on a few basic things. (You can make Porcupine Meatballs with tomato soup, with mushroom soup, with cheese soup, and call it something different every time.)

So why did she keep a recipe for eggplant stuffed with lunch meat, something our entire family (and perhaps the whole human race) would have loathed? Why did she save how-to plans for time-consuming, multi-layer tortes when she never baked? Why menus for party foods and coffee klatches written in the careful hand of a woman who rarely went to parties and never entertained? I wonder if my mother indulged in what Rosalind Coward, decades later, coined "food pornography." "All the women I have talked to about food have confessed to enjoying it," wrote Coward. "Few activities, it seems, rival relaxing in bed with a good recipe book. Some indulged in full colour pictures of gleaming bodies of Cold Mackerel Basquaise lying invitingly on a bed of peppers, or perfectly formed chocolate mousse topped with mounds of cream. The intellectuals expressed a preference for erotica, Elizabeth David's historical and literary titillation. All of us used the recipe books as aids to oral gratification, stimulants to imagine new combinations of food, ideas for producing a lovely meal."

I keep a thick folder of untried recipes too, torn from the newspaper and various magazines, handed to me by friends or scribbled from conversations. There are elaborate desserts meant to be served on linen tablecloths by candlelight, and hearty family suppers for a family I no longer have to feed. I'm still caught, like her, between what I've imagined and what I've known, what's been given and what I've been able to take. I rarely use any of them. Like impulsively chosen lovers, a lot of recipes look less appetizing in the cold light of day.

One of my mother's old recipes is on a bit of stationery from a hotel in Reno, and when I found it, I was suddenly, unreasonably glad that she went there. I could see her laughing, drinking a martini, playing slot machines, staying up late with other secretly dissident women, smoking cigarettes, and not missing their husbands. But I was struck as well by a sudden small grief that she spent even one minute there in Reno copying down a recipe.

—*Sallie Tisdale*

"That bread with ham and cheese brings back *the essence of our embraces,* and that German wine, *the taste of his lips.* **I cannot separate eroticism from food** and see no reason to do so. On the contrary, **I want to go on enjoying both** as long as strength and good humor last." —*Isabel Allende, from* Aphrodite

Naughty Little Cookbooks
Gastroporn

"Cook-books have always intrigued and seduced me. When I was still a dilettante in the kitchen they held my attention, even the dull ones, from cover to cover, the way crime and murder stories did Gertrude Stein." —Alice B. Toklas

We want to let you in on a little secret. The hottest thing in a chick's kitchen isn't her Tabasco sauce or her griddle. People in the know claim that what wets a chick's whistle are her cookbooks and that there is nothing we crave more than reading a hot recipe between the sheets. At the risk of putting our First Amendment rights in jeopardy, we wanted to share some of our favorite steamy passages so that you might understand how a chick could get a little—*ahem,* overheated. Is it the forceful yet simple directives? The luscious photos and centerfold illustrations? Or the mere suggestion of something mouthwatering scrumptious? Read on if you dare: Make sure your swooning couch is within reach—and see you at the cookbook burning!

"Golden Apple Dumplings . . . place the orbs an inch apart in an ungreased baking dish, and pour the Apple Bath around—not on—the dumplings until the bottom halves of the dumplings are relaxing in approximately 1½ inches of liquid." —*Romancing the Stove* by Margie Lapanja

"Sticky Buns . . . have the seductive flavor of caramel and pure, sweet butter and the crunch of nuts." —*The Breakfast Book* by Marion Cunningham, a.k.a. Fannie Farmer

"Arrange the bananas. . . . Drizzle the rum mixture over the top. Bake until the bananas are tender and candied. . . ." —*Celebrate!* by Sheila Lukins

Dish Fullfillment

PEOPLE GET A LITTLE WACKY AT FUNERALS, and I am no exception. During the service for my father, whom I adored, I thought suddenly—shamefully—of salad dressing. His dressing. I never asked him for his secret one last time, though he said he always intended to tell us. It would be a living memorial, we joked. The Eternal Cruet . . .

Since then, as I've struggled to replicate Dad's formula, I've come to wonder: How many families are haunted by a signature fleeting flavor? Remembered taste is a touchstone so potent, so deep, it has inspired great literature, has wafted through the recent vogue for "retrieved memories" and stoked the current passion for comfort food. The sweet longing for misspent youth has sent graying Mouseketeers off in search of Necco wafers, Maypo, and fluffernutters. I'm sure Proust would have understood—if not endorsed—the displays of gaudily wrapped Moon Pies found at Restoration Hardware. . . .

I've come up with—and discarded—a half-dozen Freudian reasons for my dad's kitchen diffidence. He was by nature a generous guy, and I'm now convinced he was simply enjoying the joke with his *spécialité de pink tract ranch*. John—Jinks to his pals—was a blue-collar worker with decidedly uptown appetites. He did all the grocery shopping, and though we kidded him for cruising the dented-can shelves, he fed us like suburban royalty. As a weekend cook, his repertoire was small but exquis-itely honed. When he grilled a steak, weimaraners whimpered a quarter mile away. His lobster stuffing, served in Pyrex custard cups alongside the broiled beasts, was a heady brown bog of crumbs, herbs, and glistening tomalley. No one recalls how he made any of it. But it is that dressing that haunts.

Family food historians date Dad's elixir back to the mid-sixties. The first batches were concocted in emptied Good Seasons cruets; he admitted to a brief seduction by Anna Maria Alberghetti, who purred about the virtues of that make-it-and-shake-it dressing on TV. The store-bought stuff sufficed until his backyard garden—doggedly carved from a development that had sold off the topsoil—finally produced veggies that deserved a custom blend.

To Dad's delight, women seemed most smitten with his brew. Sisters-in-law, nieces, and his two daughters fussed and wheedled. Jinks's Dressing was doled out to favored females in pickle jars, squat mustard glasses, margarine tubs. He was generous with the stuff itself, but not the recipe. He shooed the curious from the kitchen: "G'wan, I'll tell you before I die." Yes, he admitted, there was a Mystery Ingredient: "When I tell you what it is, you won't believe it." We would threaten to take a jarful to a lab for analysis but had to confess it was too precious to titrate. We tried an end run: My mother, placidly complicit and admittedly "not a salad person," would murmur innocently, "I just never notice what he's doing in there."

▶

"*A family is like fudge. A few nuts but mostly sweet.*"

Families carry on without their loved or long-for Missing Ingredient. I have Dad's cozy Pendleton shirts, his garden shears and tomato cages. His scrappy oregano plants are duking it out with my Siberian iris. My vinaigrettes are getting decent—almost signature, I think. But the enigma persists. After three years of experimentation, I'm no closer to the answer. And I am always looking. Recently, I thought I tasted a Jinks' note in my neighbors asparagus dip. Curry, she explained. Shall I try a pinch in the next laboratory batch? A friend makes me a lunch of sublime Italian canned tuna and cracked Sicilian olives and, knowing of my quest, she wonders aloud: Mashed green olive? I roll it around thoughtfully, on both tongue and memory. Hmmmm, he was an olive guy. . . .

Am I frustrated? Not really. I probably enjoy the chase. And I suppose I'm not quite ready to let him go. I do believe this: A remembered taste has the same satisfying genetics as a family smile. So we seek continuity in the wide grins of babies—or in the vapor of a stewpot. A family flavor's tantalizing mystery is also its immortality. And it is the most benign of hauntings.

—*Gerri Hirshey*

"He's the Cooker"

As my four-year-old daughter and I were picking herbs out in the yard the other day, she remarked, "We have to bring these in to Daddy, because he's the Cooker." I choked. But. But. I calmly asked my daughter, "But Mommy used to cook, right?" For four years nonstop, from organic mashed super I'm-such-an-excellent-mother baby food to excellent dinners at least three out of seven nights a week. "Yes, you were the cooker, but now Daddy is." She was right. My husband and I had switched parenting roles, and I was now working full-time out of the home, while he was the full-time parent. He was master of the kitchen, knew the ladies at the supermarket, made the lunches, and got ticked when I tried to tell him he left out the salt. To add insult to injury, his standard dinner repertoire—the meals we cook over and over—was better than mine. For a moment, my daughter's comment brought me down. I felt a loss. But then I heard singing in the background, and it was the tune "Hallelujah!" I let go of the apron strings to embrace my great good luck. A partner who cooks. Does dishes. Loves my kids. A cooker!

—Karen Bouris

NOTHING BLASTS YOUR FOOD WITH FLAVOR like a well-crafted marinade. Typically, marinades have three components: an acidic agent, such as vinegar or lemon juice, that tenderizes; an oily ingredient to moisturize; and a collection of herbs and spices to infuse flavor. Meat, fish, and chicken are usually the lucky recipients of these delicious soaks, but vegetables, and even fruit can also be enhanced by the right potion.

These marinades make enough to season about 2 pounds of meat or fish.

Rosemary and Balsamic Vinegar Marinade

2 tablespoons olive oil

½ cup balsamic vinegar

7 garlic cloves, crushed and chopped

½ teaspoon freshly ground pepper

4 tablespoons fresh rosemary

Salt and pepper to taste

Lemon~Thyme Marinade

3 tablespoons white wine

3 tablespoons lemon juice

2 tablespoons olive oil

2 tablespoons fresh thyme

2 shallots chopped

Salt and pepper to taste

Honey Mustard Marinade

½ cup olive oil

½ cup rice-wine vinegar

¼ cup honey

¼ cup grainy mustard

½ small onion, finely diced

2 tablespoons parsley leaves, minced

Salt and pepper to taste

Use the same technique for all marinades: Whisk all ingredients in a glass bowl. Then place the meat or fish in a heavy, resealable freezer bag, pour in the marinade, and seal it (try to get all the air out of the bag first). Gently knead and squish to distribute the marinade around the meat or fish, then place the whole thing in a shallow bowl. Turn it over periodically to ensure it marinates evenly. Before cooking, lightly salt and pepper the surface.

Timing: Fish can marinate for about an hour. Don't marinate shellfish for more than 20 minutes, as the acids can actually "cook" the tender flesh. Chicken, beef, lamb, or pork can be marinated for 4 to 24 hours in the refrigerator.

A little birdie told us . . . You can squeeze more juice from your lemons if they are at room temperature or warmed slightly in the microwave (10 to 15 seconds) prior to squeezing.

A ROASTING REVIEW

Roasting meat in the oven is such a retro move. Our families loved this method in the past, and there seems to be a real return to those slow-cooking ways. What could be better than tossing something in the oven and forgetting about it (if only for an hour)? And it fills the house with the warm, comforting smell of home cooking, too.

"No one ever conquered the world *on an empty stomach.*"

—*Susan Jane Gilman*

Chicken

One 3- to 4-pound whole chicken
1 small orange
7 cloves garlic, peeled
2 to 3 tablespoons olive oil
Salt and pepper

1. Preheat oven to 400°F.

2. Remove the chicken from the package and wash thoroughly. Remove all the gizzards (yes, you're right, this can be downright disgusting!). Set chicken on a roasting pan, breast side up. Pierce orange several times with a fork and place in chicken cavity with 3 cloves of peeled garlic. Drizzle olive oil over the chicken and scatter the remaining garlic cloves in the roasting pan under and around the bird. Lightly salt and pepper the chicken and place in the oven.

3. Julia Child suggests that you roast a chicken for 45 minutes plus 7 minutes per pound. To test for doneness, stick the thermometer deeply between the breast and thigh, but do not let it touch the bone. When the thermometer registers 165°F and the juices of the bird run clear, remove the chicken from the oven.

Serves 4

Pork

1 boneless 2- to 3-pound pork loin

2 tablespoons olive oil

2 ounces prosciutto, diced

3 tablespoons chopped fresh rosemary leaves

4 cloves garlic, peeled and crushed

2 cups light red wine (pinot noir or red zinfandel)

2 medium yellow onions, peeled and coarsely chopped

1. Preheat oven to 350°F.

2. Slice slits one inch long and ¼ inch deep over the surface of the pork loin.

3. Mix the olive oil, prosciutto, rosemary and garlic together in a small bowl.

4. Place the pork loin in a small roasting pan, and spread the olive oil mixture on it with a basting brush. Pour the wine over the pork and surround with the onions.

5. Pork loin should be roasted for about twenty minutes per pound. After an hour insert a meat thermometer to test for doneness. When the thermometer measures 155°F, the pork is done.

Serves 6 to 8

Roast Beef

One 4-pound boned beef rib roast

2 tablespoons olive oil

3 cloves garlic, peeled and crushed

2 tablespoons dried thyme

2 teaspoons salt

Freshly ground black pepper

1. Preheat oven to 350°F.

2. Mix together the olive oil, garlic, and thyme and brush on the beef. Salt and pepper thoroughly.

3. Place the roast on a rack in a roasting pan.

4. Figure about 15 minutes per pound. Check the roast with a meat thermometer after 50 minutes. For medium rare you should get a temperature reading of 135°F. Remove roast from oven and let it sit for 15 minutes before carving.

Serves 8

A little birdie told us . . . Give your chicken or roast a time-out after cooking. They will taste better if they are allowed to sit for 10 to 20 minutes before carving.

i SCREAM *for* Ice Cream

ICE CREAM CONSUMPTION WAS A PROBLEM IN OUR HOUSEHOLD. Whenever my mother bought a carton of ice cream, I would eat most of it right away. This wasn't fair to the other members of the family. My mother didn't want to increase the quantity of ice cream that I ate, but she wanted everyone to be able to have some. She decided that she would buy three half-gallon cartons at a time: one for me, one for my brother, and one for the parents. She would make this purchase once every three weeks, so I could make my half-gallon last for three weeks, or I could eat it all right away, but that was my ration.

I always got mint chip, and, never one to waste time, I ate my half-gallon in the first two days. My brother made his last, eating a scoop or two every three days. This drove me mad. One afternoon, long after my supply had dried up, I opened his carton. He hadn't eaten any yet. I figured that if I just ate around the edge, he wouldn't notice. I traced a light canal around the perimeter of the carton with my spoon. Rocky Road. After three or four laps around the carton I determined that my invasion was still undetectable. I sealed it back up and scurried upstairs.

The next afternoon, I returned to the scene of the crime. Again, I furrowed delicately around the edge of the carton. The ice cream still reached the top; it just had a neat moat around it that was certainly no cause for alarm. But that night my brother opened his ice cream.

"Mom, doesn't this ice cream look weird?" She agreed that there was something wrong with it. They stood over the carton, trying to figure out what might have happened.

"Maybe it melted in the store?" Eric suggested.

"Maybe," she said. "I'll take it back. I don't think you should eat it. Something is wrong with it."

Taking it back to the store? I panicked. If they took it back to the store, I would surely be discovered and possibly arrested. When I confessed to my crime, I was cut out of the next few rounds of ice-cream purchasing.

Some months later I came up with a new approach. Again, my mint chip was long gone, leaving me to gaze longingly at my brother's half-gallon of Oreo, which sat nearly full in the freezer. It was in a rectangular box, which opened at the small top instead of the wide side. My brother had taken a few nibbles, but the rest was intact. I spooned out a bit from the top, but knew I couldn't go much further without detection. Then I had an idea. I opened the bottom of the box and began a rear-entry sneak attack. It was subtle at first, but as the week passed, I grew bolder until I had eaten about a third of the carton, from the bottom up.

Then my poor brother, in the ordinary course of scooping his ice cream, broke through to the gaping vortex that should have been the remainder of his supply. This time there were no mysteries. My gall astounded my mother. My brother was genuinely curious.

"Did you truly believe that I wouldn't figure it out?"

I kind of did. Actually, I had hoped that the ice cream might slide down to fill the void as he served himself, the way it creeps further into an ice cream cone as you eat it. But that was the end of ice cream in our household. From then on, when we wanted ice cream, we went out to the parlor. One scoop each, no thievery, no plotting, no fun.

—*Hilary Liftin*

"Life is uncertain. *Eat dessert first.*"

—*Anonymous*

A little birdie told us . . . Here's the scoop—an ice cream scoop that has a defrosting liquid sealed inside the handle. The heat of your hand activates the defrosting agent, but we find running it under warm water for a few seconds really shifts it into high gear. No more bent spoons, and it really cuts down the serving time. Zeroll is the premier brand; you can get the scoop online at www.cooking.com and in specialty kitchen stores.

WHILE A PICNIC MAY NOT HOLD A CANDLE to Hemingway's moveable feast of Paris in the '20s, it sure can freshen up the day-to-day dining experience. And, with a little planning, the annoyances of dining alfresco—ants, sand in the food, bug bites—won't dampen the fun.

Keep it simple, silly. The most mundane meal seems like a banquet when you settle on your blanket under a bright blue sky. To make the picnic utterly carefree for everyone, have a completely disposable spread—plastic tablecloth, paper plates, plastic utensils, deli containers of food. Then, when you're sated, simply roll up the whole mess in the tablecloth and toss it out. We all love the romantic notion of a little wicker hamper, but our picnics are never that petite. A clothes basket is what we need to transport everything from car to blanket. A little gauche, perhaps, but it gets the job done. If you're really into presentation, just stash it back in the car until you're ready to pack up.

There's nothing worse than anticipating that crisp, chilled glass of chardonnay, then realizing you forgot the corkscrew. It's a real picnic buzz-kill

(and we're not talking about swatting flies). To keep such tragedies from happening, we like to consult our picnic check list before we pull out of the driveway:

Chicknic Checklist

A large blanket or cloth

Corkscrew

Eating utensils (bowls, plates, knives, spoons, forks, cups or plastic wineglasses)

Serving utensils (large spoons, forks, trays, or platters)

Sharp knife

Napkins

Wet wipes

Can and bottle opener

Small cutting board that can double as a serving tray

Condiments (mayonnaise, dressings, ketchup, relish, mustard, salt & pepper)

Plastic storage bags for leftovers

Water

Ice or frozen ice pack

Sunscreen

Bug repellent

Trash bag(s)

Cooler

"Life is a glorious banquet, a *limitless and delicious* buffet" —*Maya Angelou*

THE PRINCESS PICNIC. Think tiaras, boas, wands, or whatever makes you feel particularly queenly. Since monarchs should be regal at all times, messy food is a no-no. Keep the nibbles rich and bite-sized, with a basket of cucumber finger sandwiches (crusts removed), toast points with herbed cream cheese, bonbons, and a nice bubbly beverage for dessert. Accent the scene with pink napkins, plastic-stemmed drinking glasses, and flowers.

OOO-LA-LA PICNIC. Don sensuous slacks and a sleek blouse and tap into your inner femme fatale. The menu: baguettes, soft cheese (brie, St. Albray, goat), three types of mustards (Dijon, honey mustard, etc.), pâté, grapes, French *citron pressé* or a chilled bottle of French rosé. *Voilà!* Le French Pique-nique!

THE LADY JANE. Imagine the landscape of an estate named Pemberley. There you sit, with your parasol, nibbling daintily in the cool shade of an oak tree beside a gentle brook. Spread around you are scones, fruit preserves, sweet butter, fruit salad, and your very own Mr. Darcy.

BIG FAT GREEK PICNIC. Middle Eastern food is the perfect finger fare for outdoor feasting. Pack up some hummus, pita bread, stuffed grape leaves, falafel, cold sliced lamb, triangle spanikopitas, tabbouleh salad, olives, and baklava for dessert. To really pile it on, add an herbed rotisserie chicken to the menu and you'll be fat and happy.

THE SCARLETT O'HAMPER. Get down home—we mean *way* down home, as in south of the Mason-Dixon line. God help you, you'll never be hungry again with a picnic hamper busting with finger-lickin' fried chicken, corn bread, creamy coleslaw, and watermelon. Ambitious chicks can toss in a shaker and the fixin's for mint juleps, too.

As Martha dutifully tended to the condiments and pickled herring, Juanita helped herself to a sweet side of Antonio.

CHICK tips ... *for chicks and chow*

Pre- is the key. Prewashed, precut, prepeeled, prepackaged, pre*anything* makes your life easier and frees you up to read a book or schmooze with your friends. Employ these handy timesavers whenever you can. (We think the people who invented the salad in a bag deserve a Nobel Prize.)

Only one high-maintenance dish per meal. If you want to try a complicated recipe, pick one per menu and make sure the rest of what you cook is simple.

Encore! Encore! Sure things win rave reviews. Don't be afraid to make the same tried-and-true entrées, appetizers, and desserts again and again.

Fabulous markets are the secret weapon of every good cook. Find them, know them, and make time to use them.

Batch bake. Double a recipe and freeze half of it. That way you will always have something tasty on tap that you can defrost.

Seek out, test, and store quality frozen food entrées and sides. Everything from French fries to filo comes frozen, but it's important to separate the good from the bad by sampling.

Lie, cheat, and steal—do whatever it takes to simplify a recipe. Read them carefully beforehand and strategize to simplify.

Feed your mind with new recipes. For inspiration, buy or borrow a new cookbook, cruise recipes online, and ask good cooks to share a recipe.

Put your meal to work. Use the chicken you roasted earlier in the week to make sandwiches later, and use the carcass for soups.

part four

"I can enjoy flowers quite happily without translating them into Latin."

—*Cornelia Otis Skinner*

CHIcks
and Hoes

Scratching Around in the Garden . . .

gArden*ing* lessOns

I PLAN MY GARDEN AS I WISH I COULD PLAN MY LIFE, with islands of surprise, color, and scent. A seductive aspect of gardening is how many rituals it requires. Uncovering the garden in the spring, for example. Replacing a broken-down metal gate with a burly wooden one. Transplanting rhododendrons to a sunnier spot. Moving the holly bushes to the side of the garage, to hide them from the deer, who nonetheless find and eat them, prickles and all. (It may be like our affection for strong peppermints, hot mustards, spicy peppers—maybe the prickles add a certain *frisson* to the deer's leafy diet.) By definition, the garden's errands can never be finished, and its time-keeping reminds us of an order older and one more complete than our own. For the worldwide regiment of gardeners, reveille sounds in spring, and from then on it's full parade march, pomp and circumstance, and ritualized tending until winter. But even then there's much to admire and learn about in the garden—the hieroglyphics of animal tracks in the snow, for instance, or the graceful arc of rose canes—and there are many strategies to plan.

Surely there is a new way to outwit the marauding deer and Japanese beetles? Gardeners understand the word *pestilence* as only medieval burghers did. Gardeners can be cultured and refined. They can be earthy, big-hearted folk who love to get their hands dirty as they dig in the sunshine. They may obsess about tidy worlds of miniature, perfectly blooming trees. They may develop a passion for jungle gardens reminiscent of Amazonia. They may specialize in making deserts bloom. They may adore the weedy mayhem of huge banks of wildflowers. They may create interflowing worlds of color and greenery, in which small meadows give way to a trellised rose bed; a moon garden with blossoms all silver or white; a water garden complete with small bridge and waterfall; a butterfly garden also visited by hummingbirds; a "flamboyant" garden filled only with red, yellow, and orange flowers; a hedge of pampas grasses whose tall plumes sway like metronomes.

Gardeners have unique preferences, which tend to reflect dramas in their personal lives, but they all share a love of natural beauty and a passion to create order, however briefly, from chaos. The garden becomes a frame for their vision of life. Whether organic or high-tech, they share a dark secret, as well. Despite their sensitivity to beauty and respect for nature, they all resort to murder and mayhem with steel-willed cunning.

Nurturing, decisive, interfering, cajoling, gardeners are eternal optimists who trust the ways of nature and believe passionately in the idea of improvements. As the gnarled, twisted branches of apple trees have taught them, beauty can spring in the most unlikely places. Patience, hard work, and a clever plan usually lead to success: private worlds of color, scent, and astonishing beauty. Small wonder a gardener plans her garden as she wishes she could plan her life.

—*Diane Ackerman*

"My philosophy is: *Forget winning,* cultivate delight."

—*Diane Ackerman*

Put Your Wellies Up
Best Green Reads

Anatomy of a Rose: Exploring the Secret Life of Flowers, Sharman Apt Russell

Cultivating Delight: A Natural History of My Garden, Diane Ackerman

Deep in the Green: An Exploration of Country Pleasures, Anne Raver

Elizabeth and Her German Garden, Elizabeth Von Arnim

The Flower Gardener's Bible, Lewis and Nancy Hill

Green Thoughts, Eleanor Perényi

Mrs. Greenthumbs Plows Ahead: Five Steps to the Drop-Dead Gorgeous Garden of Your Dreams, Cassandra Danz

My Favorite Plant: Writers and Gardeners on the Plants They Love, edited by Jamaica Kincaid

Onward and Upward in the Garden, Katharine White

The Orchid Thief, Susan Orlean

The Secret Garden, Frances Hodgson Burnett

The Sweet Breathing of Plants, edited by Linda Hogan and Brenda Peterson

The Tulip: The Story of a Flower That Has Made Men Mad, Anna Pavord

Two Gardeners: Katharine S. White and Elizabeth Lawrence—A Friendship in Letters

Women of Flowers: A Tribute to Victorian Women Illustrators, Jack Kramer

COTTAGE GARDENS CHICK STYLE

In-your-face-feminine, unruly, chaotic, romantic, and exuberant, the cottage garden began as a defiant rebuttal to the structure and control of formal garden design. In short, cottage gardening is all about attitude. Not for the faint of heart, cottage gardens require dedication, attention, and lots of work to achieve a "naturally" carefree look. The cornerstone of the look is an eclectic, jumbled combination of different plants and flowers and a variety of textures, heights, and colors that somehow work together. It's like a good party—an odd yet harmonious mix of personalities that feels comfortable yet is never boring.

You need not live in a charming thatched hut in the English countryside to have a cottage garden. An abundant, intermingled collection of plants, herbs, and even vegetables can be applied to practically any space, from a grouping of pots on a deck or a window box to a small front yard or sweeping acreage. Cottage gardens are classically jam-packed, so plant densely and keep placement in mind: tall plants at the back, with shorter plants graduating to the front for a lush, spilling effect. Here are a few guests who tend to mingle well in the cottage garden. The more the merrier!

TALL, SPIKY PLANTS
Delphinium
Gayfeather
Hollyhocks
Foxglove
Daylilies
Honey bush

ROSES
English, tea, hybrid, climbing, heirloom, cabbage, China—there's room for any and all kinds of roses in a cottage garden.

AIRY, LACY PLANTS
Sugarplum geraniums
Love-in-a-mist
Santa Barbara daisies
Queen Anne's lace
Baby's breath

CLIMBING OR CREEPING PLANTS
Wisteria
Clematis
Jasmine
Climbing roses
Honeysuckle

Plant these near the backs of beds with trellises, fences, or ironwork to support them, or use them to frame gates or entrances.

"Let no one be discouraged by how much there is to learn.

ROUND, MOUNDING PLANTS
Phlox
Lavender
Scabiosa
Sweet William

SMALL, LOW-GROWING PLANTS
Primroses
Campanula
Sage
Thyme
Bergenia

With cottage gardens it is especially important to mix annuals with perennials to ensure you have color throughout the year and to limit bare spots in the garden. Naturalistic touches like stones, gravel paths, twig fencing or supports, and small water features like birdbaths all enhance the cottage look. Think shabby and rustic for your ornamental touches.

Looking back upon nearly thirty years of gardening . . . *each new step becomes a little surer, and each new grasp a little firmer,* till, little by little, comes the power of intelligent combination, the nearest thing we can know to the mighty force of creation."

—*Gertrude Jekyll*

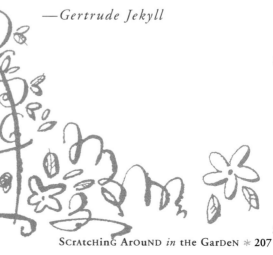

Hyde & Seek Around the Cottage

NEVER ONE TO DILLY AROUND HER DAHLIAS, Gertrude Jekyll has long been dubbed "the beautifier of England." Before the eminent Ms. Jekyll came along in the late nineteenth century, serious English gardeners favored formal gardens with flower beds arranged in precise geometric configurations with artificial color patterns and filled with many imported plants.

A diagnosis of failing vision made the young Gertrude turn from painting and embroidery to flower gardening and, like the Impressionist painter Monet, Gertrude looked at the garden in a whole new light. She helped England rediscover the rare beauty in the cottage garden—the nonprofessional gardens maintained by housewives throughout the English countryside. These gardens were filled with flowers indigenous to England that had gone out of fashion: violets, marigolds, dahlias, clematis, daffodils, cowslips, and rambling roses.

Gertrude's own expansive garden, Munstead, was meticulously designed, planted, and maintained. The work Gertrude did there, as well as her fourteen books, catapulted her into great demand as a garden designer and consultant. One of her specialties was the primrose, and she had an entire garden dedicated to this flower. To celebrate roses, her favorite, and to extend the life of their petals, Gertrude often made potpourri. Not one to do things on a small scale, Gertrude had 11,000 roses gathered one year to make her stash.

Gardening in army boots and an apron with big pockets for her tools, Gertrude left no stone unturned, no detail ignored, and upon her death at age eighty-nine, she had completed three hundred commissioned garden plans. Her belief in the power of gardening to transform was complete: "[T]here is no spot of ground, however arid, bare, or ugly, that cannot be tamed into such a state as may give the impression of beauty and delight."

"The love of gardening is a seed once sown that *never dies.*"

—Gertrude Jekyll

the $600 Tomato

AS UNSUCCESSFUL AS WE WERE WITH THE LIVESTOCK, my husband and I seemed even more ill-fated in the garden. From the first, all we reaped was a harvest of pain.

"No wonder they call it Rock Ridge," is a local saying. When we tilled the soil we found more stone than earth. It became a process of rock excavation—small pebbles, big stones, and then finally, boulders. I spent most of my time preparing the alleged garden, jumping on the end of a pickaxe, trying to tilt the tip of what might be a glacial formation that extends to the core of the earth.

When at last there was a thin strip of what we could call soil, we stuck in seeds, which were instantly lost and unidentifiable except to the birds that snacked on them. We graduated immediately to seedlings that cost as much as the finished vegetables. In this way, we worked our way up, with credit cards, to the six-hundred-dollar tomato.

There was a hallucinatory moment in the commercial greenhouse when we selected flats of tomato varieties, deluding ourselves that we would someday see the fruit they advertised—beefsteak heirloom, golden, cherry. We went for the traditionals and the exotics; we got nothing.

After months of caring for the plants, of supporting their spastic branches with all manner of vegetable crutches, we were rewarded with . . . vines. The vines were luxuriant, fragrant. I crawled on all fours between the braces supporting the weak plants to sniff their essence. Good that I inhaled the aroma that had tantalized me from my rooftop past, for it would take Herculean efforts to get a taste.

Oh, they grew, all right. Some tomatoes even became tinged with color. But before they could reach the texture appropriate for picking, the animals struck. The deer. The groundhogs. They all loved tomatoes. They didn't take the zucchini, but neither did we.

The garden became their outdoor Shop-Rite. They marched in by moonlight and munched. In the morning, I would run to the garden to find their chewed leftovers—the pale pulp and spit-out seeds. Their hoof prints were everywhere, marking the gazpacho orgy they had enjoyed, combining our fresh peppers with the tomatoes, leaving us only the woody discards, the dental impressions, their beebies.

In desperation, I searched out anti-animal remedies. Just let me have one tomato, I prayed, so I can taste it, hot from the sun, feel its juice spurt in my mouth. ▶

I got it, but only after heavy fencing, all-night stakeouts, and an expenditure in batteries to keep the boom box playing the rock music deer dislike. I briefly considered the nursery's other suggestion: gallon jugs of human urine hung from the trees, hair balls, sweaty gym shorts and socks. My garden was dispiriting enough without seeing these items. As it was, I decided to cut my losses and share with the herd. They could have 398 tomatoes if I could have one.

And so I tiptoed out before dawn one day to catch the critters in the act, their eyes red in the beam of my flashlight, enjoying their early brunch.

I made an animal sound that startled even myself—Eeeyah!—and I charged the garden. I got it: the single, semi-soft, unblemished tomato. I grabbed it and looked—no teeth marks. I bit into it—how sweet it was!—and the cost of the fence, the fertilizer, the stakes, the extended hose line system, all could be amortized. What mattered was this, the taste of my own fresh homegrown tomato.

I savored it along with a bit of extra good news. Deer do not like basil. So I had a garnish.

—*Laura Shaine Cunningham*

"A garden is evidence of faith.

It links us with all the misty figures of the past who also planted and were nourished by the fruits of their planting." —*Gladys Taber*

A little birdie told us . . . When your plants get leggy, get them some panty hose. Old hosiery is perfect for staking plants and training vines. It's soft, flexible, and, best of all, free.

Nothing should come between a gal and her buds. With a good inventory of basic garden tools, you'll have no excuse to chicken out. Be it stubborn roots, voracious weeds, frail plants, or roses gone wild, this treasure trove of tools will arm you for the worst and best of it.

GARDEN GLOVES. We love to garden, but we don't like withered hands. Get yourself a couple of pairs of gloves, a waterproof pair for muddy work and a knit or leather pair for general clipping, cutting, and digging. To preserve your manicure, don a pair of thin latex gloves underneath your gardening ones.

WATERING CAN. The quintessential tool for gardening chicks. If you want only one can, get the kind where the "rose," or shower-head, nozzle can be removed. That gives you the option of showering plants or removing the attachment and using the bare spout for a more concentrated dose of water.

WHEELBARROW. Not just for Farmer Jane anymore, use it to move dirt, heavy pots, rocks, bags of potting soil, and of course for kiddie rides.

HAND PRUNER. From cutting back plants to clipping flowers, you've got to have it.

LOPPER. Long-handled ones extend your reach, to keep trees and tall shrubs neatly pruned.

HOE. A must for weeding, prepping beds, cutting roots, and light grading.

GARDEN SPADE. The shape makes them perfect for edging lawns, flower beds, and pathways.

HAND TROWEL. A necessity for potting plants, digging small holes, and mixing soil.

STEEL-TINE LAWN RAKE. If you only want one rake, get this one. You can use it to rake grass clippings, leaves, and soil on either dirt or concrete surfaces.

LONG-HANDLED WEEDER. This back-saving tool will spare you a lot of stooping and pulling.

ROUND-POINT SHOVEL. Digging, scooping, spreading, planting, cutting sod, slicing roots—you can do it all with this multitasking tool.

KNEELING PAD. In a word: comfort.

HOSE WITH SPRAY ATTACHMENT. You'll save water, and the sprayer with different settings lets you direct just the right amount of force.

SOAKER HOSE(S). Great for when you need to water deeply and slowly. You can coil them up around a plant or weave them along a row of plants for easy, carefree watering.

OUTDOOR BROOM AND DUSTPAN. For cleaning up after yourself and sweeping the porch.

A little birdie told us . . . D-shaped handles (the kind that look like a triangle at the top) are easier for us chicks to use than traditional straight-handled tools. The D shape gives you more control, and you can use your leg and lower-body strength for power, instead of relying on upper-body force.

GOOF-PROOF PLANTING

An old gardening adage says, "Dig a $100 hole for a $1.00 plant." Translation: The success of a flower depends greatly on how well you plant it. *Where* you plant is also key—follow directions for light exposure when choosing the spot. Here's the dirt on some proper planting techniques.

SIZE MATTERS. The hole you dig should not be any deeper than the original container the plant came in, but it should be about twice as wide as the container. Set the plant, still in the container, inside your hole to make sure that you like its placement in the garden. You want the base of the plant, or the top of the root ball, to sit just below the level of the ground.

AMEND THE SOIL. Take the soil you've dug out and mix in some organic matter like compost, peat, manure, or humus until you have a mixture of half native soil and half organic matter. You can also add a time-release fertilizer to boost the soil.

SET IT FREE. If your plant is in a plastic container, tilt it at an angle, then gently roll and firmly push the sides to release it a bit. Now grasp the plant at its base and, while poking your fingers through the holes in the bottom of the container, gently pull the plant as you firmly push from the bottom through the holes. Be gentle: a shrub or tree can handle a firm tug, but pulling on small plants will leave you with a bouquet, not a viable plant. Plants in peat pots or other degradable containers can be planted directly in the ground, but first make a slit down each side and cut the lip off so that the top of the container is level with the soil.

GET TO THE ROOTS. With your plant out of its container, gently loosen the roots with your fingers. (You don't want to remove the dirt from the roots; just poke your fingers into it to free them up a bit.) Place the plant in the hole, turn it and level it the way you want, and begin filling the hole with the amended soil. Add the soil evenly around the plant, a bit at a time, and every time you add soil, push it firmly down to remove air pockets. (But don't pack it so firmly that it's unyielding to the roots as they grow.) Use extra soil to make a little berm around the plant, and fill the basin with water.

MULCH. Finish by adding organic matter such as bark or wood chips around the plant to retain moisture and stave off weeds. Don't mulch right up to the trunk of a shrub or tree, because it can keep the trunk too wet, thus putting the plant at risk of rot and mildew.

HYDRATE. To see if your plant needs watering, do the finger test: Dig your finger down about five inches into the soil. If the soil is dry, you need to water. If the leaves are wilted and perk up when you water the plant, you know you need to water more frequently. Yellowed or light green leaves mean you need to cut back on watering.

A little birdie told us . . . Avoid watering your plants during the heat of the day. Water magnifies heat and light, so your plants are more apt to get heat stroke. Early morning or late afternoon is a better time.

garDens *of the* IMaginAtion

THERE IS A CHAMBER IN THE LIFE OF A GARDENER that is not a place in the garden itself at all; it is a part of the digging of holes, the pressing in of roots securely so as to prevent pockets of oxygen from forming in the newly occupied hole in which the plant has been placed, the watering in, the anxious awaiting of the actual blooming. It is a place in the mind of the gardener where there is no garden at all, at a time when the garden exists in the imagination as the possibility of the garden, not too far in the future, in a few months according to the actual calendar. January, February, and March, which are the months in which the catalogues make their welcome appearance, seem right then to be the most important season in the life of the garden. Since one can't be in the actual garden itself—it is lying buried under mounds of snow, or simply imprisoned in the unyielding earth—the gardener makes an imaginary garden; the landscape in such a garden is ideal, level ground mostly, with perfect contours in the right places; the soil is free of rocks, it is double-dug, the pH is perfect; plants that require a lime-free soil grow side by side, thriving with a happiness that has previously been unknown to the gardener. For some gardeners, and I am among them, the garden will never be any better than it is at this time of the year, in the deep winter, when the catalogue arrives. . . .

A real gardener, to my mind, is someone who loves growing things, but this is combined with a meandering spirit, deliberate and yet haphazard, carefree and yet not, around and in a space large or small, with the world in mind, and also nothing at all in mind. A real gardener knows nothing at all of garden design; the design of the garden comes about through love. Things have been chosen, not with any regard for theory, but from love of a particular plant, an obsession with a particular plant, a particular feeling for a particular plant. This feeling, this choosing, is based on love.

—*Jamaica Kincaid*

"She was standing inside the secret garden. It was *the sweetest, most mysterious-looking place* anyone could imagine . . . and she felt she had found a world all her own."

—*Frances Hodgson Burnett,*
The Secret Garden

Flower feLon

I T'S HARD FOR ME TO ADMIT IT, but my penchant for posies borders on the criminal. With age I've gotten better: Your flowers are safe around me as long as they are not overhanging a sidewalk, behind bushes that conceal them from your front door, or dangling over the fence on my side. But I once formed a gorgeous bouquet of long-stemmed red roses from a real estate office's abundant landscaping. (It was late at night and I just happened to have a pair of garden shears in my glove compartment. . . .) I convinced a friend to hire the agency to sell her house some years later, so I consider us even.

How do other people resist the whisper of a lilac, heavy as grapes, overly perfumed, swaying in the breeze, whispering, "Pick me"? I just can't walk away; I weakly surrender and give myself up to the consequences. This bad-girl behavior—and no amount of rationalizing can make it anything but bad—began at an early age. My mother says I picked flowers as soon as my fingers formed the pincher grasp. Dandelions, daisies, dogwoods—I was indiscriminate—if it bloomed, I picked it and carried it triumphantly to her to be put in a vase. I blame her for encouraging me: She could have thrown them away or made me "put them back," but no, she displayed my ill-gotten gains and on top of that had the poor judgment to visibly enjoy them.

I felt some relief the day I realized that half the plants in my mother's yard began with a story that starts something like this, "I dug that up on the side of the road on the way to Aunt Jo's house five years ago. . . ." or "Remember that neighbor we had on St. Joseph Street? Well, that's where those buttercups came from." My aunt Nola is in on the ring as well—she has a gorgeous seven-bark that came from the woods outside of town and a garden filled with plants of questionable origins. So I'm really not bad, I'm just fulfilling a tradition, a legacy, a destiny. I come from a long line of women who heed the call of the wild—and the free. Let's face it, there's no reason we couldn't admire a flower and head to the garden center and purchase it like respectable people. But that does not make for a very exciting story.

A few years ago I had an experience that greatly reduced my blossom burglaring. My husband and I were living near the Presidio Naval Base in San Francisco. At the time the former officers' housing was vacant and the charming brick homes with million-dollar views lay abandoned—along with their gardens. Even an amateur like me could appreciate how beautiful these gardens must have been in their prime. Through the weeds and rambling vines I could picture a woman nursing the beds, pruning and gently cluck-clucking. We're talking gorgeous heritage roses, heavenly perfumed tea roses, jungle-like thickets of calla lilies and birds of paradise, and every flavor of daffodil and hyacinth. All deserted and all alone! You see where this is going. I would walk through the yards, my bag stuffed with garden

"Best in Show" or "Bad Seed?" After hours of deliberation, the garden club judges were still hopelessly deadlocked on Daisy's striking arrangement.

tools, and get lost in the reverie of gardening. Following the adage that the more you clip roses, the more flowers they produce, I did my duty to keep the rosebushes busy. I didn't just pick flowers; I pruned, divided, and shaped. This garden was no longer homeless—it was mine.

In the beginning I was furtive, popping up from my exploits with every car or jogger that passed by, to give the illusion I was just out for a stroll. Like most criminals, however, in time I became bolder, and eventually I became downright comfortable.

One day I was busy pruning back a lovely pale pink rose, when I sensed someone watching me, but I was so intent on the task at hand, I didn't turn around until I heard the deep, bass tone clearing of a throat. I knew instinctively that the disapproving sound came from under the thick mustache of a park policeman. I sheepishly turned around and saw him, his arm held out the car window, his authoritative sunglasses mirroring my open mouth. I stammered a few words as my mind frantically began going through the consequences—jail, huge fines, community service, how bad I would look in a bright orange vest, divorce. . . . Seconds felt like minutes and in that span of time his stern face transformed into a small grin. He grumbled in a deep voice, "I didn't see a thing." And with that, he slowly rolled off. I thanked my gardening angels and walked home—with my last batch of Presidio roses.

Last week I took my sixteen-month-old daughter, Grace, for a visit with my mom. I caught sight of them about halfway up the block, returning from a walk. I could see a yellow spot bobbing in front of Grace and as they got closer I realized it was a brilliant yellow dahlia clutched in her chubby little hand. Grandma said, "Mommy, this is for you," as Grace thrust the flower at me with a huge, toothy grin. I put it in water and chuckled to myself. So it begins.

—*Ame Mahler Beanland*

THE BUD SYSTEM Flower Arranging Simplified

Nothing boosts your mood like fresh flowers. So unleash your inner florist and try your hand at an arrangement. Here are a few simple do's for putting buds together.

Begin with a clean, watertight container (see opposite page) filled with cool water. A few drops of bleach or a packet of floral food will combat bacteria and extend the life of your bouquet.

Using a sharp knife, cut the flower stems at a deep angle, preferably with the stems submerged underwater as you cut. The more of the inner stem you expose, the more water the flower takes in. Remove all the leaves that will be below the water level. (They rot and will speed the demise of your bouquet.) Arrange the first few flowers by choosing taller ones and crisscrossing their stems in the vase. This "grid" creates support that will help you build the arrangement and anchor the flowers in place.

Keep adding flowers, taller ones in the center, shorter ones at the rim, until you get the effect you want. For maximum longevity, change the water every day and rinse the stems under water. Every two days, retrim the stems about half an inch. Clean up an aging arrangement by pinching off dead leaves and petals and removing spent flowers.

MORE TIPS:

• For an easy and elegant "sure thing," choose just one type of flower and arrange an abundant mass.

• Choose flowers at various stages of opening—a combination of tight buds, half-open, and fully open flowers.

• For a mixed bouquet, try to vary the types of flowers yet harmonize the colors.

• You can "fluff" rose heads that aren't fully open by easing them open a bit with your fingers. They'll fill the arrangement better and look more relaxed.

• A few bud vases featuring one flower each is a simple way to forgo any arranging at all.

• A shot of vodka added to the vase keeps tulips perky . . . works for some chicks, too!

• For plants with woody stems like hydrangeas or flowering branches, use garden pruners to split the stem at its base (make a 1- to 2-inch cut) to maximize water intake.

Vase, Schmase *Creative Flower Holders*

If it holds water, we put flowers in it. Everything from the typical teacup to our kids' galoshes—nothing is off-limits when it's time to arrange flowers. We use watering cans, pitchers, martini glasses, wineglasses, egg cups, soup cans, buckets, etc. If it doesn't hold water, we tuck a jar, a glass, or a plastic tub inside. That opens up a whole new realm of possibilities! We keep a stash of assorted jars, plastic containers, and bottles; floral moss, which hides a multitude of sins; floral tape for securing precarious containers; floral wire; and Oasis (floral foam). Some of our more unorthodox "vases" have been:

A GIFT BOX IN BLOOM. Take a box with a lid and wrap both separately. Add a bow to the lid. Fill four jars (or whatever the box will accommodate) with water and arrange your flowers. Choose some fill flowers that will cascade over the jars, which helps to disguise them. Tuck tissue or moss all around to cover the jars. Prop the lid against the box or partially wire it on for effect.

THE FLOWER CAKE. Take a plastic food container and cut a piece of soaked floral Oasis to fit flush inside, about ½ inch lower than the rim. Dry the outside of the container and wrap with a band of pretty paper, fabric, or ribbons. Stick flowers into the Oasis to cover, and keep them low and uniform to emulate a "cake." Add a few birthday candles, set it on a cake plate, and you're in business.

A HIGH-HEEL SHOE. Baby food jars tuck in perfectly to hold the flowers. Then cover the surrounding area with floral moss or tissue paper, depending on the fashion statement you want to make. For a truly unique statement, find old shoes at thrift stores, spray-paint them, and embellish.

THE VINTAGE POSY PURSE. Take an old purse and insert a glass or jar inside to hold your water and flowers. Surround with fabric or tissue to hide the container, tuck in a pretty hankie, display a small flower in a lipstick cap.

THE COWGIRL CORSAGE. We let this one go to our heads. We took a straw cowboy hat, tucked a butter tub inside filled with soaked Oasis, and arranged daisies and wildflowers in it.

Bloom wHere You're plAnted *an urban gardener's tale*

NTIL LAST SUMMER, my experience as an urban gardener was limited to growing geraniums in a window box. My various Manhattan apartments have all been small spaces with no terraces. I longed for a plot of earth.

When the Beautification Committee of my West Village complex called to tell me there was a planter box available in front of the building, I raced downstairs to check it out. My sidewalk garden was a 4' by 4' planter box with a callery pear tree in the middle, a scraggly shrub in one corner. I would make this barren space beautiful.

After several trips to the Union Square Greenmarket, I planted cosmos, daisies, zinnias, impatiens, lobelia, Dusty Miller. I was surprised how many plants it took to fill such a small plot. So many choices. I was overwhelmed and realized making a garden is like writing. You start with a few ideas but don't know how it will turn out. Add, delete, trim, clip, rearrange. Will the piece ever be finished? What effect am I going for?

Just for fun (and as a forecast?), I found the table favor from my niece's wedding—a tiny pastel green planter pot with a packet of wildflower seeds, tied with a ribbon, embossed, "Patty & Brent sowing the seeds of love." I tossed the seeds into the box—a long shot; I expected the birds to get them.

Would the spindly-stemmed cosmos survive the wicked winds off the Hudson River a half block away? Right after I installed them, it stormed. I worried, thinking, I'm glad I did not have children. I'd be fretful all the time; these are only plants, for God's sake. The rain ended and the hardy guys survived 25 mph gusts. I talked to them, my brave little soldiers. I was already too involved. Pretty soon, I'd be ordering seed catalogues.

While I was setting up, a woman walking her terrier said, "Thanks for doing this. Makes the block look great."

"It reminds me of my garden in my home country," noted another woman with an accent, who was parking her car.

"It's so nice. God bless." "Thanks, glad you like it," I smiled back, stunned. I was being blessed on the sidewalks of New York, and was awed that my tiny plot stirred memories.

As a community activist fighting against a highrise bordering our historic district, it was relaxing to make small talk with neighbors instead of ranting over development and pulling out petitions. Playing in the soil was mellow, a break from dispiriting discussions about new zoning laws.

Other gardeners from my building emerged after me, with useful information: the sprinkler system is buried in one corner of my box. For that shallow spot, they suggested a decorative stone or plants with small roots. They wished me luck and raved about my pink and lavender cosmos. I felt a bit competitive.

"The fragrance always remains

By June, my box was filled and looking good. Then I got anxious about events that bring crowds to my block, but my garden survived Gay Pride in June and Op-Sail on the Fourth of July. The box stayed remarkably clean all summer; I fished out a few soda cans and a couple of used condoms. (I wore gloves.)

One July morning, while I was removing scruffy-looking stuff that had dried up as the summer progressed, I heard a voice behind me, "Now say good morning to the lady with the pretty flowers." I turned to see a family: mother, father, little boy in a stroller.

"Good morning," a tiny voice piped up.

"Good morning," I said. "Do you know your colors?"

The mother created a lesson from my cue. "What color is this?" She pointed to a zinnia, "That's pink. Can you say pink?"

I waved bye-bye as they walked down the street.

By August, the daisies were growing like mad but not blooming; they needed more sun. After coming back from vacation, my cosmos were dead. The zinnias and impatiens looked great. Amazingly, the wildflower "seeds of love," my niece's wedding favor, were blooming profusely. A good omen.

During late summer, the Village was filled with visitors from the heartland who beamed at me when I was gardening. I imagined them thinking that city folks must be all right if we're doing what they do back home. As a sidewalk gardener, I had become an unofficial ambassador to New York.

Like dogs or babies, my flowers made people smile and stop and talk; they gave permission to drop our guards and be friendly; for a few minutes, we were not in the big city. I met tourists, neighbors, and many people from my large building who thanked me for my work.

During languid summer evenings, tending the garden gave me a reason to leave my apartment, enjoy the evening air, and watch the sun set into the Hudson River. Gardening became a cure for urban claustrophobia.

This spring, I'm trying out new flowers, having learned from my mistakes—forget anything that needs full sun. I'm hoping for bright colorful surprises and can't wait to see who and what pops up.

—*Kate Walter*

in the hand that *gives the rose.* " —*Heda Bejar*

Contain Yourself

With carefully chosen plants, creative containers, and artistic placement, you can give your yard, patio, deck, or garden a fresh punch of color, interest, and personality. Go Tuscan Villa with a grouping of terra-cotta pots planted with Mediterranean favorites like rosemary, lavender, and ornamental grasses. Get downright down-home by planting a wheelbarrow with petunias and ivy. Put your nose up in the air and outfit some urns with formal topiaries and ferns. Or brighten up a dark spot in your garden with some pots of shade-loving white impatiens. Here are some tips for container gardening:

PERENNIALS AND ANNUALS ALIKE DO WELL IN CONTAINERS. When choosing plants, try to combine different textures, contrasting colors, and a mix of heights—a tall plant, a mid-height plant, and a trailing variety or vine.

IF YOUR CONTAINER DOESN'T HAVE DRAINAGE HOLES, MAKE THEM, using an ice pick or pickax. Or insert another container inside it that does have drainage holes. That way you can remove the plant to water it, let it drain, and then pop it back into the decorative container.

USE A RICH, WELL-DRAINING SOIL MIX: equal parts potting soil, peat moss, and perlite or vermiculite. Stick your finger into the soil and, if it feels dry about one inch down, water it. Fertilize regularly according to directions for potted plants.

WHEN PLANTING, START IN THE MIDDLE (if you want a mounded look) or the back (for a stair-step effect) with taller plants. Choose shorter plants for the edges and end with trailing varieties. Don't be afraid to pack in plants for a full, lush effect that doesn't look "just planted."

POTS IN THE LANDSCAPE OR PATIO CREATE VISUAL INTEREST. You can spread them out to draw your eye across a space, or group them for more impact and focus. When grouping, remember that odd numbers are more interesting, and vary the height. If you want a more formal, balanced look, go for pairs placed symmetrically to frame an entryway, gate, or sitting area. Create connections between the indoors and outdoors by placing container gardens inside your home or on your patio where they can be seen from inside.

For more information on container gardening, check out Rebecca Cole's book *Potted Gardens: A Fresh Approach to Container Gardening.* We especially love some of her ideas for containers— toy dump trucks, dresser drawers, tea kettles, and vintage metal containers, to name a few.

A little birdie told us . . . To fill in areas or cover the dirt in a potted plant, use dried green moss or some small stones. Add a small piece of statuary or an architectural fragment for interest.

Dirty Diva

AS THE FOUNDER AND CHIEF FUND-RAISER for the New York Restoration Project, guardian of the city's parks and neglected public spaces Bette Midler is not afraid to get down and dirty. "When I moved to New York, I was very disappointed in how parts of the city looked. I was so upset, I didn't sleep for weeks. I love New Yorkers, and I'm like them—I'm noisy, I have my opinions—but I'm not used to the kind of carelessness and waste that I was seeing. People were throwing their garbage out the window, leaving their lunches on the ground. Finally, I realized I needed to actually do something—even if I had to pick up the stuff with my own two hands."

The Divine Miss M started in her own backyard by cleaning up the street area around her Tribeca loft and planting crab apple trees. That barely scratched the surface, so she approached the New York City Parks Commissioner at the time, Henry Stern, and asked what she could do. As she tells the story, "He told me that if I wanted to help, that was fine, but not downtown. There were already enough rich, stupid, white women like me who could save their own parks. He told me to go do the work uptown, where rich people don't live."

So Bette took the fight uptown. Never one to follow the beaten path, she mapped a new route to restoration by establishing her own foundation. Whether it was in an effort to circumvent bureau- cracy, or just to keep her own hands on the plow, Bette's decision was expedient. "I felt that if I didn't complain to the city or ask for its money, the work would get done more smoothly." And it is getting done. From parks, open spaces, and trails, to coves, cottages, and community gardens—Bette and her legions of volunteers are beautifying the Big Apple.

Behind this successful chick is one proud rooster, her husband, Martin von Hasselberg. Martin once gave Bette a grappling hook on the end of a long aluminum pole for her birthday—not exactly the kind of gift you'd expect a hubby to bestow on a celebrity wife, but perfect for her. He had the tool custom-designed for removing plastic bags and other trash caught in the high branches of her beloved trees. Now, that's romantic!

> "I'd rather have roses on my table *than diamonds* on my neck."—*Emma Goldman*

A little birdie told us . . . It's not all dirt and mudslinging at the NYRP. Green goes glam with celebrity picnics, famous fetes, and alfresco festivals to celebrate and raise money for the foundation. For more information on Bette's garden party, log on to www.nyrp.org.

Pick a Palette

When it comes to color in the garden, a chick has unlimited choices. But just because you can do it doesn't always mean you should. Garden designers swear that a carefully chosen, somewhat limited palette translates into a cohesive, artful space as opposed to a chaotic mishmash. The trick is to pop in some unexpected things here and there so that it doesn't look overthought or contrived. Choosing color in your garden is no different than choosing color in your wardrobe or other surroundings—pick what makes *you* feel good. In homage to some of our favorite chicks, we've come up with some garden palettes based on personalities. Dig deep, find yourself, and get planting.

Color tips

Dark colors make distant areas look farther away. By keeping vibrant colors near your home and darker colors at outlying landscape points, you can make your garden look larger and more sweeping.

Use white flowers with restraint to create dramatic contrasts in the garden. A little sprinkle works better than a mound. It's kind of like salt in cooking —too much ruins the broth, but none at all makes it bland.

To brighten shady areas, use paler shades of flowers and foliage.

For a unified, harmonious feeling, and to keep the eye moving, repeat colors and textures throughout your garden. Use the colors, shapes, and textures of foliage to create continuity.

Drama Queen

Bold, luxurious, and never garden-variety, the chick who inhabits this deep, lush, colorful, and exotically textured paradise loves to loll about on her chaise lounge. We dare you to catch *her* without her dark glasses!

Palette
Red, burgundy, deep purple, dark green, hot pink

Plants to ponder
Fuchsia
Deep red roses
Chocolate cosmos
Bleeding heart
Giant-leaf coleus
Bearded purple iris
Bird of paradise
Cannas (red, burgundy)
Calla lily (purple)
Passionflower
Helleborus
Lisianthus (purple)
Amaranthus caudatus (Love Lies Bleeding)
New Zealand flax
Hollyhocks (Crème de Cassis variety)
Salvia

Accessories
Mirrors
Lanterns
Candles
Canopies or netting
Chaise lounge

Lady of the Manor

Cool, calm, and collected but never stuffy, this is the garden for the gal who digs the good life. This well-heeled garden is manicured, elegant, and eschews rough edges on the hedges. She may not have a penthouse perch but this royal retreat more than makes up for it.

Palette
Green, pale pink, white

Plants to ponder
Ivy, both standard green and varie-
    gated varieties
Topiaries
Boxwood hedges
Ferns
Spruce trees
Rubrum lilies
Casa Blanca lilies
Peonies (pale pink)
Lily of the Valley
Hydrangeas (white, pale pink)
Azaleas (white)
Rhododendrons
Narcissus
Lemon trees
Orange trees

Accessories
Urns
Statuary
Sundial
Fountain
Stone walls

Buddha in Bloom

For the chick who likes to meditate, procrastinate, sleep in late, time seems to stand still in her garden sanctuary. This is an outdoor haven that's spare, simple, and peaceful. Take a deep breath and don't forget to exhale.

Palette
Green, plum, gray, white

Plants to ponder
Juniper
Bamboo
Cypress
Moss
Japanese maple
Waterlilies
Hostas
Sedum
Burrow's tail
Licorice plant
Star jasmine
Aloe vera
Agave
Sage
Fountain grass
Black mondo grass

Accessories
Reflecting pool
Small bubbling fountain
Boulders
Bamboo fencing
Sand garden
Spiritually inspired statuary
Stone lantern or bench

Wildflower

If the world is your playground, why shouldn't your garden be your very own amusement park? Filled with color, intensity, and whimsical detail, this is an enchanted landscape where fairies (and irreverent chicks) frolic with abandon. Social butterflies welcome!

Palette
Orange, yellow, chartreuse, hot pink

Plants to ponder
Nasturtium
Black-eyed Susan
Dahlias (orange, hot pink)
Geraniums (hot pink)
Zinnias (chartreuse, hot pink, orange)
Catnip
Sunflowers
Euphorbia
Bells-of-Ireland
Sweet potato vine
Nicotiana (lime green)
Calla lily (Green Goddess variety)
Poppies
Coneflower

Accessories
Gazing ball
Mobile
Wind chimes
Birdhouse
Kitschy statuary
Hammock
Brightly colored umbrella

Up Close and Personal

To say that GEORGIA O'KEEFFE HAD AN EYE FOR DETAIL is a gross understatement. "You know how you walk along a country road and notice a little tuft of grass, and the next time you pass that way you stop to see how it is getting along and how much it has grown?" she once asked. Given that passion for nature, it's not surprising that it fell to Georgia to show the world what a flower is really all about.

Flora and fauna have inspired artists for centuries, but until Georgia O'Keeffe came along, no one really looked closely enough. She credits two things for inspiring her unique view of flowers and her ensuing paintings: a small still life by Fantin-Latour and the hectic pace of life in New York in the Roaring '20s. "Everything was going so fast. Nobody had time to reflect. . . . There was a cup and saucer, a spoon and a flower. Well, the flower was perfectly beautiful. It was exquisite, but it was so small you really could not appreciate it for itself. So then and there I decided to paint that flower in all its beauty. If I could paint that flower in a huge scale, then you could not ignore its beauty," she wrote.

In this case, bigger was better; petite wallflowers suddenly took center stage, and the art world took notice. Georgia honored the flowers that so inspired her and had dominated her childhood in the prairies of the Midwest. She took the sweet, the overlooked, the retiring bloom, and blew it up to epic proportions. She showed the world what flowers must look like to each other!

It just so happened that Georgia's genius collided with a time in history when the subject of flowers was controversial. Previously, flowers had connoted femininity, virtue, and innocence, and were appreciated as purely decorative objects. But in the Freud-obsessed world of 1920s New York, flowers had become the

"When you take a flower in your hand and really look at it, it's your world for a moment. *I wanted to give that world* to someone else."

—*Georgia O'Keeffe*

new sex symbols. The artist was offended and surprised by critics who characterized her work as sexually charged, provocative, and even pornographic. She vehemently denied the accusations and resented the focus on a singular aspect of her art. Years later when an interviewer asked her about the "vulval character" of her flowers, the feisty artist snapped back that she would not speak of "such rubbish."

Next time you are in the garden, gaze deeply into the face of a pansy. Prim and proper, or bad seed? You decide. And offer up a little thank-you to Georgia O'Keeffe, who made you look.

State of Grace

"My attention to a flower can help me rediscover my true self, the self I lose to forces I'm responsible for but often do not completely understand. That centered staring helps erase the robot self of Lists, Calls, Chores, Duties, Dampened Desires.

"The frailest of nature's objects, these most female emblems, have staying power. Staying power has healing power, too. You can stand in front of flowers and look them in their many eyes and see *just them,* and for a moment you are doing only one thing fully, being in the presence of their tart soil and tender personalities, and connecting with the tart and tender within yourself."

—Molly Peacock

Garden Latin, Chick Style

DIVADIGGER MAXIMUS: A chick who loves to garden

POOPOO PERPETUA: A chick who loves to garden organically

FAUNA FEMFESTUM MAGNUS: Garden Party Princess

FECUNDUS CUCUMBUS AMONGUS: The chick who showers her friends with endless garden bounty, most of which is disturbingly phallic shaped

OPTIMUS BLOSSOMUS GRANDSTANDIUM: The chick who brags endlessly about the size of her peonies

BONITAS ROSARIUS: The chick whose roses never suffer black spot, aphids, or mildew

MASCULUS CLUELESS: He who tramples the clematis and is oblivious to the garden path

HERBA ODIUM: A spiteful, hateful plant that refuses to grow under the most loving conditions

ARACHNE ATTACKME: Drama queen discovers spider in the garden

FATALIS UNSPADIBUS: The garden dead zone, a place of absolute blight

FLORIDIS VIRIDIS CERES: Goddess with a green thumb

Enchanted Elizabeth How Royalty Pulls Weeds...

COUNTESS ELIZABETH VON ARNIM DESPERATELY LOVED TO GARDEN, and was determined not to let anything come between her and "the happy flowers I so much love."

As a young bride and an inexperienced gardener, Elizabeth moved to a family estate with a long-neglected garden, and was instantly smitten with it. Her husband, the count, was decidedly uninterested in their garden, and not eager to provide extra funds for its support. The indomitable Elizabeth rose above her budget crisis and managed to save for new flowers by "not indulging all too riotously in new clothes" and hoarding her "pin-money" for supplies, particularly good manure.

More problematic than the countess's meager funds, however, was overcoming the rigid rules of nineteenth-century society that forbade women, particularly "respectable" women, from doing anything with flowers but pointing and cooing at them. "If I could only dig and plant myself! How much easier . . . to make your own holes exactly where you want them and put in your plants exactly as you choose," complained Elizabeth. Instead, she had to rely upon hired help to do her dirty work. She tirelessly trained and coached her gardeners: Once, the countess even decided to read passages from gardening books to her gardener as he planted. The disgusted gardener took to going about with a spade in one hand and a revolver in the other. After that, Elizabeth addressed him in only the sweetest of tones and stopped reading to him, but eventually he was sent away, after he turned on her when she "mildly asked him to tie up a fallen creeper."

Never one to sit on her hands, Elizabeth declared, "I never could see that delicacy of constitution is pretty, either in plants or women." She did occasionally slink out and surreptitiously tend to her plants while the servants were at dinner hour. She described how she had to then "run back very hot and guilty into the house, and get into a chair and behind a book and look languid just in time to save my reputation."

> "I wish with all my heart I were a man, for of course the first thing I should do would be to *buy a spade and go and garden*."
>
> —*Countess Elizabeth Von Arnim, 1898*

Garden Garb *What Hoers Wear*

Whether we're potting a houseplant, digging a trench, or tying up a creeper, a chick needs the right garb to get the job done. Here are some fashionable flower girls:

THE SWEET PEA. Jane Austen, eat your heart out; this little blossom flaunts ruffles, a floppy sun hat, and pastel-colored gardening gloves. A parasol completes the look.

THE BIRD OF PARADISE, a.k.a. Buffy the Weed-Slayer. Not since Eve lived in paradise have the *fashionistas* been so abuzz. You can leave your hat on, but take off everything else. (Don't forget the sunscreen.)

THE HYBRID. Chanel meets L. L. Bean in this coveted look inspired by gardener/poet Vita Sackville-West, who dared to don pearls and jodhpurs while spiking her lawn.

THE HOT POTATO. This lovely number would make Daisy Mae blush. With cut-off blue jeans, pink bandanna, and a halter top, this is a great outfit for striking the posterior pose.

THE PRIMROSE. For the woman who refuses to dress down to garden—tweed suit, pressed white blouse, and Ferragamo shoes—a perennially professional look worn exclusively by garden writer Katharine White until now.

Mary Louise always managed to get someone else to do her dirty work.

"Don't wear perfume in the garden—*unless you want to be pollinated* by bees."

—*Anne Raver*

THERE'S NOTHING LIKE A LITTLE WARM WEATHER to make a chick want to fluff her feathers and strut around the garden with some of her favorite pals. Here are some inspirational garden party suggestions that will turn even the biggest wallflower into a preening GPP! Don't be afraid to mix and match these festive ideas and bring your own favorite recipes to the table.

The Hoedown

GIRLFRIEND GARDEN PARTY

The ultimate occasion to get chicks scratching around in the dirt! Have each guest bring her favorite flower or plant: after the festivities you have a garden that honors all your best gal pals. What to wear? Overalls, tool belts, floppy hats. What to sip? Dirty Martinis (see page 231). What to dig into? Fried Green Tomato and Basil Sandwiches. What to hold back? Nothing.

Chicks dig it.

fried Green Tomato and Basil Sandwiches

2 cups all-purpose flour

2 teaspoons salt

¼ teaspoon freshly ground black pepper

8 medium unripe tomatoes, sliced

1⅓ cups buttermilk

2–3 tablespoons vegetable oil

16 slices sourdough bread, toasted

4 tablespoons mayonnaise

2 teaspoons balsamic vinegar

About 40 basil leaves, plus extra for garnish

1. Combine flour, salt, and pepper in a shallow bowl.

2. Pour buttermilk into another shallow bowl.

3. In a large skillet, heat oil on high until a drop of water sizzles when it hits the pan.

4. Dunk the tomato slices in the buttermilk, then coat each side in flour. Place the slices in oil, lower heat to medium, and fry each side until golden brown. With a slotted spatula, remove and drain on paper towels.

5. In a small bowl, mix the mayonnaise and balsamic vinegar together and spread on the 8 slices of toasted sourdough bread. Top with basil leaves and fried tomatoes. Cut each sandwich on the diagonal.

Makes 8 sandwiches

Garden Goddess Gathering

SOME ENCHANTED EVENING

A flight of fancy awaits your guests when you invite them to create fantasy formalwear in honor of their favorite flower, nymph, or other nature-inspired creature. Goddesses and fairies may be escorted by their favorite rakes (dressed as humble gardeners, of course!). Greet your guests with exotic corsages and trailing boutonnieres. Host this fete at night and illuminate your trees and landscape with white twinkle lights, lanterns, and glowing luminaries. Tempt revelers with "nectar of the goddesses" (Champagne punch), Ambrosia Salad with Poppy Seed Dressing, cucumber sandwiches, and chocolate fondue served with exotic fruits and nuts for dipping and feeding to one another.

Ambrosia Salad with Poppy Seed Dressing

Two 12-oz bags of prepared mixed greens with arugula
Poppy Seed Dressing (recipe follows)
3 blood oranges (or 2 Ruby Red grapefruits), peeled and sectioned
1 cup fresh rose petals* (Harvest flowers early, wash carefully and keep them in the refrigerator between damp layers of paper towel.)
¼ cup shredded coconut

1. Place greens in a large salad bowl.

2. Lightly coat with Poppy Seed Dressing (recipe below) and top with orange sections.

3. Garnish with rose petals and shredded coconut.
Serves 8 to 10

Poppy Seed Dressing

1 teaspoon dry mustard
¼ cup sugar
1 teaspoon salt
⅓ cup tarragon white wine vinegar
½ cup vegetable oil
½ cup olive oil
¼ cup finely chopped sweet onion
1½ tablespoons poppy seeds

1. In a nonmetallic bowl, whisk together the mustard, sugar, salt, vinegar, and vegetable and olive oils until well blended. Add the onion and poppy seeds.

2. Pour mixture into a salad dressing shaker or jar with a tight-fitting lid, and refrigerate for 2 hours. Shake well before serving.

Eat only flowers and petals that you are sure have not been exposed to pesticides. Never assume that flowers from a florist, nursery, or garden center are edible unless they are labeled for food crop.

The Pot Party

PLANTING OUTSIDE THE BOX

This adventure begins with an intriguing invitation to bring the most creative vessel you can find—from old shoes to flea-market furniture—that you don't mind getting dirty and that won't leave you distraught if it gets ruined. Using flats of wheatgrass and assorted plants that you provide, you can all garden amidst Grateful Dead tunes. Munchie suggestions include hummus, pita bread, tabouli salad, baked beans, stuffed "bell-bottom" tomatoes, and, of course, scrumptious brownies.

Stuffed Bell-Bottom Tomatoes

6 large ripe tomatoes

salt and pepper to taste

1 tablespoon olive oil

2 cloves garlic, peeled and finely diced

1 small yellow onion, diced

2 cups sliced mushrooms

4 slices bacon, cooked and crumbled

2 tablespoons bread crumbs

1 cup freshly grated parmesan

1. Preheat oven to 400°F. Lightly grease a cookie sheet and set it aside.

2. Cut the top off each tomato. Using a teaspoon or melon baller, scoop out the centers of the tomatoes and set aside 1 cup of the pulp. Salt and pepper the inside of the tomatoes.

3. Heat olive oil in a saucepan over medium heat and sauté garlic and onions until soft and transparent, about 3 minutes. Add sliced mushrooms and cook until tender.

4. In a large mixing bowl, stir together the onion and mushroom mixture with the bacon, bread crumbs, and reserved tomato. Stuff each tomato with mixture and sprinkle with parmesan.

5. Place on cookie sheet and bake for 30 minutes or until cooked through.

Serves 6

🐦 *A little birdie told us . . .* If your roses are holding back before your garden party, troll the aisles of your local craft store and buy some convincing silk imposters to dress up those stingy bushes. Today's silk flowers are amazingly lifelike, and who knows? Maybe the impersonators will make your lazy roses so envious they'll bloom out of sheer spite.

Martini Garden

Martinis are festive and easy to make, and we love the way we look holding the glass. Serve your party guests one of the garden-themed martinis from the recipes below. Careful, these little ladies pack a punch, so make sure your chicks have a safe place to roost after imbibing!

DIRTY MARTINI

Test your grit with this spicy favorite of gardening chicks everywhere.

    6 parts gin
    2 parts dry vermouth
    I part olive brine
    Cocktail olives

Pour gin, vermouth, and olive brine into a shaker with ice. Shake well. Strain into a chilled martini glass and garnish with three olives.

HONEYDEW MARTINI

Your honey will do just about anything once plied with this delightful cocktail.

    6 parts vodka
    I part Midori
    I part Triple Sec
    Twist of lemon

Pour the vodka, Midori, and Triple Sec into a shaker with ice. Shake well. Strain into a chilled martini glass and garnish with lemon.

STRAWBERRY BLONDE

We all know one and we all love her. Cheers to chicks!

    6 parts strawberry vodka
    2 parts Lillet blanc
    Slices of fresh strawberry for garnish

Pour vodka and Lillet together into a shaker with ice. Shake well. Strain into a chilled martini glass and float a slice of fresh strawberry to finish.

You're Invited to a Weeding

BRIDESMAIDS GONE BAD

"You may now diss the bride." Under the guise of home improvement, gather all your best buds to don those oh-so-unattractive bridesmaid frocks from the past and revel in your attempts to trash them. Dig, give each other mud facials, and have a hose-down! The theme gives a nod to nuptials with "wedding"-inspired invites and decor. Serve "crab grass" appetizers (mini crabcakes with a side of cole slaw), turnip greens, dandelion wine, and even a tiered "weeding" cake to celebrate.

Dandelion Wine

This is a classic punch to serve when all your favorite chicks flock to your garden.

4 ounces brandy

2 ounces sugar

1 pint strawberries, washed, stemmed, and sliced

2 lemons, thinly sliced

2 oranges, thinly sliced

1 bottle chilled white wine

2 sprigs mint

4 dandelion flowers

1 pint club soda

2 cups ice

1. Combine the brandy and sugar; stir until sugar has dissolved.

2. Add the fruit slices and allow to stand for one hour.

3. When ready to serve, add the wine, mint, and dandelions and stir together. Then pour in club soda and ice.

Serves 6

"We want to smell like a rose. We want to smell like a henna flower. *But we don't want to smell like the largest inflorescence in the world,* the nine-foot-tall titan arum, *mythically pollinated by elephants,* which gives off a stench so revolting it has made men faint." —*Sharman Apt Russell*

Preparty Primping

If your hands and nails look, well, like a dirt grub-ber's, try these pampering treatments a day or two before your garden party. And, of course, you'll need to repeat the process after you've gotten down and dirty with your gardening gang.

THE GREEN THUMB ELIXIR

Soak your hands in a luxurious hand-softening, dirt-banishing bath. To a bowl of warm water add:

2 drops chamomile essential oil
2 drops geranium essential oil
2 drops lavender essential oil

Soak your hands for about 10 minutes, scrub gently with a nail brush, rinse, and pat dry. Now you're ready to really clean up your act.

SALTY TALON SCRUB

This makes a tough yet gentle hand scrub for after-garden cleanup. (The chicks like to mix up a batch of this and keep it in a jar by the sink.)

1 cup coarse sea salt
2 drops peppermint essential oil
3 drops lavender essential oil
½ ounce sweet almond oil

Combine salt and oils in a bowl and mix well with your fingers. Massage your hands, concentrating on the stained and rough spots. Rinse with warm water and pat dry. Now you are ready for the irresistible softening treatment.

"NEVER PULLED A WEED" SOFT HANDS

Blend 1 tablespoon sweet almond oil with ½ teaspoon castor oil. To this mixture add:

4 drops clary sage essential oil
2 drops geranium essential oil
4 drops lavender essential oil
2 drops rosemary essential oil

Rub this heavenly mixture vigorously into your hands, paying special attention to cuticles. Use a soft towel to gently push back your cuticles. (For a truly intense treatment, don a pair of cotton gloves and let the potion sink in overnight.)

Rinse hands thoroughly with warm water, and scrub nails with a brush and gentle soap to remove oil in preparation for nail polish. Dry thoroughly with a soft towel.

PINK POSY POLISH

Call attention to your newly soft and supple hands by treating your nails to some beautiful blooming color. Apply a clear base coat, follow with two coats of your favorite shade of pink, then dot on some simple daisies in white and yellow polish using a fine artist's brush or a toothpick. Seal the deal with a shiny top coat and you'll have oh-so-kissable hands to extend with abandon.

JaMaica *in my* LiVing RoOm

IN THE MIDDLE-CLASS JAMAICAN COMMUNITY in which I was reared, men and women, equally, toiled in their gardens in the early mornings or evenings after work, often talking across fences, over the sounds of the flow of water and children playing. Although many of them could afford a gardener, working in their gardens kept them in touch with a part of themselves that was decent and wholesome and gave greater meaning to their lives than whatever white-collar job they had did. The great joy was being able to share the products of one's garden with neighbors. We never bought flowers, but our vases were always filled with fresh-cut flowers; and seldom did we purchase fruits or vegetables. One's garden was a mark of pride, a visible sign of one's humanity. The belief was that having a garden kept one sane and honest.

My mother had a splendid garden. It was said she had a green thumb, and could make anything grow. In truth our house was surrounded by a wild blend of plants, flowers, vegetables and fruit trees. On the enclosed front veranda were my mother's prized African violets in varying shades of purple, pink, and white flowers. Often she instructed me in how to water them, cautioning me to not get the leaves wet. Fat African violets with shiny green leaves, many of which my mother had grown from a single leaf, sat proud. In the front and side of the yard were anthuriums, gerbas, oleander, sun flowers, red ginger, bird-of-paradise, crotons, hibiscus and many more, the names of which I never learned. There were also mango, sweetsop, sour-sop, breadfruit, ackee and guava fruit trees. Gungo peas hedged the side of one fence that separated our yard from our neighbors to the right, and banana and plantain trees hedged the left side. Our yard was nestled in green.

Some evenings, immediately upon coming home from work, even before my mother went inside the house to change out of her work clothes, she would stop in the garden, pull off dead leaves and bulbs, fuss over a plant, then reach for the hose and begin to water. I remember spending many long hours with my mother outside as a child, even after dusk had fallen. This was particularly the case if she was upset or troubled about something. No telling how long we would be out in her garden, me jumping about, slapping at the mosquitoes and enjoying the sound of water seeping into the soil,

> "It is only when my mother is working on her flowers that she is radiant. . . . She is involved in work her soul must have. Ordering the universe in the image of her personal conception of Beauty."
>
> —*Alice Walker*

"A little garden, all one's own, is a real Eden.

and my mother talking to the plants as if they were people. By the time my mother was through, her voice would always be raised in song, the melody floating through the air. She was always happy after nurturing her flora.

I did not think I had inherited my mother's penchant for gardening, but many years ago, before I was married and with children, Judy, a friend visiting my apartment for the first time said, "Wow! You've brought Jamaica to Oakland!" She walked around and counted close to forty plants in my one-bedroom apartment. I was surprised that there were so many, as I had not thought to count them, but I had been collecting them over the years. Many of my female friends bought clothes or shoes to congratulate themselves for some accomplishment, but I would buy a plant to celebrate another poem published. My plants thrived: the palm and rubber trees clambered to the ceiling. The ferns and spider lilies draped the windows. My favorite corner, where I often curl up in my wicker chair and listen to soft music in the semi-darkness, was enclosed by Dragon Tree, Striped Corn Cane, Ficus Benjamin, Bamboo Palm, Weeping Fig, and Dieffenbachia. When Judy declared that it must be quite a job caring for all these plants, I could only shrug no, not really.

I didn't feel as if I had been investing a great deal of time caring for them; yet I must have, as they were healthy and flourishing.

That was the moment I understood how essential plant life was to my existence. I felt great satisfaction after a Saturday afternoon or Sunday morning spent transplanting plants on my tiny balcony. I loved the damp sweet smell and gritty, porous texture of soil. I realized then that whenever I was frustrated, felt betrayed or angered by insensitivity or racism, I would wander to a plant store and stroll around; seldom would I leave without purchasing a plant. Plants and flowers became my lifeline; they helped me to unwind, to find my way back to my inner peace. More importantly, I now know that plants and flowers, in a very private and perhaps strange way, keep me in touch with my Caribbean heritage, where the land and what it yields is still essential to the masses of people who inhabit that shore.

—*Opal Palmer Adisa*

Earth possesses *no greater charm.*" —*Anonymous*

* A birdhouse

* Plenty of pink flowers in her garden

* A fabulous straw hat that perfectly shades her face and makes her feel like a professional

* A favored flower or plant obtained through questionable means

* Well-worn, mud-caked gardening clogs or wellies by the back door

* A vintage copy of *The Language of Flowers*

* Something in her garden planted by a friend

* A seed catalog subscription to get her dreaming of spring in the dead of winter

* A birdbath to welcome and refresh her feathered friends

* A cozy perch where she can take an alfresco break

* Serious garden tools to get the dirty work done with style and efficiency

* A moss-covered, aged-to-perfection piece of statuary

* A dog-eared gardening book specific to her geographic zone

* An abandoned bird's nest tucked into a tree or plant

* A few stones collected from a cherished trip, beachcombing excursion, or walk

* A gardening journal for musings, sketches, and a record of past mistakes and victories

HOUSEPLANT HOW-TO

Having an indoor Eden requires quite a bit of commitment from a chick. Searching for simple houseplant tips is like asking for advice on how to get a baby to sleep. Everyone has a different technique, a sure thing, a fail-safe method—until someone else tries it on a different baby. There are chicks who swear that ficus trees are as hardy as two-hundred-year-old redwoods, while others bemoan the fickle nature of ficus and their hateful propensity to drop leaves. What we do know for sure is that there is a houseplant for every chick. You just have to keep buying them, babying them, and, yes, on occasion burying them. Hopefully you'll come across the dream partner before you begin to feel like a horticultural serial killer. Here are a few bits of houseplant insight:

LOCATION, LOCATION, LOCATION. It's true for real estate, and it's true for houseplants. Plants are very sensitive to light, temperature, and how dry or humid a place is. Work with the space you've got and pick a plant that will be happy in that space. How much light will it get? Is it in a cooler or hotter part of the house? Dry or humid? Are there windows or vents nearby? Armed with that info, head for the nursery to choose a houseplant.

PLANT DIET. Just like people and animals, plants need the right nourishment. Whether it's a commercial fertilizer or a specialized blend of organic nutrients, plants need customized, regular feeding. Your nursery or plant seller can tell you what your individual plant needs.

Unable to bear the ridicule after losing yet another African violet, Sandy buried it amidst the annual border just before her bridge club arrived.

PLANT HYGIENE. Everyone appreciates a nice trim, although plants don't need them as often as we chicks do (thank goodness). Plan on being your plant's stylist as needed—pruning off dead or dying leaves and branches or pinching back leggy sections so the foliage will stay full. It will leave them looking refreshed and revived. Don't forget to turn your plants frequently so they will get sun exposure on all sides and grow evenly.

GIVE THEM A TRIP TO THE SPA. Plants need to get away sometimes too. Take them outside regularly (weather permitting), for some nice sun or cool shade, depending on what they like. Water them thoroughly at this time, letting water flow completely through their pots to let salts run out.

LET THEM SOCIALIZE. "Does this new cachepot make my bud look too big?" Just like chicks, plants need some time to get together for some healthy competition and blithe chatter. They appreciate being grouped together and will grow better with stimulating company.

INVEST IN A "BUD DOUBLE." If you are going to spend the time and effort to raise and get to know a certain type of plant, why not invest in two? That way you can rotate them—one goes outside while the other brightens your interior, or send them to different areas of your home.

Houseplants from Hell (High-Maintenance Plants)

We want to be surrounded by lush, green, flowering houseplants, but all too often we are seduced by sly flora that die on a whim. Here are the most offensive culprits—the houseplants from hell:

Maidenhair ferns: Don't be lured by this fair maiden who soon reveals her true form—a tangle of hairless tendrils and brittle stems.

Gardenia: They die so regularly that some gardeners claim they are suicidal.

Orchids: These little alien dragons are thought to have come from soil irradiated by a meteor—and the silk versions look SO real.

Mini roses: Nip the impulse to buy them in the bud, otherwise nipping buds is all you'll be doing.

African violets: Though some chicks have success with them, these beauties demand proper lighting, a "constant-feed fertilization program," and a new home every 9 to 12 months.

MVPs (Most Valuable Plants)
Almost Sure Things

These hardy plants are great guinea pigs for the indoor gardener even if you're black-thumbed. Keep these guys happy, then you can proceed to more demanding houseplants. Then again, why would you want to?

BROMELIADS. These exotic-looking beauties generally do well in low light or filtered sun. The ones with gray leaves can usually tolerate more light. Water the plant itself according to nursery directions for the variety and keep the soil moist too. Maintain by fertilizing only in spring and summer.

GRAPE IVY. This lovely, deep green, trailing plant likes to loll about in bright light. Don't soak this one. Let the dirt dry out a little in between watering. Maintain by fertilizing regularly. For a bushier plant, pinch off the tips of the vines. Take it outside or in the tub and shower the leaves every once in a while.

GERANIUM. These sun goddesses revel in the bright light of windowsills. There's huge variety of these flowers both in color and foliage. Scented geraniums have leaves with wonderful herbal fragrances like lemon, rose, and even chocolate. Overwatering can cause deadly rot, so let the soil dry out between showers. Low maintenance is key. Fertilize when you think of it; if they get pot bound, that's okay—they bloom more in a smaller pot. For a fuller, bushier plant, simply clip off some stems.

PARLOR PALM OR CHAMAEDOREA ELEGANS. This classic palm grows up to four feet tall, with full, feathery fronds, and gives high-impact garden style to a room. They need consistent watering, regular fertilizing, and good drainage, but they are very tolerant of low light and tight pots. They need to be repotted every two or three years.

PIGGYBACK PLANT OR TOLMIEA MENZIESII. The name alone makes us want to buy this happy houseplant, with its bright green, heart-shaped leaves. When buying, go for the smaller plant, which will adapt more easily to its new home and will amaze you with its fast growth. As for care, piggyback plants like filtered or low light, consistently moist soil, and regular fertilizing in the spring and fall. In winter let the top layer of soil dry out between waterings and lay off the feeding schedule.

"There is no use trying to grow houseplants *unless one is willing to be a nurse.*" —*Katharine White*

sNaiL *Bait*

SOMETIMES YOU HAVE TO GO TO EXTREMES TO MAKE A GARDEN PRETTY—or at least to keep it from turning into the most hideous one on the street.

Take my garden snail problem. Eight months pregnant with my first child, I set out on a mission to eliminate garden snails from the flowerbeds in front of our new California home. The little suckers and their slug friends had chewed through two dozen pansies and at least as many marigolds in less than two weeks.

I was at my wit's end. My first attempt at establishing a garden in California (I'm from Chicago originally) was failing miserably. Between the rosebush that had attracted thousands of aphids and the chewed-up annuals, my flowerbeds looked like piles of litter.

So I began to read up on how to eliminate snails without the use of chemicals. I was, after all, about to have a baby and had no desire to expose my child to even a hint of a toxic product.

The best advice I found was that snails and slugs love beer. Apparently they'll slither into a bowl of beer, imbibing by osmosis until their drunken, slimy bodies get stuck in the alcohol and they die.

It was late Sunday night when I read this encouraging news.

I had already learned that snails do most of their creeping and sliming in the middle of the night when conditions are cool and moist, so I knew I had to take advantage of the opportunity to kill—that night.

Having quit my job a month earlier, I did not have to get up early to go to work the next morning, so I set out on my mission as Snail Assassin. There was no way I was going to waste any of the three bottles of ale from a local microbrewery that my husband loves, so out I set—at 10 P.M. on Sunday!—to a twenty-four-hour grocery store nearby.

My hair pulled back in a stringy ponytail and my face free of makeup, I donned gray maternity shorts, sneakers, and a worn-out T-shirt proclaiming, BABY ON BOARD, with a drawing of a smiling, full-term fetus in utero. I walked in and headed toward the liquor section.

I picked up two six-packs of Budweiser that was on special for "club card" holders. Having forgotten to get a grocery cart on my way in, I slipped the middle finger and thumb of each hand under the plastic rings of a six-pack and waddled up to the checkout aisle.

The man behind the register in the express lane and the lady checking out in front of me—who was buying a gallon of milk and some Cheerios—looked at me horrified as I dropped the beer on the conveyor belt with a thud.

At that moment I realized what I must have looked like. Their incredulous looks flattened my resolve and I began to stutter my way through a long-winded explanation about snails and beer, all the while giggling nervously.

The woman with the milk left without a word. The young man at the register hesitated and offered a gratuitous laugh, but scanned my beer anyway.

I wondered if they actually believed my snail story, but I decided I didn't care. I was on a mission.

Though I picked up more slimeballs in three weeks than a dumb blonde picks up at a college bar, I soon had abandoned snail genocide in favor of motherhood. The snails come back every year. Must be the happy hour specials.

—*Cameron Sullivan*

Bug Off!

Aphids are the bad girls of the garden. They eat all the good stuff, ruin the aesthetic of the place, and are pests with a capital P. (Sound like some people you know?) If aphids are ransacking and pillaging your paradise, it's time to call in the very elite, highly trained Aphid Assassins. You can go with the ultrapolite and well-dressed ladybug. She is a classic choice of organic gardeners and she will politely devour the little buggers. Or, if you are past the Ms. Nice Guy stage and really want to wipe them out, green lacewing larvae are your new best friends. Baby lacewings are called aphid lions. They earn that name by literally hunting down and attacking aphids—voraciously. You can introduce green lacewings as eggs or as larvae. Eggs are cheaper, but larvae are immediately hungry, ticked off, and ready to clean up the joint. About 500 larvae can take care of about 500 square feet of garden, depending on how bad the infestation is. Look to your local or online organic pest control sources for places to buy them.

"I don't mind Japanese beetles having sex on the roses, *I just wish they wouldn't eat* at the same time."

—*Diane Ackerman*

Roses aRe *dead*

THE ROSEBUSHES WERE THE BIGGEST PROBLEM OF ALL. They were dormant when we moved in and I hate to admit it, but I didn't like them from the start. I just couldn't find anything to love about my rosebushes. The old adage about politics and sausage is true of roses as well: People who like roses should not watch them grow. Those gnarled, thorn-covered branches and mean, prickly leaves looked like some horrible monster that had just crawled out of the earth and colonized the flowerbed.

And they were so fickle and difficult to care for! I had already learned to identify whitefly, rust, and mildew, thanks to them. I was afraid to go back to the nursery and find out what kind of chemical warfare I'd have to engage in to save them. The flowers just didn't seem worth the effort. If I want some roses, I'll call the florist and order a dozen. This was one case where homegrown was not necessarily better.

My neighbor Charlie, on the other hand, had a beautiful rose garden that he planted for his wife, Beverly—a dozen or so bushes, in shades of red, pink, and yellow. After he planted them, he found out that she was allergic to roses. But he still took care of them, pulling weeds, pruning, and fertilizing. He offered me roses every time he saw me, saying, "I can't even bring them in the house, she sneezes so much. Take some."

I adore roses as cut flowers, and will gladly accept a dozen any time Charlie wants to hand them over the fence. Scott brings me roses from time to time, the lavender Sterlings with their wild sharp scent, or tiny antique roses, white with the barest hint of green around the petals' edge. But I neglected my own rosebushes, and over time, as they got uglier and thornier and sicklier, I developed an outright revulsion toward them. The more I neglected them, the hardier they became, the stubborn things. Clearly, they were not going to wither away on their own. If I wanted them gone, I was going to have to take action. . . .

I think the roses felt a little nervous around me, like stepchildren left in the care of their evil stepmother. They hunched low to the ground and they tried their hardest not to bloom so as to avoid drawing attention to themselves. They look uncomfortable and out of place among the plants I'd brought home so far, my natural-born children, the blowsy cosmos and sunny calendula. I'm pretty sure they knew they were doomed as soon as they met me. It was only a matter of time.

Everyone has a time to die. For my roses, that time came one fine May afternoon, when they were at their sickly, thorniest, pest-ridden peak. I got my pruning shears and walked outside, holding them behind my back. It was the kind of day on which no one in their right mind would think to prune a rose, exactly the wrong time of year. Even a beginning gardener like me would know better. I looked around to make sure I was out of sight of the neighbors. I didn't want to arouse suspicion. Without a word, I knelt down next to the roses, lay the blade of my pruning shears against their scrawny green necks, and cut them right down to the ground. It only took one clean cut through the base of the plant, and the whole thorny mess toppled. I threw them over the back fence into the alley, feeling a little like a gardening mob boss, dumping the bodies of those who had become inconvenient. I stood over the stumps and warned them that if they put out so much as a single leaf, I'd be back.

There's something to this murder racket, I realized, as I looked at the bare spot where the rose bushes had been. It felt good. Rubbing them out gave me real satisfaction. Now all I needed was a mob name, like Mundo or The Shredder. Or how about the Pruner? I looked over at Charlie's roses, innocently blooming in the spring air. I could take them down in a minute. Charlie was out adjusting the sprinklers. Hey Charlie, I wanted to say, in my hoarse Godfather voice, a man can't be too careful about his roses these days. Would be a real tragedy if anything happened to them. A man in your position might want to arrange for some protection.

But I didn't say any of that. Sometimes you need to keep a low profile with the neighbors. I waved, and he waved back, and I went inside, my pruning shears concealed in my pants pocket, the steel blade hard against my hip.

—*Amy Stewart*

Dirty Ditties
TUNES WE DIG

- *The Rose:* Bette Midler
- *Garden Party:* Ricky Nelson
- *La Vie en Rose:* Edith Piaf
- *I Feel the Earth Move:* Carole King
- *Take Me to the River:* Al Green
- *Here Comes the Sun:* George Harrison
- *Scarborough Fair:* Simon and Garfunkel
- *A Day Without Rain:* Enya
- *Soak Up the Sun:* Sheryl Crow
- *Motherland:* Natalie Merchant
- *Alabama Rain:* Jim Croce
- *Blackbird:* The Beatles
- *Wildflowers:* Tom Petty
- *Willow:* Joan Armatrading
- *Sunshine on My Shoulders:* John Denver
- *Waitin' on a Sunny Day:* Bruce Springsteen
- *You Don't Bring Me Flowers Anymore:* Barbra Streisand
- *Long Time Gone:* The Dixie Chicks
- *Inch by Inch:* David Mallett
- *Somewhere Over the Rainbow:* Judy Garland
- *Love Is a Rose:* Neil Young

She's No fleur~de~Lis

EMPRESS JOSEPHINE BONAPARTE CULTIVATED A LEGENDARY GARDEN that was anything but prim. Seven miles west of Paris, at Château de Malmaison, this royal diva created a luxurious novelty garden dedicated to a single flower—the rose, her passion.

With an aristocratic shopping fervor usually reserved for shoes or jewelry, she hired personal shoppers to canvass the globe in search of the rarest and loveliest varieties. She immortalized her treasures by commissioning her friend and court artist Pierre-Joseph Redouté to paint them. (A folio of Redouté roses recently sold at Sotheby's for more than $400,000.)

You don't have to have a royal pedigree or a league of professional gardeners to consort with some of the same roses that Josephine enjoyed. Though many of her originals have vanished, the following rose varieties that graced Malmaison are readily available today:

Cabbage Rose (*Rosa centifolia*). Though their abundant petals make their flowers look like cabbages, they smell heavenly and are a prime source of rose oil.

Austrian yellow rose (*Rosa foetida*). Keep this beautiful, sparsely petaled yellow rose away from other roses, as she may be the genetic source for black spot.

The Seven Sisters Rose (*Rosa multiflora platyphylla*). Paris nurseryman Louis Noisette gifted Josephine with this showy purple-pink variety (which probably originated in Japan), but, sadly, the empress died before the plant ever bloomed.

Damask Roses (*Rosa damascena variegata*). These bold beauties are fashion forward with their striped or variegated petals.

> *Rosa gallica officinalis* is known as the apothecary's rose and was grown in medieval herb gardens. The darker the color of the flower, the more prized oil it contained in its petals.

Pierre-Joseph Redouté

Hen ScrAtcHes *competition in the garden*

UNDER COVER OF DARKNESS, a solitary figure crept toward a small stand of yellow mums. In her hands were the tools of her deception: a large spoon and a premixed bottle of Miracle-Gro.

With stealth and furtiveness, my grandmother silently approached her little flower garden, planted that very day in a chummy session with her dear friend and neighbor, Mrs. Blue. Across the driveway, Mrs. Blue's similar newly planted garden stood yearningly in the cool evening light.

With precision, Nana placed a tablespoon of the miracle elixir under each flower, working into the soil the evidence of her duplicity.

In the weeks that followed, my grandmother's garden became an ad-worthy profusion of riotous blooms. Across the way, Mrs. Blue's garden seemed to languish, hopelessly undernourished and outflanked.

Week after week, my grandmother's secret nighttime forays into her garden continued and the blooming disparity between the two gardens grew. Finally, toward the end of the summer, Mrs. Blue, overcome with public horticultural humiliation, gave in to displaying pink plastic flamingoes and placed a troll strategically in front of her plants.

The lushness of my grandmother's garden was certainly aided by her furtive feedings, but this one additive cannot completely explain the glorious denseness of her foliage. Perhaps some of the stronger offshoots of Mrs. Blue's envious blossoms decided to jump the border and stow away in my grandmother's garden to partake of the evening buffet? Or maybe Mrs. Blue's deprived plantings simply became dispirited in their subsistence existence, and gave up. Whatever the reason for her garden's largesse, my grandmother, unapologetically, but with seeming modesty, accepted her crown to rule that summer as a true garden diva.

—*Karen Miles*

A Gardener's Confession

I confess that . . .

I like the taste of hose water.

Several geraniums in my garden make me feel guilty when I recall how I got them.

I once hollered, in public, how fond I am of decollate snails.

When I heard urine was good for roses, I tried it.

I don't go anywhere from 6 to 8 P.M. in midsummer, because that's when the garden cools off just right.

I pretended to sympathize when my husband told me that running the chipper-shredder is bad for his allergies.

I'm ridiculously proud of fist-sized knots of red worms in my compost pile.

I snuck into the neighbors' yard and planted narcissus bulbs and geranium cuttings.

I'm scheming on a magenta pelargonium I saw on Country Club Lane.

—*Debra Lee Baldwin*

IT'S WHAT EVERY GARDEN CHICK NEEDS—personalized garden tools and irresistible places to plant. Whip some up for your gardening buds and don't forget yourself. You'll all have much more fun in the dirt with these flashy accessories, and your plants will just fall all over themselves blooming when you set them up in a fabulous polka-dot pot.

Gold Diggers and Hip Hoes

We recommend doing this project outside because it involves spray paint. Cover your work surface with newspaper or a drop cloth. (Trust us, we have a hot pink spot in the driveway.)

You'll need:

Newspaper or drop cloth to protect your work area

Medium-grit sandpaper (100 grit works well)

2 handheld gardening tools with wooden handles

Tack cloth

Painter's masking tape

A box or pot of sand or dirt

Spray paint in metallic gold

Assorted Spouncers—round sponges with stick handles—used for stenciling but also the perfect tool for making polka dots. They usually come two to a pack with various-sized sponges, and can be found at any craft store.

Spray paint in hot pink and lime green

Acrylic paint in hot pink and lime green

Polyurethane spray

Using the sandpaper, rough up the surface of the tool handles. Wipe well with the tack cloth to remove dust. Use the tape to cover the metal part of the tool, and sink the metal part of the tool into the sand or dirt. This enables you to spray paint the handle without touching it or needing to move it around.

Spray a coat of hot pink on the handle. Let this dry completely according to manufacturer's directions. After the hot pink coat dries completely, use your Spouncer to apply lime green polka dots randomly around the handle. Now do the reverse on the other tool: Spray it green, let it dry, and Spounce on hot pink dots.

After the handles are completely dry, use the tape to mask off the handles, then spray-paint the metal parts of the tools gold. To seal and protect your tools, give them two coats of polyurethane spray, letting them dry between coats.

These garden tools are stylish and virtually impossible to lose in the garden.

Polka Pots

We chicks have a soft spot for polka dots—to the distress of our husbands, who've coined the phrase "chick pox." But dots are fun and festive—two things we can't get enough of—and they are brainlessly easy to master once you get a Spouncer in your hand. Take all the pots that are languishing in the garden shed, dust them off a bit, and give them a face-lift. If you are making this as a gift, you might want to splurge on a new pot.

You'll need:

Newspaper or drop cloth to protect your work area

Spouncer in desired size

Flowerpot (clay, plastic, it doesn't matter)

Spray paint for base color

Acrylic paint for polka dot color

Polyurethane spray

Spray the pot with your base color paint. (Be sure to go around the inside rim, too, and down about 3 inches, because that rim shows even when the pot is no longer empty.) Let the base color dry. Use your Spouncer to make polka dots randomly all over the pot. Let those dry. Protect it from weather and water by giving it at least two coats of polyurethane spray. Let dry between coats.

From Dirt Poor to Dirt Rich

If prospecting for gold or oil in your backyard has tanked as an excuse for garnering more dig time, do not give up on the fantasy that you'll reap what you sow. Take the case of Evelyn Gage, an unassuming British chick who picked up some foxglove seeds for a song at a garage sale. Evelyn planted the seeds and felt more than compensated simply by the fact that they came up and actually bloomed. She happily gardened alongside her pretty investment until one day a garden-savvy friend noted that there was something a little different about her new foxgloves. Certain of their uniqueness, she insisted that Evelyn investigate. Seed merchants Thompson & Morgan confirmed that Evelyn's bargain foxgloves were anything but ordinary—she had discovered a new variety. The next year, Digitalis purpurea "Primrose Carousel" adorned the front of Thompson & Morgan's catalog and was their best-selling seed. Since she discovered them, Evelyn earns royalties for all sales of the seeds—a literal return on her garden investment.

Thanks to plant patent laws, American gardeners can also strike it rich with the discovery of a new variety. If you think you've found the next seed catalog cover girl, contact PlantHaven at 612-551-1384 or planthaven.com.

DarWiniAn garDen*ing*

AGAIN I HAVE JUMPED THE VERNAL GUN: annuals lounging in window boxes, hanging baskets dangling from shiny new hooks on the front porch, tomato plants cringing under their cages. In the yard, sprouts, like pieces of cut glass, have jumped along with me, nudging their way into the open air. We are all in a rush to put winter behind us.

And then the death knell: frost warnings announced on the evening news. I run to the front porch and remove all the baskets, filling the front hall with ivy geranium. Armored in a green Burpee apron, I rush to the garden shed to continue my fight. Out come dozens of gallon milk jugs, their bottom halves recruited in my battle against the indifferent elements.

In the yard, I search for buds. Some have already grown too high for the jugs and need to be swathed in plastic bags. As the sun begins to recede, I am still hard at work. Behind me, the ghostly bags seem to snicker. I even think I hear one ask, "What in the world are you doing?" But it's only my neighbor, peering down over our shared fence. An ardent gardener herself, she knows exactly what I'm doing.

"I am a firm believer in Darwinian gardening," she says from her vantage point. "Survival of the fittest."

"But these little jewels are all exposed!"

"They look sort of sexual to me," she says.

My little buds sexual? And I hear her laughing as she curls up with a cup of coffee, giving herself permission to enjoy the approach of another frost spring night.

The next morning, I check for survivors. Once more I have laughed in the face of the elements: not one casualty amongst the buds.

"Time for coffee now?" asks my neighbor.

"Yes, now that I know that everyone is safe. How did yours do?"

"Most made it. Some succumbed. The ones that survive will be hardier, and the ones that didn't probably shouldn't have anyway."

Late that night, I ponder our gardening philosophies. My neighbor's garden is a marvel: tucked in her tiny city yard is a frenzy of color, texture, smell. She weeds at will, thinning her plants without so much as a wince. I suffer with every one that I pull from the earth. I feel guilt at my omnipotence. She's at home with it. I do my own mulching, afraid a gardener might smother one of my emerging blooms. She orders truckloads to be dumped on bed after bed.

What my neighbor makes look easy, I work hard at. In her garden, it's more than a green thumb: she's an artist at work with seed and soil. She's relaxed, but enthusiastic. "Let's go after the poison ivy!" she often cries. And together we spend an entire afternoon attacking the villain that has insinuated itself between the fence posts. We laugh and talk, saying some of the best things we've ever said. Or I'll find bunches of daylilies on my porch, with a note—"Give them a good home." I never seem to have extra, or else I can't seem to let go of what I have.

So whose philosophy is the right one? Is my garden more work than play? Am I being overprotective? By shielding my plants from frostbite, have I somehow been interfering in the great scheme of things?

In the middle of my midnight musings, the phone rings. It is our son, calling from college. I hold my breath. "I'm fine, Mom," he says. And I begin to breathe again. "I just called to say thanks."

Thanks?

He had spent the evening with his friends, all of whom had been complaining about their parents. They had described insult, injury, anger, and injustice.

"What did you say?" I asked.

"I told them that you guys are okay, even if you are a little overprotective. I was thinking when everyone was complaining that you pay attention to me. Anyway, I just called to say thanks."

"Darwinian gardening," I murmur into the pillow after I replace the receiver on its cradle and pull the comforter up to my chin. "Darwinian parenting."

"What did you say?" asks my husband, curling up beside me.

"Nothing," I say, smiling. "Actually everything . . . oh wait! Did you hear the weather report? Any frost warnings tonight?"

"It's too late," he says, "They're all on their own."

—*Barbara Kaplan Bass*

Jennie Butchart *"It Was the Pits"*

Most of us chicks have had to rescue a plant or two smooshed by a member of the male breed, but horticulturist Jennie Butchart saved an entire scarred landscape created by her husband's business—a limestone quarry in Ontario, Canada. Hanging precariously from the sides of the quarry in a sling, Ms. Butchart tucked hundreds of beautiful flowers and plants into the cracks and walls of the former quarry until the formerly bleak wasteland became a spectacular sunken garden. The garden, later known as Butchart Garden, became a stunning and unprecedented model of how to refurbish a pit. These days Butchart Gardens is a well-known tourist site, attracting more than fifty thousand visitors a year. Until very recently Ms. Butchart herself served tea to her guests.

"Oh, let it go. Let the *plants fight their own battles.*"

—*Katharine White*

Window Dressing

Just as the perfect sunglasses can take you from ho-hum to whoa-baby, a window box can sweeten the view and boost your home's curb appeal. Styles vary from ornate ironwork to rustic wood, so choose one that fits the look of your home and garden. Between the local nursery, home-improvement store, do-it-yourself options, and online sources you're sure to find one that fits just right. Remember that window boxes need to drain, so if your box doesn't have them, drill some holes and pay attention to what's going to be dripped on below.

Once you've chosen the right container, it's time for the fun part—filling it up. Add loam or a soil polymer to the potting mix to help the box retain water, and add a time-release fertilizer to boost blossoms. Choose plants that aren't overzealous about expanding in the limited space, and pick three varieties of plants: something tall and vertical, something medium, and something that trails over the edge. Good window box plants include geraniums, impatiens, snapdragons, coleus, and fuchsia. For trailing varieties, try ivy, bacopa, alyssum, licorice plant, and dwarf periwinkle. Consult with the nursery to choose plants that are right for your light conditions. Water your window boxes every other day in hot weather. Unlike soil in the garden, they dry out very quickly.

When cold weather zaps your window garden, think outside the box for seasonal displays. In autumn fill them with pumpkins, gourds, wheat, dried leaves, and grapevines for a harvest touch. In winter, go faux, with fake snow, silk greenery, Styrofoam snowmen, and lights for a festive winter-wonderland look. Pick a theme and stage a scene in your window box, where decor is limited only by your imagination. We assure you the plants will understand that a chick needs to stay amused during a deep freeze.

Enid found her conversations with the magnolias far more stimulating than those she had with Charles.

A little birdie told us . . . Windowbox.com is an excellent resource for buying containers, and their "Floracle" link is an awesome tool for helping you choose plants.

EnDless SeasOns

SOME OF OUR CHILDHOOD MEMORIES DRIFT IN AND OUT, often in fragmented vignettes embellished with the passage of years. Others transcend time, preserved in vivid detail. That's the way it's been when thoughts have turned to my paternal grandmother, Daisye Pearl Kern Miller. I was too young to realize that she was well known in Austin, Texas, as a published author and church and civic leader. I knew her as the source of unconditional love, and believed she had the most beautiful garden in the whole world.

Tiny seeds, covered by soft soil, emerged magically as green shoots and soon turned her yard into a sea of color. There were Queen Anne's lace, larkspur, poppies, daisies, nasturtium, and zinnias. A fence supported morning glory, honeysuckle, and coral vines. One house separated us and I traveled a well-worn path for my frequent visits. On warm, sunny days we would sit in the garden, motionless, voices lowered to whispers, as bees, hummingbirds, and butterflies swirled past, seeking out nectar concealed in the blossoms. Spiders ignored our presence, intent on trapping their next meal in intricate webs.

One morning I was surprised to find Grandmother on her knees weeding the flowerbeds. I asked why she didn't let the yardman take care of this task. She put down the trowel, motioning me to sit beside her.

"I need to do this myself. It's impossible to remain angry when you're on your knees pulling weeds."

"But you don't look angry."

"Well, then, it works just like I said," she replied with a smile. "Would you like to help?"

I liked the feel of the soft earth as it stuck to my fingers. I got the hang of it without much trouble, yet a few roots were missed in the excitement of this grown-up activity. She patiently explained the importance of removing the entire weed as I watched her carefully, expecting a frown. I decided she must have made it up about being angry since her smile continued to broaden.

Grandmother died in June of 1942, two months before my twelfth birthday. I couldn't cry, although I felt lost and abandoned. When my dad sold her home and the beautiful garden slowly disappeared, I clung to tangible reminders that kept her memory alive. I read poems and stories she'd written for me. I planted a Victory Garden that covered our backyard, although few crops made it to our table. I told myself she would've grown bushels of vegetables. Gardening was hard work and no fun. My body ached. I was angry. She *had* made up a story that wasn't true.

It wasn't until I was in high school that I read her novel, ▶

"garden and you are not likely to regret it." —*Hildegarde Hawthorne*

The Year—Four Seasons of a Woman's Life, and gained a new perspective and respect for the woman I'd adored. Several years later a box containing her diaries, poems, papers, and unpublished manuscripts brought dim memories into clear focus, changing my life forever. Tears of guilt blurred my vision as I recalled the anger and betrayal I'd felt after her death. *"Think of life as a garden. . . . God has provided everything we need and put us here as care-takers. . . . Anger and weeds crowd out beauty if they're not controlled. . . . It's hard to explain, but I find it's impossible to remain angry when I'm on my knees pulling weeds."*

I recently stepped over the threshold into my seventh decade, but I haven't made the journey alone. Grandmother's words have accompanied me. Many houses, gardens, and broken, dirty fingernails later, I now live with my youngest son, daughter-in-law, and three inquisitive grandchildren, our residences separated by a breezeway. While I no longer climb the tallest ladder to reach intruding vines, or clamber across rooftops to prune tree limbs, I continue to pull weeds and content myself by planting annuals preferred by ladybugs, butterflies, and hummingbirds, which delight my grandchildren. They are learning about plants that attract different species, and beginning to identify other birds that gather at feeders or find temporary relief from the Texas heat by dunking their bodies in a birdbath.

I've come full circle. As I watch my grandchildren, I understand the joy my grandmother experienced. What a privilege it was to be part of my life as my world expanded beyond her garden. When my grandchildren ask why I don't let the yard service remove the weeds, I'll put down the trowel, motion for them to sit beside me, and share the words of their great-great-grandmother.

—*Beth Lynn Clegg*

Did I hear that tulip sneeze?

For the last three hundred years the tulip has ruled as one of the world's most coveted flowers. Dramatic red and white stripes are the signature markings of one of the most rare and popular types of prize tulip. For decades growers tried to cultivate this tulip and failed. Finally, in 1874, Dorothy Cayley figured out that the strikingly beautiful stripes were actually caused by a virus spread by aphids.

THE KINDERGARDEN

For many of us, our fondest memories of baby chickhood revolve around chasing butterflies and making mud pies in the garden. Kids and gardens go together like ants and picnics, and although kids might not be ideal worker bees, there is a host of ways to have a fun and fruitful time with the little buggers in your garden.

DRESS 'EM UP. Kids love to accessorize—hats, sunglasses, gloves, and rain boots are great garden wear for kids and help to get them excited about a garden excursion. If you want to be more ambitious, you can even dig out old Halloween costumes (insects and animals, for instance) they can don to do a little digging and rooting around "in character."

THE TOOLS. Big and little kids alike love gadgets. Petite trowels, rakes, hoes, watering cans, buckets, and wheelbarrows give mini gardeners a sense of motivation. Just be sure to steer the little diggers away from your prize beds.

DIRTY WORK. The garden is the perfect spot for those messy activities you can't do inside—so take advantage of it. Make sand art in discarded jars, bury "treasures" in a special bed or container and let them dig for them, wash garden tools, or have them help you repot some houseplants. Make mud pies and dirty lemonade in an imaginary kitchen. Kids can amuse themselves for hours with a hose and a few containers. Provide watering cans and various cups to be filled and emptied over and over again or make puddles and simply splash about.

GET BUGGY. Hide plastic bugs amid your garden or let your young friends look for the real things and document their findings in a special journal. Provide ventilated plastic containers for catching ladybugs and sow bugs (roly-polies) temporarily, and stake out a special habitat in the garden to release them back into. Teach them that some bugs are dangerous and none of them like to be touched. Buy a guide to bugs and a magnifying glass, and let children indulge in a bit of backyard detective work.

A REAL KINDERGARDEN. Let them plant their own garden. Through a child's eyes, a garden is nothing short of magic—a few seeds and some careful attention will yield flowers to pick or veggies to eat. Help them paint special pots to plant their seedlings in, and make garden markers to identify the plants. Let kids mark their turf by staking out a sunny spot and planting marigold seeds three inches apart to spell out their initials or a simple design like a star or heart. Fun plants for kids to grow include sunflowers, nasturtium, runner beans, lettuce, strawberries, carrots, cherry tomatoes, pumpkins, and squash.

OUR POSY PATCH

A ROSY POSY PARTY. Set the scene for a very special kiddie occasion with ladybug tablecloths (red cloths appliqued with black felt dots and eyes), crustless sandwiches cut into flower shapes, "ants on a log," which are simply celery sticks filled with cream cheese or peanut butter and sprinkled with raisins, and mud pies for dessert. Serve sandwiches from plastic kiddie wheelbarrows and pour lemonade from watering cans. For a fun craft, let them make stone ladybugs by painting small round stones red and adding black dots. For an activity and a keepsake, provide each child with a small flowerpot and set up stations with paints, soil, "mystery seeds" (a selection of unmarked sunflower seeds, marigolds, nasturtium, etc.), chalkboard paint, and chalk. Have the kids paint the pots as they want and then paint the rim of the pot with chalkboard paint. After it dries, they can write their name or a fun message, or draw a design. The surprise of what they've planted will be revealed in a few weeks.

Mud Pies

I box (16 ounces) brownie mix
1½ cups heavy cream, cold
¼ cup sugar
I gallon vanilla ice cream
One 16-ounce jar fudge, heated until warm and runny
½ cup chocolate cookie crumbs
8 gummy worms

1. Bake the brownies according to instructions on the box.

2. Whip cream and sugar together in small bowl until firm.

3. While brownies are still warm, cut into squares. Place 1 square in each dessert bowl. Top each brownie with 1 scoop vanilla ice cream, dribble warm fudge on the ice cream, and finish with a dollop of whipped cream and a sprinkle of cookie crumbs. Garnish each portion with a gummy worm and serve immediately. *Serves 8*

Lett*ing* it GrOw!

UNTIL ABOUT A YEAR AGO, gardening used to be a deep love of mine. One Saturday in March, I was decked out in hat and gloves, rubber clogs, and stretch pants, trying desperately to save my perennials, which were being strangled by invasive weeds. I looked around the garden and felt completely overwhelmed. Even if I spent every weekend for the next three months, I could not keep up with the demands of my garden—so I peeled off my gloves, stomped resentfully into the house, made a cup of tea, and let my garden go.

When I created our garden out of a half acre of dead grass, I envisioned our family working together, planting bulbs in the fall and enjoying the beauty of daffodils, tulips, and iris in the spring. I even assigned each of the kids a plot that they were responsible to weed, with high hopes that they'd enjoy digging in the earth. What happened in reality was that everyone was too busy—when I asked for help all I got was a lot of complaining—to the point where it was more work for me to ask for their help than it was to do it myself.

Summer rolled around and everyone asked where the snap peas, tomatoes, cucumbers, and strawberries were. Nobody even noticed that the vegetable garden, which was overgrown with weeds, had been left untouched. I did not spend five minutes working in the garden that whole summer.

Last week I had a delightful conversation with a woman who loves to garden. We talked about how pretty blueberry bushes look in the fall with their colorful leaves, and the delicious, full taste of home-grown tomatoes. I could hear my love and enthusiasm for this topic. While we talked something inside started screaming to get out. . . . I knew that I would plant a vegetable garden this summer. I missed the dirt. Yesterday I slipped on my rubber clogs and weeded; then I planted only a small part of the vegetable garden, enjoying every minute. That may be all I do—which is finally okay with me.

—*Sheila Ellison*

A little studied negligence *is becoming* to a garden.

–*Eleanor Perényi*

CHICK tips ... *for chicks and hoes*

The garden is an extension of your nest, an outdoor room. Whether you have access to acres or have room only for a pot by the front door, make your mark.

Grow something wild and unruly. Plant lettuces among your flower beds, line a walkway with teacup saucers, grow pumpkins in a vacant lot, plant tomatoes in a window box.

Contain your enthusiasm. Be ever on the lookout to add to your stash of unconventional things to display flowers and plants in.

Hunt and gather a bouquet every day. Even in the dead of winter, bring an evergreen sprig or a branch of berries or some new flowering bulbs into your nest.

Stop to smell the roses—every chance you get. Gardening inspiration and lessons can be found all around you, from your neighbors and family to museums and strip malls.

Don't be afraid to weed things out. If you've inherited a plant or grown one you don't like, don't waste your mercy on it. Gardening isn't always pretty—dig up the offender and move on.

Know when to throw in the trowel. If there is an area where you just can't cajole anything to grow, come at it from a different angle. Make a cobblestone pattern, install a birdbath, or show off your collection of vintage watering cans.

Mother Nature is the best decorator. Garner inspiration from your garden and bring it indoors and vice versa. Love that golden dandelion in your lawn? Paint your kitchen wall green and dress your window with sunny yellow curtains. Enjoy curling up by the fire? Furnish your patio with a chimenea.

Cultivate a sense of community. Be generous with the fruits of your labors—give flowers, fruits, vegetables, cuttings, and advice to friends and neighbors.

acKnowleDgments

The chicks humbly thank all the peeps who so generously supported us and shared their talents and enthusiasm to get this book hatched:

Jenny Bent, our agent, who so excitedly and graciously introduced us to all the right people

Ruth Sullivan, our editor, the queen chick whose extraordinary vision shaped this book and gave it wings

Rebecca Schiff, for generously helping us weave it all so tightly and beautifully together

Anne Cherry, production editor, for overseeing the book and making invaluable fine-tuned corrections

Peter Workman, for inviting us to rest on such a privileged perch

Katie Workman, for her wise counsel and marketing savvy

Kimberly Hicks and Sarah O'Leary, whose publicity prowess inspires us to take it on the road

Janet Vicario, our art director, for sharing her fabulous chick style and amazing design gifts

Jarrod Dyer, for tirelessly wading through and perfecting the seemingly endless tide of pink art and copy

Martha Newton Furman, our illustrator, whose artwork and attitude make the book sing

from Ame

Thank you to Peter and Grace Anne—you are my heart and my home. To my mother hen, Bootsie, who always weaves such a welcoming nest and who told me I could be anything I wanted to be—even a writer. To my sister Kathy, a true domestic goddess, who keeps me on the straight and narrow and tolerates my wide swerves to the left. To Joan Hansen, Renée Turcott, and Theresa Mahler for being the best "chick-in-laws" a gal can have. To Kim Nichols and Justina Radcliff, who stick with me through thick and thin. And to Emily, the ultimate best friend, partner in crime, and nesting buddy—thank you for standing by me and, more often than not, holding me up.

from Emily

Thank you to my husband, Dave, and my children, Julia and Henry, for their limitless love, patience, and support. To the original chick, my mother, Karen, whose love, encouragement, vision, and domestic know-how brought out the spirit of this book and kept our voices true. To my brother John, for always being a bright spot and a good listener. To my grandparents, Emily and Hans, for their constant support. To my chick-sisters, Aimee, Karen, Linda, and Mary, who always make everything more fun. To Leslie Rossman and Linda Phelan for their vast generosity. And to Ame, the true queen of Chick-dom, for ruling the roost and being the best friend a gal could ever have.

Boundless gratitude to everyone who has shared their nesting advice and not-so-domestic attitude with us. You make it happen.

a Susie Albert • Susan and Andy Archer • Cheryl Atkins b Donna and Steve Bagby • Adrienne Baker • Shirley Baker • Aimee Barille • Patricia Barille • Wendy Barner • Kathleen Beaulieu • Leah Bird • Leigh Bordelon • Jill Conner Browne • Kristen Bush c Mary Carlomagno • Celia Carrasco • Sally Chicotel • Cindy Cooper and Michelle Torrey at 560 Main • Sue Ellen Cooper and the Red Hats Society • Kathy Cordova • Cindy Cutlip d Denise Davock • Victoria Deguara and everyone at Victoria's Salon • Michelle and Peter DeGiglio • Laura Deitrick • Jim Denham and everyone at The Wine Steward at the Roxy • Mimi Doe • Noreen Doherty • Claire Donovan • Peggy Dorris • Kristen Dreyer e Jimmy Eng • Kory Eng • Mary Eng • Matt Engels f Ilene Feldman • Paola Fernandez-Rana • Jody and Phil Fidler • Sarah Freels • Kay Freeman • Dr. Paul Furman g Leanne and Tom Garcia • Liz Glenn • Will Glennon • Linda Graetz • Susan Groshans • Ellen Groustra h Lisa Hammond • Joan Hansen • Tracy Heisler • Joan Hemm • Donna Hendrix • Jayne Hess • Nola and John Hicks • Pam Himes • Deborah Hollings j Jeri and Bob Jackson • Susan Janosky k Suzy Kallo-Heitzman • Karen and Bill Kastigar • Kris King • Brenda Knight • Tammy Knight • Emily Kuvin l Adair Lara • Anne and Curt Large • Donna and Matt Lord • Mary Lou Mackin-Low • Sue and Mike Lyon m Butch and Bailey Mahler • Jason Mahler • Sheena and John Mahler • Karen McCarthy • Fran McCullough • Marie McEnery • Nicole Meunier • Nancy Milla and Brad Penner • Kim Mishler • Amanda Morales • Jim and Patti Morgenroth and the Morgenroth Development star crew • Carrie Morris • Kelly Morris n Jeanette and David Nichols o Jan O'Dell • Mark and Allison O'Dell • Ollie Oden • Kim Harris Ortiz • Carolyn and Mark Otto p Frank Pappalardo and Denine Reignier • Catherine Patience • Maureen Petrosky • Linda Phelan • Lesa Porché • Alicia Powell q Grace Quick • Jamie Quinn r Carrie and Dave Reichenberger • Debra Roberts • Jennifer Roberts • Nancy and Jay Roberts • Janna, Jonathan, Shane, and Pat Robertson • Leslie Rossman • Marly Rusoff • Mary Jane Ryan s Claudia Sadlon • Meredith Saillant • Peter Shutts • Thea Singer and Henry Santoro • Cyndi Snyder • Elisabeth Socolow • Autumn Stephens • Janice Sturchio t Kristen Tankersley • Renita Tankersley • Barbara Trafficanda • Renee Turcott • Catherine Tyler v Theresa Vargo and Keith Brauneis • Karen, John, Rebecca, and Nick Vifian w Kristina Washington • Amy Weinreich • Judy Wheeler and Bob Ditter and everyone at Towne Center Books • Nancy Wheeler • Sherry Wickwire • Jacqueline Williams-Courtright and everyone at Alden Lane Nursery • Laura Wood

CoNtribuToR BioS

And we thank the talented writers who shared their stories:

DIANE ACKERMAN is an award-winning poet and essayist whose books include *Cultivating Delight, A Natural History of the Senses,* and *A Natural History of Love.* In June 2004, Scribner will publish her *An Alchemy of Mind.* Her Web site is: www.diane ackerman.com.

OPAL PALMER ADISA is a Jamaica-born poet and educator. She is the author of *It Begins With Tears* and *Tamarind and Mango Women,* the 1992 American Book Award winner. Her new poetry collection, *Caribbean Passion,* is due out in April 2004.

DEBRA LEE BALDWIN has authored one book and is a regular contributor to *Better Homes and Gardens* Special Interest Publications, *Sunset,* and *San Diego Home/Garden Lifestyles.* Her Web site, www.debra leebaldwin.com, includes a photo tour of her own "glitter garden" in San Diego.

BARBARA KAPLAN BASS, PH.D., is director of the Maryland Writing Project at Towson University in Baltimore, where she teaches writing and American literature. She is currently working on a book of personal essays for her granddaughters.

KAREN BOURIS is a writer, publisher, and mother of two children. Most recently, she is the author of *Just Kiss Me and Tell Me You Did the Laundry: A Couple's Guide to Negotiating Parenting Roles.*

JILL CONNER BROWNE is THE Sweet Potato Queen and author of *The Sweet Potato Queens' Book of Love, The Sweet Potato Queens' Big Ass Cookbook and Financial Planner,* and *God Save the Sweet Potato Queens.* Her Web site is: www.sweetpotatoqueens. com.

BETH LYNN CLEGG writes from her Houston home. Her fiction, nonfiction, poetry, and prose have appeared in various publications, been read on public radio, and been performed on stage.

LAURA SHAINE CUNNINGHAM is a novelist, playwright and journalist, and the author of the memoirs *Sleeping Arrangements* and *A Place in the Country,* both of which first appeared as excerpts in *The New Yorker.* Laura is a native New Yorker and the mother of two young daughters.

ELLEN DEGENERES is a groundbreaking comedian and actress. Her bestselling books include *My Point . . . And I Do Have One,* and *The Funny Thing Is.* After doing the voice for the character of "Dory" in *Finding Nemo,* Ellen began hosting her own TV talk show, *The Ellen DeGeneres Show.*

LOUISE DEGRAVE is the product of a conservative French Catholic father, a liberal Protestant ex-DAR mother, and a self-made Jewish husband. She lives with her husband and two sons in La Jolla, California.

DEBORAH VIVIEN FREEMAN-MITFORD CAVENDISH DEVONSHIRE, THE DUCHESS OF DEVONSHIRE, is the youngest of the famous Mitford siblings. Her English home, Chatsworth, hosts four hundred thousand visitors each year. She has authored two books, *Counting My Chickens* and *Chatsworth, The House.*

KATE DUBE lives in Portsmouth, New Hampshire, where she is a writer and a lecturer at the University of New Hampshire.

JILL BAUER DUNNE is the host and creator of *You're Home with Jill,* a creative-lifestyle show, on the QVC Shopping Network. She dines with her husband and daughter in Pennsylvania.

SHEILA ELLISON is the author of nine books, including, *How Does She Do It? 101 Life Lessons from One Mother to Another.* Her Web site (www. CompleteMom.com) is dedicated to helping and motivating mothers.

M. F. K. FISHER was born in 1908 and is one of America's best-known food writers. The recipient of the James Beard Award, M. F. K. Fisher has authored several books, including *The Gastronomical Me, The Art of Eating,* and *How to Cook a Wolf.*

MAUREEN TOLMAN FLANNERY, who was raised on a Wyoming ranch, has raised her own four children in Chicago. She is eagerly awaiting the birth of her first grandchild—in the home where her children were born. Her third book, *Ancestors in the Landscape: Poems of a Rancher's Daughter,* is due out in 2004.

INA GARTEN founded the Barefoot Contessa, a gourmet take-out shop in East Hampton, New York. Her cookbooks include *The Barefoot Contessa Cookbook, Barefoot Contessa Parties!,* and *Barefoot Contessa Family Style.*

ELLEN GOODMAN is a Pulitzer Prize–winning *Boston Globe* columnist. Her books include *Paper Trail, I Know Just What You Mean, Keeping in Touch,* and *At Large.*

GERRI HIRSHEY's most recent book is *We Gotta Get Out of This Place: The True, Tough Story of Women in Rock.*

ANN HODGMAN is a former food editor from *Spy* magazine and the mother of two finicky eaters. Her cookbooks include *One Bite Won't Kill You, Beat This!,* and *Beat That!*

JULEIGH HOWARD-HOBSON lives on the West Coast with her husband, three kids, and two bathrooms full of mismatched towels.

JAMAICA KINCAID was born and raised in Antigua. She was a regular contributor to *The New Yorker* for nearly twenty years and is the author of several books, including *My Garden, A Small Place,* and *Autobiography of My Mother.* She resides in Vermont with her husband and children.

LISA KOGAN is the writer-at-large for *O, the Oprah Magazine.* She lives in New York City with her new baby daughter.

MARGIE LAPANJA is the author of four books, including *Romancing the Stove* and *Food That Rocks.* She lives at Lake Tahoe with her husband-consort and their daughter.

HILARY LIFTIN is the author of *Candy & Me* and the co-author of *Dear Exile.* She lives with her husband, Chris Harris, in Los Angeles. Her Web site is: www.hilaryliftin.com.

KAREN MILES is a retired educator, writer, and grandmother. She nests bountifully and prunes her petunias in southern California.

ELLEN BIRKETT MORRIS is a writer and essayist living in Louisville, Kentucky. Her work has appeared in *The Girls' Book of Friendship, The Girls' Book of Love,* and *The Writing Group Book.*

DOLLY PARTON is a country music legend and actress, whose movie credits include *9 to 5* and *Steel Magnolias.* Dolly has authored *Dolly* and *Coat of Many Colors.* In 1986 her company opened Dollywood, a theme park celebrating her Smoky Mountain upbringing in Tennessee.

MOLLY PEACOCK is the author of four volumes of poetry and the memoir *Paradise, Piece by Piece.* She is poet-in-residence at the Cathedral of St. John the Divine and president emeritus of the Poetry Society of America. She lives in London, Ontario, and New York City.

JOSEPHINE PHILLIPS can be spotted at tag sales in Connecticut, where she lives with her husband and two sons.

JILL POLLACK is a writer and recovering TV producer currently living in Los Angeles. She still likes throwing big events, but has learned to have a group of eight over for wine and cheese.

TRACY PORTER is the author of *Dreams from Home, Tracy Porter's Inspired Gatherings,* and *Tracy Porter's Home Style.* She and her husband, John, run a nationally recognized design business out of Stonehouse Farm in Princeton, Wisconsin.

PRISCILLA PRESLEY is best known as Queen to the "King" (Elvis Presley). After Elvis's death, Priscilla led Elvis Presley Enterprises into great profitability, appeared in several TV shows and movies, and authored *Elvis and Me*.

ANNA QUINDLEN is a Pulitzer Prize–winning writer and bestselling novelist. Her books include *Blessings, Black and Blue, One True Thing, Object Lessons,* and *A Short Guide to a Happy Life*.

JESSIE RAYMOND lives with her family in a still-unfinished farmhouse in Middlebury, Vermont. Her humor column, "Around the Bend," appears in the local paper, as well as on her Web site, www.jessie raymond.com.

RUTH REICHL is the former restaurant critic of *The New York Times* and editor-in-chief of *Gourmet*. She has authored *Comfort Me with Apples* and *Tender at the Bone*.

SUE SENATOR lives in a shabbily elegant, or elegantly shabby, big old house in Massachusetts with her husband, where she writes about all manner of things, particularly those inspired by raising her three very different boys.

NORA SETON is the author of *Kitchen Congregation* and lives in Connecticut with her husband and two children.

LINDSLEY ARMSTRONG SMITH is an attorney and a research assistant professor at the University of Arkansas. Her articles have been published in the *Free Speech Yearbook, The Speech Teacher,* and *Early Encounters in North America*.

AMY STEWART is the author of *From the Ground Up* and *The Earth Moved*. Amy lives in Eureka, California, and recently ripped out all the grass around her Victorian home to replant plants from her first garden in Santa Cruz.

MARTHA STEWART is the founder of the magazine *Martha Stewart Living* and author of many books, including *The Martha Stewart Cookbook, Entertaining,* and *Martha Stewart's Hors d'Oeuvres Handbook*.

ALEXANDRA STODDARD is the author of more than twenty books, including *Living a Beautiful Life, Grace Notes, Open Your Eyes,* and *Feeling at Home*. She lives with her husband in New York City and Stonington Village, Connecticut.

JULIA PRODIS SULEK has been a reporter for her hometown paper, the *San Jose Mercury News,* since 1998. Before that, she worked as a regional correspondent for the Associated Press and was named a Pulitzer Prize finalist in feature writing.

CAMERON SULLIVAN is a wife, mother of three, freelance writer, and competitive swimmer from Pleasanton, California. She prefers a glass of fine cabernet sauvignon to the cheap beer she feeds her garden snails.

BETH TEITELL is a columnist at the *Boston Herald* and the author of *From Here to Maternity,* which will be released in 2005. Her Web site is www.teitell.com.

MELANIE THERNSTROM is the author of *The Dead Girl* (a memoir) and *Halfway Heaven: Diary of a Harvard Murder* (a work of investigative journalism). She is a contributing writer for *The New York Times Magazine.* Her journalism also has appeared in *The New Yorker, Vanity Fair,* and *New York Magazine,* among other places. She lives in New York City, where her baking ambitions have been scaled down to cupcakes.

KATIE THOMPSON is a mother of three, a producer and talk-show host for a local community television station, and a former English teacher. Katie loves to wear animal prints and baseball hats and likes to drink cosmopolitans with her high school girlfriends.

SALLY TISDALE is the recipient of an NEA fellowship, a James Phelan Award, and a Pope Foundation fellowship. She is the author of five books, including *Talk Dirty to Me* and *The Best Thing I Ever Tasted* and has contributed to such publications as *The New Yorker, Vogue,* and *The New Republic.*

JANE UNDERWOOD is the owner and director of The Writing Salon, a school of creative writing in San Francisco. Her writing has been published in numerous periodicals and anthologies, performed on stage, and featured on public radio. She is currently at work on a memoir about living the writing life.

KATE WALTER is a freelance writer living in the West Village in New York City. Her essays have appeared in *The New York Times, New York Daily News, Newsday,* and many other publications.

BAILEY WHITE teaches first grade in south Georgia. Her essays and stories have appeared in several magazines, and she is a regular commentator on National Public Radio. She is the author of *Mama Makes Up Her Mind* and *Sleeping at the Starlite Motel.*

PAT WILLARD is the author of *Secrets of Saffron, Pie Every Day,* and *A Soothing Broth.* She lives in Brooklyn, New York.

biBliOgrapHy

The Alice B. Toklas Cookbook by Alice B. Toklas (Harper & Row, 1954; 1986).

Anatomy of a Rose: Exploring the Secret Life of Flowers by Sharman Apt Russell (Beacon Press, 2002).

Aromas and Flavors of Past and Present by Alice B. Toklas (The Lyons Press, 1958).

Aphrodite: A Memoir of the Senses by Isabel Allende (HarperFlamingo, 1998).

The Barefoot Contessa Cookbook by Ina Garten (Clarkson Potter, 1999).

Becoming O'Keeffe: The Early Years by Sarah Whitaker Peters (Abbeville Press, 1991).

The Best Recipes by the editors of *Cook's Illustrated* magazine (Boston Common Press, 1999).

Better Homes and Gardens Color Solutions edited by Vicki Ingham (Meredith Books, 2002).

Betty Crocker's Cookbook by Betty Crocker (Prentice Hall, 1990).

Bohemian Style by Elizabeth Wilhide (Watson-Guptill Publications, 2001).

Breaking the Rules: Home Style for the Way We Live Today by Christy Ferer (Simon & Schuster, 2001).

Candace Wheeler: The Art and Enterprise of American Design by Amelia Peck (Metropolitan Museum of Art, 2001).

Charmed Circle: Gertrude Stein and Company by James R. Mellow (Praeger Publishers, 1974).

Chez Panisse Vegetables by Alice Waters (Harper-Collins, 1996).

Contemporary Decorating by Elizabeth Wilhide and Joanna Copestick (SOMA Books, 2004).

Country Living Country Chic: Country Style for Modern Living by Liz Bauwens and Alexandra Campbell (Hearst Books, 2001).

Creating Beds and Borders: Creative Ideas from America's Best Gardeners by the editors of Taunton Press (Taunton Press, 2001).

Cultivating Delight: A Natural History of My Garden by Diane Ackerman (Perennial, 2002).

Decorating Is Fun! How to Be Your Own Decorator by Dorothy Draper (Doubleday, Doran and Company, Inc., 1939).

Deep in the Green: An Exploration of Country Pleasures by Anne Raver (Vintage, 1998 reprint).

Designing Women: Interiors by Leading Style Makers by Margaret Russell (Stewart, Tabori & Chang, 2001).

The Divine Sarah: A Life of Sarah Bernhardt by Arthur Gold and Robert Fizdale (Alfred A. Knopf, 1991).

BIBLIOGRAPHY *(continued)*

Dorothy Parker: A Biography by Marion Meade (Villard Books, 1987).

Dreams by Cassandra Danz (Three Rivers Press, 1999 reprint).

Eclectic Style in Interior Design by Carol Meredith (Rockport Publishers, 1998).

Edith Wharton: An Extraordinary Life by Eleanor Dwight (Harry N. Abrams, Inc., 1994).

Elizabeth and Her German Garden by Elizabeth von Arnim (Virago, 1898; 1938).

Entertaining by Martha Stewart (Clarkson Potter, 1982).

Entertaining Is Fun! How to Be a Popular Hostess by Dorothy Draper (Doubleday, Doran and Company, Inc., 1941).

Essential Cuisines of Mexico by Diana Kennedy (Clarkson Potter, 2000).

The Flower Gardener's Bible by Lewis and Nancy Hill (Storey Books, 2003).

From Seed to Bloom: How to Grow over 500 Annuals, Perennials and Herbs by Eileen Powell (Storey Communications, 1995).

Garden Color: Annuals and Perennials by the editors of *Sunset* and Sunset Books (Lane Publications, 1981).

Gardenhouse: Bringing the Outdoors In by Bonnie Trust Dahan (Chronicle Books, 1999).

The Gardens of Gertrude Jekyll by Richard Bisgrove (Little, Brown and Co., 1992).

Georgia O'Keeffe: A Life by Roxana Robinson (Harper & Row, 1989).

Gertrude Jekyll: A Vision of Garden and Wood by Judith B. Tankard and Michael R. Van Valkenburgh (Harry N. Abrams, Inc., 1989).

The Gift of Southern Cooking: Recipes and Revelations from Two Great Southern Cooks by Edna Lewis and Scott Peacock (Alfred A. Knopf, 2003).

Good Fat Cookbook by Fran McCullough (Scribner, 2003).

Green Thoughts: A Writer in the Garden by Eleanor Perényi (Random House, 1981).

Home Comforts: The Art and Science of Keeping House by Cheryl Mendelson (Scribner, 1999).

The House in Good Taste by Elsie de Wolfe (The Century Company, 1914).

House Plants by the editors of *Sunset* and Sunset Books (Lane Publications, 1983).

How to Be a Domestic Goddess: Baking and the Art of Comfort Cooking by Nigella Lawson (Hyperion Press, 2001).

How to Cook Everything by Mark Bittman (John Wiley & Sons, 1998).

How to Decorate by Martha Stewart (Clarkson Potter, 1996).

Invitations by Marc Friedland (Clarkson Potter, 1998).

Jane Cumberbatch's Pure Style Living by Jane Cumberbatch (DK Publishing, 2001).

Julia's Kitchen Wisdom: Essential Techniques and Recipes from a Lifetime of Cooking by Julia Child (Alfred A. Knopf, 2000).

Lidia's Italian Table by Lidia Bastianich (William Morrow, 1998).

Marie Antoinette: The Journey by Antonia Fraser (Anchor Books, 2002).

Mastering the Art of French Cooking by Julia Child, Louisette Bertholle, and Simone Beck (Alfred A. Knopf, 1961).

Mediterranean Cooking by Paula Wolfert (Harper-Collins, 1996 reprint).

Moosewood Cookbook by Mollie Katzen (Ten Speed Press, 2000).

Mrs. Greenthumbs Plows Ahead: Five Steps to the Drop-Dead Gorgeous Garden of Your Dreams by Cassandra Danz (Three Rivers Press, 1999 reprint).

My Favorite Plant: Writers and Gardeners on the Plants They Love edited by Jamaica Kincaid (Farrar, Straus & Giroux, 1998).

The New Basics Cookbook by Julee Russo and Sheila Lukins (Workman Publishing, 1989).

The New Joy of Cooking by Irma Rombauer (Scribner, 1997).

New York Cookbook by Molly O'Neill (Workman Publishing, 1992).

One Bite Won't Kill You: More than 200 Recipes to Tempt Even the Pickiest Kids on Earth by Ann Hodgman (Houghton Mifflin, 1999).

On Flowers by Kathryn Kleinman and Sara Slavin (Chronicle Books, 1992).

Onward and Upward in the Garden by Katharine S. White (Beacon Press, 2002).

The Orchid Thief by Susan Orlean (Ballantine Books, 2000).

Potted Gardens: A Fresh Approach to Container Gardening by Rebecca Cole (Clarkson Potter, 1997).

The Power of Style: The Women Who Defined the Art of Living Well by Annette Tapert and Diana Edkins (Crown Publishers, 1994).

BIBLIOGRAPHY *(continued)*

Romancing the Stove: Celebrated Recipes and Delicious Fun for Every Kitchen Goddess by Margie Lapanja (Conari Press, 2003).

The Secret Garden by Frances Hodgson Burnett (HarperTrophy, 1998 reprint).

Shabby Chic by Rachel Ashwell (HarperCollins, 1996).

The Shabby Chic Home by Rachel Ashwell (Regan Books, 2000).

Silver Palette by Julee Rosso and Sheila Lukins (Workman Publishing, 1982).

Stitch 'n Bitch by Debbie Stoller (Workman Publishing, 2003).

Southern Living Homestyle Cooking by Julie Fisher Gunter (Oxmoor House, 2002).

The Sweet Breathing of Plants edited by Linda Hogan and Brenda Peterson (North Point Press, 2001).

Tracy Porter's Dreams from Home by Tracy Porter (Andrews McMeel Publishing, 1998).

Two Gardeners: Katharine S. White and Elizabeth Lawrence—A Friendship in Letters edited by Emily Herring Wilson (Beacon Press, 2002).

The Tulip: The Story of a Flower That Has Made Men Mad by Anna Pavord (Bloomsbury Publishing, 1999).

The Ultimate Casserole Cookbook: 175 Great One-Dish Recipes by Barbara Jones (Sterling, 2002).

The Victorian Garden by Allison Kyle Leopold (Clarkson Potter, 1995).

Wabi Sabi: The Japanese Art of Impermanence by Andrew Juniper (Charles E. Tuttle Company, 2003).

Wabi Sabi Style by James and Sandra Crowley (Gibbs Smith, 2001).

Wild Women by Autumn Stephens (Conari Press, 1992).

Wild Women in the White House by Autumn Stephens (Conari Press, 1997).

Women Gardeners: A History by Yvonne Cuthbertson (Arden Press, Inc., 1998).

Women of Flowers: A Tribute to Victorian Women Illustrators by Jack Kramer (Stewart, Tabori & Chang, 1996).

peRmisSioNs

PART THREE

"My Best Friend's Wedding Cake" by Melanie Thernstrom. Copyright © 2001 by Melanie Thernstrom. Reprinted by permission of Melanie Thernstrom.

From *Last House: Reflections, Dreams, and Observations* 1943–1991 by M. F. K. Fisher, copyright © 1995 by Robert Lescher, as Trustee of the Literary Trust u/w/o M. F. K. Fisher. Used by permission of Pantheon Books, a division of Random House, Inc.

From *The Kitchen Congregation* by Nora Seton. Copyright © 2000 by Nora Seton. Reprinted by permission of Picador.

From *Elvis and Me* by Priscilla Beaulieu Presley and Sandra Harmon, copyright ©1985 by Graceland Enterprises, Inc. Used by permission of G. P. Putnam's Sons, a division of Penguin Group (USA) Inc.

"Alice Waters" by Ruth Reichl ©2000. This essay originally appeared in *American Greats* by Robert Wilson and Stanley Marcus (Perseus Book Group, 2000). Reprinted by permission of the author.

From *One Bite Won't Kill You* by Ann Hodgman, copyright © 1999 by Ann Hodgman. Reprinted by permission of Houghton Mifflin Company. All rights reserved.

From *My Life and Other Unfinished Business* by Dolly Parton (HarperCollins 1994), copyright ©1994 by Dolly Parton, used by permission of the author.

From *The Best Thing I Ever Tasted* by Sallie Tisdale, copyright © 2000 by Sallie Tisdale. Used by permission of Riverhead Books, an imprint of Penguin Group (USA) Inc.

"The Secret Ingredient" by Gerri Hirshey. Copyright © 2003, Gerri Hirshey. Reprinted by permission of SLL/Sterling Lord Literistic, Inc. and *O, The Oprah Magazine.*

From *Candy and Me: A Love Story* by Hilary Liftin, copyright © 2003 by Hilary Liftin. All rights reserved. Reprinted with the permission of The Free Press, a Division of Simon & Schuster Adult Publishing Group,

PART FOUR

From *Cultivating Delight: A Natural History of My Garden* by Diane Ackerman, copyright © 2001 by Diane Ackerman. Reprinted by permission of HarperCollins Publishers Inc.

From *A Place in the Country* by Laura Shaine Cunningham, copyright © 2000 by Laura Shaine Cunningham. Used by permission of Riverhead Books, an imprint of Penguin Group (USA) Inc.

From Jamaica Kincaid's Afterword to *Onward and Upward in the Garden* by Katharine White, copyright © 1979 by Jamaica Kincaid. Reprinted with the permission of The Wylie Agency, Inc.

From *State of Grace* by Molly Peacock. Copyright © 1995, Molly Peacock. Reprinted by permission of Molly Peacock.

From *From the Ground Up: The Story of a First Garden* by Amy Stewart. © 2001 by Amy Stewart. Reprinted by permission of Algonquin Books of Chapel Hill.

PHOTOGRAPHS

Page ix ©Retrofile.com; page xi ©Superstock; page xiii ©Superstock; page xiv ©Retrofile.com; page xvi ©Superstock; page 2 ©Retrofile.com; page 7 ©Retrofile.com; page 18 ©Retrofile.com; page 33 ©Superstock; page 50 ©Retrofile.com; page 60 ©Superstock; page 78 ©Benelux Press/ Retrofile.com; page 96 ©Superstock; page 109 ©Superstock; page 126 ©Superstock; page 142 ©Retrofile.com; page 150 ©Retrofile.com; page 164 ©Superstock; page 173 ©Superstock; page 199 ©Retrofile.com; page 202 ©Hulton/ Getty Images; page 215 ©Superstock; page 227 ©Retrofile.com; page 237 ©Retrofile.com; page 250 ©Hulton/Getty Images

Cover, pages ii, 286 © Theresa Vargo Photography, www.vargophotography.com

Original illustrations © Martha Newton Furman, www.newtonfurman.com

GeNerAL iNDex

Presley, Priscilla Beaulieu, 170–71
Priming, before painting, 15
Primroses, 207, 208
Pruning tools, 211
Pumpkins, as serving containers, 122
Purses, arranging flowers in, 217

Q

Quarry, refurbished as garden, 249
Queen Anne's lace, 206
Quindlen, Anna, 120–21
Quinn, Sally, 103
Quizzes:
    Pick a Palette, 223–24
    What Kind of Dish Are You?, 167
    What's Your Style-Q?, 10–12
    Who's Your Party Persona?, 99

R

Radner, Gilda, 66
Rakes, 211
Raver, Anne, 205, 227
Rawlings, Marjorie Kinnan, 129
Raymond, Jessie, 65–66
Recipes:
    mother's collection of, 188–89
    signature, of family member,
        191–92
    see also Recipe Index (page 282)
Red Hat Society, 107
Redouté, Pierre-Joseph, 244
Reichl, Ruth, 174–75

"Reminder-binder," 6–7
Retreats, in home, 40–41
Richards, Ann, 129
Roasting, 194–95
Rombauer, Irma, 158, 160
Roosevelt, Alice Longworth, 129
Rooster, 178
Roses, 206, 208, 242–44
    cut, "fluffing," 216
    in Empress Josephine Bonaparte's
        garden, 244
    miniature, 238
    silk, dressing up real roses with, 230
Rosso, Julee, 158
Rosy Posy Party, 254
Rothschild, Pauline de, 142
RSVP, 132
Russell, Lillian, 116
Russell, Margaret, 19
Russell, Rosalind, 121
Russell, Sharman Apt, 205, 233

S

Sackville-West, Vita, 227
Saffron, 178
Sage, 207
St. Patrick's Day, 108, 117
Salads, 177
San Francisco Herb Company, 71
Santa Barbara daisies, 206
Scabiosa, 207
Scents:
    candles and, 71, 75

faux cooking and, 165
    sweetening home with, 71–72
Seasonal displays, in window boxes,
    250
Seasons, of a woman's life, 251–52
Secondhand furnishings, 18–21,
    30–31
    flea market shopping and, 20–21
Secret Garden, The (Burnett), 213
Senator, Sue, 31
Serving containers, fruits and
    vegetables as, 122
Seton, Nora, 169
Sheets, lavender-scented, 72
Shoes, arranging flowers in, 217
Shopping:
    at flea markets, 20–21
    at only one retailer, 36
    for secondhand furnishings,
        18–22
Shovels, for garden, 211
Signature recipes, 191–92
Silk flowers, 230
Simpson, Wallis, 59
Skinner, Cornelia Otis, 202
Slugs, 240–41
Smith, Lindsley Armstrong, 46–47
Smith, Liz, 129
Smith, Margaret Chase, 33
Snail problems, 240–41
Snapdragons, 250
Soaker hoses, 211
Soaps, scented, 72
Sofa-beds, for guests, 139

Y

ReCipE iNdEx

A

B

C

TOGETHER Ame Mahler Beanland (*left*) and Emily Miles Terry (*right*) comprise Chick Ink—a partnership dedicated to celebrating friendship, hospitality, personal style, and all things chickcentric. They co-authored the bestselling *It's a Chick Thing: Celebrating the Wild Side of Women's Friendship* and host the Web site www.chickstyle.com.

AME is an award-winning editor and art director and would rather garden than eat (but dining alfresco is also very high on her list of favorite things). Her other books include *Celebrating Motherhood* and contributions to the Simple Pleasures series. She lives in Pleasanton, California, with her husband and baby girl.

EMILY is a public relations specialist, a decorating-on-a-dime diva who loves imperfect homes full of laughter and (sometimes) makes a mean lasagna (see page 171). She lives in Brookline, Massachusetts, with her husband and two children.